T0305556

Front and Back Stage of Tourism Performance

As more people travel for pleasure than ever before, host communities and intermediaries are presented with tourism opportunities that all too often become flashpoints for local contestation and mechanisms for displacement. *Front and Back Stage of Tourism Performance: Imaginaries and Bucket List Venues* explains why by situating our travel imaginaries, those dream destinations on our travel bucket lists, as co-constructed by the tourist industry, state development policies, and community negotiations, and as framed by modernity's new global cultural economy.

The ethnographically grounded chapters describe tourist encounters shaped by geopolitics, complicated by war, and troubled by and enacted within the economic inequities of neocolonialism. The points of contact afford a unique vantage from which to view cultural identity, entrepreneurial strategizing, and natural resource management as global politics and relations of difference. They also illustrate the power of social networks, cultural display, and artistic performance as collective presentation, management apparatus, and structural critique.

Drawing on a range of international case studies, this book will appeal to those interested in tourism, anthropology, global studies, environmental issues, microeconomics, and identity studies.

Frances Julia Riemer is a Professor in Educational Foundations and Associate Faculty in the Women's and Gender Studies Program at Northern Arizona University. Her work focuses on tourism, development, and sustainable communities, gender, equity, and access, and the culture and social organization of community, school, and workplace.

Routledge Advances in Tourism and Anthropology

Series Editors:
Dr Catherine Palmer (University of Brighton, UK) C.A.Palmer@brighton.ac.uk
Dr Jo-Anne Lester (University of Brighton, UK) J.Lester@brighton.ac.uk

To discuss any ideas for the series please contact Faye Leerink, Commissioning
Editor: faye.leerink@tandf.co.uk or the Series Editors.

This series draws inspiration from anthropology's overarching aim to explore
and better understand the human condition in all its fascinating diversity. It
seeks to expand the intellectual landscape of anthropology and tourism in relation to how we understand the experience of being human, providing critical
inquiry into the spaces, places, and lives in which tourism unfolds. Contributions
to the series will consider how such spaces are embodied, imagined, constructed,
experienced, memorialized and contested. The series provides a forum for cut-
ting-edge research and innovative thinking from tourism, anthropology, and
related disciplines such as philosophy, history, sociology, geography, cultural
studies, architecture, the arts, and feminist studies.

Everyday Practices of Tourism Mobilities
Packing a Bag
Kaya Barry

Everyday Practices of Tourism Mobilities
Packing a Bag
Kaya Barry

Tourism and Indigenous Heritage in Latin America
As Observed through Mexico's Magical Village Cuetzalan
Casper Jacobsen

Tourism and Embodiment
Edited by Catherine Palmer and Hazel Andrews

Front and Back Stage of Tourism Performance
Imaginaries and Bucket List Venues
Edited by Frances Julia Riemer

For more information about this series please visit: www.routledge.com/Routledge-
Advances-in-Tourism-and-Anthropology/book-series/RATA

Front and Back Stage of Tourism Performance

Imaginaries and Bucket List Venues

**Edited by
Frances Julia Riemer**

Routledge
Taylor & Francis Group

LONDON AND NEW YORK

First published 2020
by Routledge
2 Park Square, Milton Park, Abingdon, Oxon OX14 4RN

and by Routledge
605 Third Avenue, New York, NY 10017

Routledge is an imprint of the Taylor & Francis Group, an informa business

First issued in paperback 2021

Publisher's Note
The publisher has gone to great lengths to ensure the quality of this reprint but points out that some imperfections in the original copies may be apparent.

British Library Cataloguing in Publication Data
A catalogue record for this book is available from the British Library

Library of Congress Cataloging-in-Publication Data
A catalog record has been requested for this book

ISBN 13: 978-1-138-34786-1 (hbk)
ISBN 13: 978-0-429-43684-0 (ebk)
ISBN 13: 978-1-03-223878-4 (pbk)

DOI: 10.4324/9780429436840

Typeset in Times New Roman
by Taylor & Francis Books

Contents

Figures

Acknowledgements

Editing this book has been a dream. As a lifelong traveler, I couldn't be more delighted to bring together this group of trenchant ethnographies on tourism. The opportunity to engage with tourism imaginaries is propitious in this time of overtourism, and I want to thank each of our authors for their important contribution.

We thank the American Anthropology Association's (AAA) Anthropology of Tourism Interest Group (ATIG) for hosting the panels that gave birth to the edited text, and to our editor, Faye Leerink, and editorial assistants, Ruth Anderson and Nonita Saha, at Routledge, for shepherding it through publication. We also acknowledge anthropologists of tourism Valene Smith, Erve Chambers, John Urry, Dean MacCannell, and so many others who first took tourism seriously. Their research and writing provides the groundwork for our scholarship and the chapters in this text.

Editing this book is also a disruption of dreams. We acknowledge the communities in Nepal, Mali, Ecuador, Indonesia, India, Morocco, Mexico, Haiti, and Botswana, whose members hosted us and who negotiate the everyday challenges of 21st century mass tourism. They helped us understand that what began as hopeful opportunities all too often became mechanisms for contestation and displacement. Yet they also showed us the power of social networks, cultural display, and artistic performance as collective presentation, management apparatus, and structural critique.

More and more of us are tourists at some point in our lives. I first ventured out into the larger world at the age of eight. My recently widowed grandmother took me as travel companion on a trip to Switzerland, Germany, and Austria, where she was raised and where her sisters and brothers farmed. We visited family, took a bus tour through the Swiss Alps, and sightsaw Schönbrunn Palace in Vienna. I dedicate *Front and Back Stage of Tourism Performance* to my grandmother, who showed me the big glorious world, made me a traveler, and taught me we are all human.

To those of you who also consider yourself tourists, travelers, and guests, those of you who study tourism, and those of you who keep travel bucket lists, we hope you appreciate our troublings.

Frances Julia Riemer, Ph.D.
Sedona, AZ

Introduction

Frances Julia Riemer

Travel bucket lists

Travel bucket lists, those inventories of places to see before you die, are filled with the stuff of wonder. They are catalogues of imaginaries, shared images that exist on our lists and in our cultural and social imaginations (Strauss 2006). An African safari, a backpacking trek in Nepal, a visit to Mayan ruins evoke images of places "that we might like to visit or worlds that we might like to inhabit" (Gravari-Barbas & Graburn 2016, 1). In this book, we both examine and trouble those places of our imagination. Building on what Graburn and Gravari-Barbas (2016) described as a recent concept in anthropological inquiry, we look at the way tourism constructs and complicates our travel imaginaries. In ethnographically grounded chapters, we view bucket list destinations as confounded by war, framed by geopolitics, and troubled by and enacted within the economic inequities of neocolonialism.

Tourism is the stuff of modernity. Before the 19th century, only the elite traveled. Visits to drink and bathe in spring water were popular health prescriptions among the upper class in the 18th and 19th centuries (Urry 2002). The Grand Tour of Europe's classic antiquities in the mid 18th to early 20th century was a rite of passage largely for sons of wealthy English families (Craik 1997; Withey 1997). It wasn't until after World War II, when the new global economy, workers' paid vacations and holidays, increased train and air travel, and rise of middle-class mass consumption in the West "elevated tourism from the pastime of select individuals to a billion dollar industry" (Duggan 1997, 46). More and more of us are tourists at some point in our lives. According to estimates by the United Nations World Tourism Organization (UNWTO), 1.2 billion tourists traveled in 2016, a 49-fold increase since 1950 (Roser 2019). France, the United States, Spain, China, and Italy are our top five destinations; Bangkok, London, Paris, Dubai, and Singapore, our top five cities to visit (Smith 2018).

Many of us travel or dream of traveling, yet many of us also contest the term "tourist." Harkening to Valene Smith's (1977) seminal typology, we might prefer to call ourselves "explorers" or "offbeat travelers" in the attempt to separate ourselves from the mass tourism industry of cruise ships and tour groups. Or perhaps we prefer to think of ourselves as Nomads, Jet Setters, Safarists, Cruisers, Flâneurs, Oenophiles, Trekkers, Bon Vivants, Adventurers, Glampers, Wanderlusters, or Gastronomes, terms offered by *The New York Times* (2019) to advertise its annual Travel Show.

The inchoate stigma of and distancing from "tourist" as nomenclature may have something to do with growing effects of all this travel. In more than 51 destinations, tourists outnumber locals (Smith 2017). Many are small municipalities—Andorra, Macao—or island archipelagos—British Virgin Islands, Turks and Caicos Islands—places without much room to spare. Venice is overtouristed. Long-time residents can no longer afford to live in the city, and cruise ships cram the canals (Ellwood 2018). "Venice is dying, slowly, slowly, but it is dying," and "crowds of tourists" are to blame, explained Matteo, a Venetian archeologist, tour guide, and official resident of Venice (Becker 2013, 77). My own small town of Sedona, Arizona, nestled in the high desert red rock canyons and buttes of the Mogollon Rim, has a year-round population of 10,000 and tourist population of three million visitors a year. I can attest that a ratio of 300 tourists to one local creates traffic logjams and fuels frustrations that surface in local elections.

The tourism industry is "overbooked" (Becker 2013), and "overbooked" has led to a backlash to tourism across the planet. "Tourists go home" has become ubiquitous graffiti in Barcelona and other tourist destinations around Spain (Burgen 2018). New Zealand's tourism boom, the result of the country's marketing of its "Lord of the Rings" Middle Earth scenery, has become a cause of concern for its residents. The government recently imposed a "visitor tax" and deported an English family for their bad behavior (Graham-McLay 2019, A9). Overtourism was the topic of 2018 at both a UN co-organized gathering of more than 60 tourism ministers and private-sector leaders and at ITB Berlin, a major industry convention (Pannett 2018).

This then is a perfect moment for an anthropology of tourism. To quote Erve Chambers, "Where and how we travel, who travels and why are by nature anthropological questions" (2009, 13). The study of tourism is multidisciplinary and has been a concern of geographers, sociologists, and historians. Anthropologists alone ask what tourism is and how tourism is imagined, experienced, and practiced, questions that are as, if not more, important now as they were when Valene Smith (1977) posed them 42 years ago.

The anthropology of tourism

I have had the good fortune and have always loved to travel. I have fond childhood memories of the occasional Sunday afternoon when my mom and dad would take us to the local airport just to watch planes take off and land. Along the way, I have been also been tourist. But like Chambers (2009, 5), I find

> I make little distinction … between the terms *travel* and *tourism*. Obviously tourism is a kind of travel, and … modern tourism is a fairly

recent phenomenon that is distinct in several respects from earlier travel traditions. More often than not, such distinctions seem to me to be heavily invested in some 'local prejudices' of class and privilege. Despite considerable evidence to the contrary, there is still a tendency to think of tourism as a mindless and frivolous activity and of travel as an avenue to great adventure and self improvement.

Anthropologists of tourism take tourism seriously; they frame our travels culturally, historically, and theoretically. They situate us not only as tourists but as a global movement of peoples engaged in mediated activities with human consequences, where culture is produced and reproduced, and where power is organized, negotiated, and re/produced. They remind us tourism is pilgrimage (Chambers 2009), dating back to Chaucer's pilgrims and the larger movement of 12th to 14th century Europeans who walked long miles in pilgrimage to St. Thomas Becket's shrine in Canterbury and other sites of saints' relics. Tourism remains pilgrimage for those 300,000 hikers who walked Santiago de Compostela to the shrine of St. James in 2017, just as it does for the 300,000 fans who visited the National Baseball Hall of Fame in Cooperstown, New York that year.

Anthropologists also propose that tourism divides the extraordinary from the ordinary (Urry 2002). As tourists, we visit extraordinary sites (e.g. the Grand Canyon, the Eiffel Tower, the Empire State Building), we conduct quotidian tasks (e.g. drink, eat, shop) in unusual settings, and we see the unfamiliar in the familiar (e.g. in museums, ruins). Tourism is the opposite of "regular and organized work" (Urry 2002, 2); it is a flight from the routines and practices of everyday life (Neumann 1999, 245).

Tourism is a relatively new focus for anthropologists. The disciplinary attention is officially traced to Valene Smith's 1974 American Anthropological Association symposia on tourism and the resultant *Hosts and Guests: The anthropology of tourism* (1977). With a second edition (Smith 1989) look at the longer-term effects of tourism and Smith and Brent's (2001) treatment of tourism in a globalized 21st century, the host/guest binary has played a significant role in the theoretical trajectory. A corresponding pro-tourist/anti-tourist binary is also woven through the literature (Chambers 1997; MacCannell 1976). Grounded in economics, the pro-tourist stance is attributed to planners who advocate tourism as local revenue enhancement and poverty antidote. Anti-tourism advocates, wrote MacCannell, "are urban and modernised liberals and Third World radicals who question the value of touristic development for the local people" (1976, 162).

MacCannell (1999) offered another binary—drawing on Erving Goffman's (1956) front and back stage—as a way to think about co-construction of the traveling experience both as tourists (i.e. front) and as hosts (i.e. back stage). The distinction of front and back stage, in terms of wealth, nationality, and social or cultural distance, presented opportunities for anthropological inquiry on the coping strategies of host communities. "It is assumed that as long as tourists' expectations are fulfilled at the front stage (often by tourist-oriented, partially inauthentic products of performances), authentic social life remains intact in the back stage" (Skinner & Theodossopoulos 2011, 4). Anthropologists develop typologies, and along with these binaries came typologies of tourists (Chen & Huang 2018; Cohen 1979; McKercher & du Cros 2003; Nyaupane & Andereck 2016; Plog 1972; Smith 1977), of tourism (Smith 1977; Smith & Eadington 1992), and of tourism sites and hosts (Butler 2006; Dogan 1989; Stone 2006; Urry 2002). We are now in the age of "adjective tourism," which Skinner (2011, 117) described as "the exoticization and re-branding [of] tourism itself." At the very least, we have (and related studies of) death tourism (Lennon & Foley 2000), diaspora tourism (de Santana Pinho 2016; Reed 2017), romance tourism (Pruitt & LaFont 1995), eco-tourism (Stronza 2001), medical tourism (Speier 2011), adventure tourism (Cater & Cloke 2007), and poverty tourism (Frenzel, Koens, & Steinbrink 2012).

The publication of Urry's 1990 *The Tourist Gaze* shifted the disciplinary analysis to the "gaze." Urry was interested in "the development and historical transformation of the tourist gaze" (5), that is, the ways that "the images generated of different tourist gazes come to constitute a closed self perpetuating system of illusions which provide the tourist with the basis for selecting and evaluating potential places to visit" (7). Anthropologists wrote about the performative understandings and practices of tourism workers (Crang 1997), and the photographic eye and "selling dreams" (Crawshaw & Urry 1997, 188). Ethnographers continue to build on and complicate Urry's notion of the gaze, acknowledging that tourism is a "multidimensional and complex practice and that the tourist is more than a disembodied sightseer" (Iles 2011, 157).

More recently, anthropologists have supplanted "cultural beliefs," "cultural schemes," and "collective ideologies" with "imaginary" in the study of tourism (Graburn & Gravari-Barbas 2016; Salazar 2012; Strauss 2006). Drawing on the work of French post-structuralists (Lacan 1977), political scientists (Anderson 1991), and philosophers (Taylor 2003), imaginaries, the "intangibles, vague or specific mental concepts whose exact nature and boundaries are hard to nail down: commonly related to dreams, legends, or narratives," provide a way of studying our travels (Gravari-Barbas & Graburn 2016, 3). Framing imaginary as both object of study and as analytical concept (Appadurai 1996), anthropologists investigated how tourist imaginaries are re/invented (Garcia-Fuentes 2016; Laverdure 2016; Regnault 2016; Ross 2016; among others) in literature, photographs, and handicrafts, and by public relations firms and nation builders.

This analysis of the construction and negotiation of imaginaries also brought intermediaries into focus (Chambers 2009; Urry 2002). Ethnographies (Gelbman & Maoz 2012; Mancinelli 2014; Salazar 2010) expanded our understanding of all the go-betweens—from public relations firms and safari companies to government departments and local guides—to include their fundamental role as cultural mediators, instrumental in the production of those imaginaries.

With this postmodern turn to invented imaginaries, authenticity became a concern for tourists and a revisited analytical heuristic for anthropologists. The notion of back stage led MacCannell (1973) and others to an analysis of the importance tourists placed on "authenticity," and the ways "staged authenticity" organized tourist spaces like that of Fred Harvey's Hopi House, where "live Indians" displayed their traditional culture for visitors to the Grand Canyon (Dilworth 2001, 145). Ritzeron and Liska (1997) offered a compelling counterpart, writing that in a postmodern world, many tourists were actually interested in "inauthenticity" (107) that is, in "highly predictable, efficient, calculable (cost), controlled vacations" (99). Think Las Vegas and Disney World. Forty years later, however, the tourist continues to be framed as "a modern man in search of authenticity," asserted Girard & Schéou (2016, 134). Anthropologists argued that authenticity was "the imaged real" in the rural countryside of the Catalan Pyrenees (de Marmol 2017, 31), in the poverty of highland Bolivia (Sammells 2014, 125), and as myth, imperiled by modernity (Girard & Schéou 2016, 131).

Another theoretical shift came with postcolonial anthropologists, who drew on Appadurai's (1996) cultural study of globalization to focus on "disjunctures between tourist anticipation and local social realities" (Skinner & Theodossopoulos 2011, 16) in sites that range from WWII battlefields (Iles 2011) to the wildly popular *Body Worlds* touring exhibit (Desmond 2011). Appadurai's (1996, 31) five elementary "scapes," (i.e. *ethnoscapes, mediascapes, technoscapes, financescapes,* and *ideoscapes*) have been useful heuristics in the analysis of tourism as global cultural flows and the interplay of global and local practices and processes (Appadurai 1990). With these frames, studies of tourism became the study of the ways images, money, ideas, people, and technologies cross national borders. That is, tourism became a focus of transnational studies, and transnationalism became a methodology and theoretical frame through which to view tourism practices and policies (McKay 2018; Xiang, Toyota, & Chee 2013). In this research, tourists are actors who "take up and participate in transnational space" (Batchelor 2017, 320), and tourist sites are products of transnational forces (Torres & Momsen 2005). Mobility studies are also relevant here. Approaching tourism as embodied mobility and mobility as embodied practices, tourism, studied as deep rich accounts of movement, disrupted the host/guest and work/leisure binaries of previous scholarship (Hannam 2009; Rickly, Hannam, & Mostafanezhad 2017).

Viewing tourism as transnational process also highlights uneven development and stark power and economic inequities. Researchers argued that tourism creates dependency on unpredictable external income sources, and increases income and resource inequality (Azhar & Masood 2018; Doner 2009). We are also reminded that tourism is a form of imperialism: former colonial powers advise, own, and manage tourism for tourists, who are most often from those former colonizing nations and who create bucket lists based on imaginaries popularized by these very same former colonizers.

This political-economy approach views tourism from the periphery rather than the center, and frames tourism as mirroring "historical patterns of colonialism and economic dependency" (Burns 2004, 6–7). As theorists documented colonialism's construction of tourism imaginaries and neocolonialism's production and maintenance of tourist sites, they positioned tourist sites as "growing venues for the cultivation of a 'hegemonic gaze' that reproduced representations of alterity in contexts of inequality and exploitation" (Meiu 2011, 97). These neocolonial representations of the "Other" and growing income disparities between visitors and host countries complicate development platforms (World Tourism Organization 2019) that promote tourism to reduce poverty and contribute to a country's socioeconomic development (Burns 2004; Lea 1988).

Troubling imaginaries

The ethnographies in this book draw on and build from these anthropologies of tourism. We employ tropes of front and back stage and tourist imaginaries, and we also move the conversation forward theoretically by focusing on the enactment of power in these global contacts. Seeded by an ATIG (Anthropology of Tourism Interest Group) sponsored panel at the 2015 American Anthropology Association annual meetings, *Front and Back Stage of Tourism Performance* further unfolds the ways tourism is co-constructed and imagined within state development policies and global structures, and troubles the imaginaries of our travel bucket lists by recognizing the ways power is structured and practiced in tourism encounters. Authors examine tourist performance, tourism mediators, tourism imaginaries, tourism flows, and tourism authenticity in markets at Agra and Fez, on beaches in Mexico and the Caribbean, at Mayan ruins of Tulum, on safari in Botswana, at the Festival in the Desert outside Timbuktu, and on backpacking treks in Nepal. They show how global encounters play out in Kichwa cultural displays in Ecuador and Komodo dragon walks in Indonesia.

Five overlapping themes rotate around tourism and global politics. We begin with managing tourism during war time, a relevant starting place in this time of endless war as US "pragmatic military strategy" (Bacevich 2016). While tourist safety is of particular concern to the tourist industry, travel warnings can be fatal to local tourism. During armed struggle, tourism space (and related imaginaries) is constructed and organized as ongoing negotiation. Hepburn highlights the ways authenticity and inauthenticity blurred in the culture of silence and climate of fear, suspicion, and security that surrounded Nepal's Maoist insurgency. Montague investigates tourism mobilities as the global musical Festival in the Desert in Timbuktu, Mali, a "melding of modernity and tradition," was disrupted by supporters of Al Qaeda of the Islamic Maghreb separatist movement.

In Part 2 we look at performing tourism imaginaries, those mesmerizing dance and cultural displays that authors argue are both staged exhibitions and structural critique. Quick's focus is on Kichwa dance and visual art in highland Ecuador as constructed both for tourist audience and as indigenous identity and community. Erb takes us to Flores, in eastern Indonesia, to examine the presentation of violent *caci* cultural display as complement to the area's Komodo dragon, the largest lizard in the world, and response to the intrusive development that accompanied the creation of and subsequent 1991 UNESCO World Heritage Site status of Komodo National Park.

Mediation and mediators of tourism are the focus of Part 3, as authors complicate the work of guides, photographers, shop owners, and other tourism intermediaries. Grounded within the commodifying logics of neoliberalism, the ethnographies describe the essential role and the power and powerlessness of, and the relationships among these go-betweens, negotiators, and convincers. Bhandari's research with tour guides and photographers who work from the parking lot outside the Taj Mahal in India reveals their rational negotiating practices at the intersection of government regulations and public–private partnerships. Dizard follows Fez's unofficial tour guides and argues that their formation of syndicates offered the kind of security and informal control mechanisms previously provided by families and neighborhoods.

We move to the production of imaginaries of place in Part 4. The focus is on the negotiation, resistance, denial, and, at times, ambivalent acceptance of tourism as socially and financially constructed place. Jensen describes local Mayas' estrangement from their own historical identities, as produced by the government and private sector at the Tulum Ruins, a walled ancient Mayan city in Mexico's eastern Yucatan. Nelson shifts our attention to a private enclave resort in the Caribbean, created by a cruise ship enterprise, to examine the colonially shaped interactions among expatriate tourists, Haitian tourists, and Haitian nationals in what he calls "bubbles of tropicality."

Our final section looks at sustainable tourism initiatives and the negotiation of global politics, international agendas, and national and local government policies. Fueled by transnational economic influences and a cultural shift in environmental awareness, sustainable and eco-friendly tourism are gaining popularity among tourists, tour operators, and national governments. The chapters reveal both the neocolonial footprint of Western sustainable philosophy and aesthetics and the resultant implementation, financial, and ontological challenges confronting local communities. Fischer and Pierce take us to Isla Mujeres, Mexico, where tourists, expats, and local Isleño communities opposed the local government ordinance banning beach and street vendors. Riemer, Velempini, and Maruatona close the section with a theoretical look at safari and community-hosted safari tourism in Botswana, and the dislodging effect of the government's internationally supported hunting ban on local communities.

As a whole, *Front and Back Stage of Tourism Performance* reminds us that those items on our travel bucket lists are complicated when we expand the frame of our inquiry. The inclusion of power as anthropological analytic shreds the veil of romance and reveals neocolonial relationships around race and class, mapped by Global North and South, and driven by global flows of finances, ideas, people, and images. Places on tourist bucket lists and items on state development priorities, these points of contact afford a unique vantage from which to view the negotiation of cultural identity, entrepreneurial strategizing, and natural resource management as global politics and relations of difference.

References

Anderson, B. (1983/1991/2006). *Imagined Communities: Reflections on the origin and spread of nationalism*. London: Verso.

Appadurai, A. (1990). Disjuncture and difference in the global cultural economy. *Theory, Culture & Society*. 7, 295–310.

Appadurai, A. (1996). *Modernity at Large: Cultural dimensions of globalization*. Minneapolis: University of Minnesota Press.

Azhar, M.u.R., & Masood, S. (2018). Tourism causes uneven development: A case study of natural and cultural heritage tourism in Pakistan. *Journal of Advance Research in Social Science & Humanities*. 4(7), 6–14.

Bacevich, A.J. (2016). Ending endless war. *Foreign Affairs*. 95(5), 36–44.

Batchelor, B. (2017). Thinking through tourism in San Cristóbal de las Casas, Chiapas: Transnational as a methodology. *Transnational Social Review*. 7(3), 320–324.

Becker, E. (2013). *Overbooked: The exploding business of travel and tourism*. New York: Simon & Schuster.

Burgen, S. (2018, June 25). "Tourists go home, refugees welcome": Why Barcelona chose migrants over visitors. *The Guardian*. Retrieved November 20, 2018 from https://www.theguardian.com/cities/2018/jun/25/tourists-go-home-refugees-welcome-why-barcelona-chose-migrants-over-visitors.

Burns, G.L. (2004). Anthropology and tourism: Past contributions and future theoretical challenges. *Anthropological Forum*. 14(1), 5–22.

Butler, R.W. (2006). *The Tourism Area Life Cycle, Vol. 1, Applications and Modifications*. Clevedon, UK: Channel View Publications.

Cater, C., & Cloke, P. (2007). Bodied in action: The performativity of adventure tourism. *Anthropology Today*. 23(6), 13–16.

Chambers, E. (1997). *Tourism and Culture: An applied perspective*. Albany: State University of New York Press.

Chambers, E. (2009). *Native Tours: The anthropology of travel and tourism*. Longrove, IL: Waveland Press.

Chen, G., & Huang, S.S. (2018). Towards an improved typology approach to segmenting cultural tourists. *International Journal of Tourism Research*. 20(2), 247–255.

Cohen, E. (1979). A phenomenology of tourist experiences. *Sociology*. 13(2), 179–201.

Craik, J. (1997). The culture of tourism. In Rojek, C., & Urry, J. (eds.) *Touring Cultures: Transformations of travel and theory* (pp. 113–136). New York: Routledge.

Crang, P. (1997). Performing the tourist product. In Rojek, C., & Urry, J. (eds.) *Touring Cultures: Transformations of travel and theory* (pp. 137–151). New York: Routledge.

Crawshaw, C., & Urry, J. (1997). Tourism and the photographic eye. In Rojek, C., & Urry, J. (eds.) *Touring Cultures: Transformations of travel and theory* (pp. 176–195). New York: Routledge.

de Santana Pinho, P. (2016). *Mapping Diaspora: African American roots tourism in Brazil*. Chapel Hill: University of North Carolina Press.

del Marmol, C., Morell, M., & Chalcraft, Jasper (2017). *The Making of Heritage: Seduction and disenchantment*. New York: Routledge.

Desmond, J.C. (2011). Touring the dead: Imagination, embodiment and affect in Gunther Von Hagens' Body Worlds exhibitions. In Skinner, J., & Theodossopoulos, D. (eds.) *Great Expectations: Imagination and anticipation in tourism* (pp. 174–195). New York: Berghahn.

Dilworth, L. (2001). Tourists and Indians in Fred Harvey's Southwest. In Wrobel, D.M., & Long, P.T. (eds.). *Seeing and Being Seen: Tourism in the American West* (pp. 142–164). Lawrence: University Press of Kansas.

Dogan, H.Z. (1989). Forms of adjustment: Sociocultural impacts of tourism. *Annals of Tourism Research*. 6, 216–236.

Doner, R.F. (2009). *The Politics of Uneven Development: Thailand's economic growth in comparative perspective*. Cambridge: Cambridge University Press.

Duggan, B.J. (1997). Tourism, cultural authenticity, and the native crafts cooperative: The Eastern Cherokee experience. In Chambers, E. (ed.) *Tourism and Culture: An applied perspective* (pp. 31–58). Albany: State University of New York Press.

Ellwood, M. (2018, October 24). The underside of Venice's overtourism problem. *Conde Nast Traveler*. Retrieved December 15, 2018 from https://www.cntraveler.com/story/the-other-side-of-venices-overtourism.

Frenzel, F., Koens, K., & Steinbrink, M. (2012). *Slum Tourism: Poverty, power and ethics*. New York: Routledge.

Garcia-Fuentes, J.-M. (2016). Reinventing and reshaping Gaudí: From nation and religion to tourism, architecture, conflict and change in Barcelona's tourist imaginary. In Gravari-Barbas, M., & Graburn, N. (eds.) *Tourism Imaginaries at the Disciplinary Crossroads*. New York: Routledge.

Gelbman, A., & Maoz, D. (2012). Island of peace or island of war: Tourist guiding. *Annals of Tourism Research*. 39(1), 108–133.

Girard, A., & Schéou, B. (2016). Fair tourism and the "authentic" encounter: Realization of a rite of recognition in the context of the myth of authenticity. In Gravari-Barbas, M., & Graburn, N. (eds.) *Tourism Imaginaries at the Disciplinary Crossroads* (pp. 130–146). New York:Routledge.

Goffman, E. (1956). *Presentation of Self in Everyday Life*. New York: Anchor Books.

Graburn., N., & Gravari-Barbas, M. (2016). Introduction: Tourism imaginaries at the disciplinary crossroads. In Gravari-Barbas, M., & Graburn, N. (eds.) *Tourism Imaginaries at the Disciplinary Crossroads*. New York: Routledge.

Graham-McLay, C. (2019). Bad guests push New Zealand to rethink its welcome mat. *The New York Times*. A9.

Gravari-Barbas, M., & Graburn, N., eds. (2016). *Tourism Imaginaries at the Disciplinary Crossroads*. New York: Routledge.

Hannam, K. (2009). The end of tourism? Nomadology and the mobilities paradigm. In Tribe, J. (ed.) *Philosophical Issues in Tourism*. Bristol, UK: Channel View Publications.

Iles, J. (2011). Going on holiday to imagine war: The Western Front. In Skinner, J., & Theodossopoulos, D. (eds.) *Great Expectations: Imagination and anticipation in tourism* (pp. 155–173). New York: Berghahn.

Lacan, J. (1977). *Écrits, a selection* (A. Sheridan, trans.). New York: Norton.

Laverdure, J. (2016). Crafting archaism, cultural entrepreneurs, indigenous masks and the political and tourist imaginaries of heritage in Central America. In Gravari-Barbas, M., &

Graburn, N. (eds.) *Tourism Imaginaries at the Disciplinary Crossroads.* New York: Routledge.

Lea, J. (1988). *Tourism and Development in the Third World.* London: Routledge.

Lennon, J., & Foley, M. (2000). *Dark Tourism: The attraction of death and disaster.* New York: Continuum.

MacCannell, D. (1973). Staged authenticity: Arrangements of social space in tourist settings. *American Journal of Sociology.* 79(3), 589–603.

MacCannell, D. (1976/1999). *The Tourist: A new theory of the leisure class.* Berkeley: University of California Press.

Mancinelli, F. (2014). Shifting values of "primitiveness" among the Zafimaniry of Madagascar: An anthropological approach to tourist mediators' discourses. *Journal of Tourism and Cultural Change.* 12(3), 224–236.

McKay, J. (2018). *Transnational Tourism Experiences at Gallipoli.* New York: Springer.

McKercher, B., & du Cros, H. (2003). Testing a cultural tourism typology. *International Journal of Tourism Research.* 5, 45–58.

Meiu, G.P. (2011). On difference, desire, and the aesthetics of the unexpected: The White Masai in Kenyan tourism. In Skinner, J., & Theodossopoulos, D. (eds.) *Great Expectations: Imagination and anticipation in tourism.* New York: Berghahn.

Neumann, M. (1999). *On the Rim: Looking for the Grand Canyon.* Minneapolis: University of Minnesota Press.

The New York Times (2019). Calling all travelers advertisement. January 16, A7.

Nyaupane, G.P., & Andereck, K.L. (2016). A typology of cultural heritage attraction visitors. *Travel and Tourism Research Association: Advancing Tourism Research Globally.* 63.

Pannett, R. (2018, May 22). Anger over tourists swarming vacation hot spots sparks global backlash. *Wall Street Journal.* Retrieved November 1, 2018 from https://www.wsj.com/articles/anger-over-tourists-swarming-vacation-hot-spots-sparks-global-backlash-1527000130.

Plog, S.C. (1972). Why destination areas rise and fall in popularity. *Cornell Hospitality Quarterly.* 14(4), 55–58.

Pruitt, D., & LaFont, S. (1995). For love and money: Romance tourism in Jamaica. *Annals of Tourism Research.* 22(2), 422–440.

Reed, A. (2017). *Pilgrimage Tourism of Diaspora Africans to Ghana.* New York: Routledge.

Regnault, M. (2016). Tourism imaginaries and political discourses of Mayotte Island. In Gravari-Barbas, M., & Graburn, N. (eds.). *Tourism Imaginaries at the Disciplinary Crossroads.* New York: Routledge.

Rickly, J., Hannam, K., & Mostafanezhad, M. (2017). *Tourism and Leisure Mobilities: Politics, work, and play.* New York: Routledge.

Ritzeron, G., & Liska, A. (1997). "McDisneyization" and post-tourism: Complementary perspectives on contemporary tourism. In Rojek, C., & Urry, J. (eds.) *Touring Cultures: Transformations of travel and theory* (pp. 96–109). New York: Routledge.

Roser, M. (2019). Tourism. OurWorldInData.org. Retrieved from https://ourworldindata.org/tourism.

Ross, R. (2016). Evangeline, Acadians, and tourism imaginaries. In Gravari-Barbas, M., & Graburn, N. (eds.) *Tourism Imaginaries at the Disciplinary Crossroads.* New York: Routledge.

Salazar, N.B. (2010). *Envisioning Eden: Mobilizing imaginaries in tourism and beyond.* New York: Berghahn.

Salazar, N.B. (2012). Tourism imaginaries: A conceptual approach. *Annals of Tourism Research.* 39(2), 863–882.

Sammells, C. (2014). Bargaining under thatch roof: Tourism and the allure of poverty in highland Bolivia. In Picard, D., & DiGiovine, M.A. (eds.) *Tourism and the Power of Otherness: Seductions of difference* (pp. 124–137). Bristol, UK: Channel View Publications.

Skinner, J. (2011). Displeasure on "Pleasure Island": Tourist expectation and desire on and off the Cuban dance floor. In Skinner, J., & Theodossopoulos, D. (eds.) *Great Expectations: Imagination and anticipation in tourism* (pp. 116–136). New York: Berghahn.

Skinner, J., & Theodossopoulos, D. (2011). *Great Expectations: Imagination and anticipation in tourism.* New York: Berghahn.

Smith, O. (2017). The 51 destinations where tourists outnumber locals. *The Telegraph.* Retrieved December 15, 2018 from https://www.telegraph.co.uk/travel/maps-and-graphics/countries-where-tourists-outnumber-locals/.

Smith, O. (2018, October 2). World's most popular cities for tourists 2018 named. *Traveler.* Retrieved December 15, 2018 at http://www.traveller.com.au/worlds-most-popular-cities-for-tourists-2018-named-h164d2.

Smith, V.L. (1977/1989). *Hosts and Guests: The anthropology of tourism.* Philadelphia: University of Pennsylvania Press.

Smith, V.L., & Brent, M. (2001). *Hosts and Guests Revisited: Tourism issues in the 21st century.* Elmsford, NY: Cognizant LLC.

Smith, V.L., & Eadington, W.R. (1992). *Tourism Alternatives: Potentials and problems in the development of tourism.* Philadelphia: University of Pennsylvania Press.

Speier, A.R. (2011). Health tourism in a Czech health spa. *Anthropology & Medicine.* 18(1), 55–66.

Stone, P.R. (2006). A dark tourism spectrum: Towards a typology of death and macabre related tourist sites, attractions, and exhibitions. *Tourism.* 54(2), 145–160.

Strauss, C. (2006). The imaginary . *Anthropological Theory.* 6(3), 322–344.

Stronza, A. (2001). Anthropology of tourism: Forging new ground for ecotourism and other alternatives. *Annual Review of Anthropology.* 30, 261–283.

Taylor, C. (2003). *Modern Social Imaginaries.* Durham, NC: Duke University Press.

Torres, R.M., & Momsen, J.D. (2005). Gringolandia: The construction of a new tourist space in Mexico. *Annals of the Association of American Geographers.* 95(2), 314–335.

Urry, J. (1990/2002). *The Tourist Gaze.* London: SAGE.

Withey, L. (1997). *Grand Tours and Cooks' Tours: A history of leisure travel, 1750–1915.* New York: William Morrow.

World Tourism Organization (2019). Webpage. Retrieved February 11, 2019from http://www2.unwto.org/content/who-we-are-0.

Xiang, B., Toyota, M., & Chee, H.L. (2013). Global track, national vehicle: Transnationalism in medical tourism in Asia. *Journal of Transnational Studies.* 5(1), 27–53.

Part 1

Managing Tourism during War Time

1 Loose lips can sink tourism

True lies and evasion during Nepal's Maoist insurgency

Sharon J. Hepburn

What if lies, evasions, and credible denials could constitute an authentic encounter?[1] I would say that during the People's War in Nepal they did. Sometimes what can be said and seen, and what must be silenced and hidden, is not just a matter of performing for tourists; it can be a matter of life and death. During the People's War between the Communist Party of Nepal-Maoist (CPN-M) and the state security forces (1996–2006), a culture of silence pervaded the social life of non-aligned citizens. Much of Nepali life was lived on front stages where people were silent about the war and wary of who might overhear their conversations. Likewise, with war-curious tourists, Nepalis were usually similarly reticent, playing the role of "person who knows nothing." In such circumstances, maybe a lie can be truthful to the reality of an encounter between the tourist and the toured. Maybe in some circumstances a lie is the only sensible option the toured has.

I arrived in the town of Pokhara, Nepal, in December 2001, a month into a national state of emergency in which most human rights were suspended. Maoists usually concealed their presence from tourists, but there was one location—on the trails near Pokhara—in which they openly interacted with tourists. Tourists generally singled out these encounters as—in our terms—their authentic back stage experiences of the war. And yet the real war was all around them, in the lives of civilians the tourists encountered. This was hidden by a pervasive secrecy born of fear, and hidden so effectively that many tourists thought "everything seems fine here" when really it was not. Bruner discards the idea of "authenticity" as a red herring, to be examined only when tourists or locals evoke the concept (2004, 5). Many tourists valued and talked about their meeting with "real" (i.e. authentic) insurgents on the trails. But in the end, perhaps ironically, the most authentic encounter they experienced was in the town, when much was concealed. Here the local's "little lie" (MacCannell 1976, 93) is not a

---

1   This chapter has no photos. The research concerns people who guarded information closely. Likewise, and in respect for this, I was cautious about what notes I had on me at any time that could possibly have been read or confiscated. I emailed my notes from and to various accounts each day, and then deleted them from my laptop. I took no photos.

show or mystification, but is practice coterminous with the rest of their life, given the constraints and dangers they faced.

Pokhara is a popular tourist destination with a subtropical climate, a lake, and fine Himalayan vistas. Most non-Indian tourists stay by the lakeside with its array of hotels, restaurants, boats for hire, and trekking agencies. Although this chapter is about the conditions of December 2001 and January 2002, it is informed by my residence in Nepal for a total of four years over the past 30, including five one-month trips during the war. I told people I was researching tourists and travel writing. I only directly asked Nepalis about the conflict if I knew them quite well. I extensively talked to tourists about their assessment of risk, their motives, and their experiences.

Meeting a real insurgent: The Maoist as tourist attraction

Maoists met tourists on the mountain trails, and asked for money to support the insurgency and nascent regime. Maoists and tourists performed almost routinized interactions that tourists recognized as "meeting the Maoist." These became the key incidents in their traveler's stories about their mountain trek during the war. The encounters were routinized as the cadre had their orders of what to say and do. The tourists also knew their role, having consulted other tourists, online information sources, and Maoist pronouncements. This then is a front stage interaction, between (after Smith 1987) "hosts" (albeit insurgents with guns), and "guests" (those who would pay to be able to stay).

The tourists came to trek during the war despite embassy warnings and worldwide security concerns. Many found reassurance in the Nepal Tourism Board's announcement (2001) that "visitors experience near normalcy in most of the prominent tourist destinations." Many knew that the Maoist leader, Prachandra, had announced that tourists were safe provided they gave money when asked. Once convinced of their own immunity, many tourists considered this an ideal time to visit Nepal, especially with low prices and empty lodges.

By December 2001, police north of Pokhara were unable to defend themselves against surprise attacks, and police posts along the trails were abandoned. On these unpoliced trails tourists met Maoists and their demands for a "donation." The Maoists carried guns and grenades, and the groups had one member who could speak at least rudimentary English. In exchange for cash the tourist received a "Maoist visa" granting permission to travel in the area. This served as a receipt that other Maoists in the area would recognize as proof that payment (one to three US dollars per day) had been made. The receipts bore images of communist leaders including Stalin or Mao, and some commentary about the cause. While some tourists feared meeting Maoists, others wanted to. Although toward the end of the war, tourist encounters with Maoists became more strained (Baral 2013), in 2002 many enjoyed meeting the Maoists, and some sought them out as an extra perk of travel in wartime. These visitors heard firsthand about their cause, and came away with both an authentic Maoist visa, the one material souvenir of the insurgency, and an encounter with a "real insurgent" to add to their store of travel experiences. The encounter also yielded a story to tell, as tourists in trekking lodges and restaurants compared adventures and Maoist visas. Some tourists actually wanted to give, inspired by the social justice concerns of the "very nice young men" with guns by the trailside. These guns, though: even the pleasant interactions sometimes sparked dissonance as the young insurgents generally held a weapon, and tourists often suspected that other cadre stayed hidden nearby, slightly off the "stage."

Where are the back stage and front stage here? The Maoists encounters with tourists on the trails were framed by an historically deep back stage. Rallies, idealism, the history of oppression in Nepal, and how that has played out in thousands of lives formed the hidden backdrop of these interactions. Maoists described this political context to tourists to justify their armed requests for money. What they did not tell—what was unseen and unsaid—was that Maoists controlled the countryside by fear and the threat of bodily harm (see below). That was all tidily hidden though hinted at by the weapon clearly in sight. The situation could change quickly if a tourist resisted; there might be threats, or a tourist's porter with an acute understanding of the situation might encourage them to pay. Maoists rarely harmed tourists, but they certainly obstructed their way and frightened their porters. Ongoing and potential violence shaped the encounter between tourists and Maoist Nepalis, but a cooperative tourist would generally have a friendly encounter. The tourist had the frisson of excitement of being close to the authentic, the real insurgent, and got a real Maoist visa. As one told me: "Where else do you get that? And safely?" In these encounters between clearly identifiable Maoists and tourists, only the tourist who resists paying fees risks harm.

The rest of this chapter concerns encounters tourists had with other Nepalis, and the conditions, largely unseen and untold, in which they took place. The "stage" exists any time a tourist says to a Nepali that "everything seems fine here" and the Nepali says "yes no problem here," or "the problem is off in other places." In asking their questions the tourist risked nothing, but Nepalis potentially risked much in answering. The ephemeral stage is formed in that moment of asking, exists as the Nepali answers, and effectively dismantled as the tourist is reassured, and the Nepali (and Nepali tourism) are protected.

Nepalis were variously situated in the conflict, and likewise in encounters with tourists. Some worked in the tourist industry, some fought as insurgents, some worked in the security forces, and some were simply non-aligned civilians trying to survive between two warring forces. Nepalis of all kinds encountered other Nepalis of course, with or without tourists around. In these encounters, to see, speak, or remain silent in part depended on the audience and the stakes. Behavior is always adapted to context, and much of Nepali life itself at this time was particularly influenced by the very thing MacCannell (1973) argued characterizes tourist experiences: performances that hide and performances that reveal—or selectively reveal—truth.

Thus, tourists and Nepalis met in contexts shaped by the conditions of war—conditions of wary silence in which it was often prudent to act as "someone who knows nothing." The complexity of the interface between tourists and Nepalis during the decade-long People's War was marked by silences and a "nod" (from Nepalis) to what tourists see as their authentic encounters (described above), implicitly confirming that the tourist saw the "back stage" and what was really going on. There was no fixed stage—as in a staged cultural performance—for these tourist–Nepali encounters, but there was the unsaid and unseen. There was potential violence, and there was the ever-present fear that formed the back stage of these encounters, much as it did when Nepalis encountered other Nepalis.

A culture of fear and silence: Historical, geopolitical trajectories

Why the fear when Nepalis encounter other Nepalis? In 1996 the Communist Party of Nepal-Maoist launched the People's War to establish a communist republic. The conflict lasted a decade. An Amnesty International (2002) report documenting the period covered in this chapter notes the widespread use of arbitrary arrest, illegal detention, disappearance, torture, and extra-judicial killings by the Royal Nepalese Army (RNA). Maoists frequently killed or maimed people who did not cooperate with their cause. Through this time a culture of silence emerged (Gautam 2004). People on both sides and non-aligned citizens caught in the middle all feared the consequences of being overheard by the "wrong" people.

"Loose Lips Sinks Ships" was a slogan used in United States propaganda supporting World War II efforts. This, and the British equivalent, "Careless Talk Costs Lives," admonished people to avoid indiscretion, especially involving any information that the enemy could use. Posters to discourage reticence were not needed during Nepal's war. Loose Lips during the conflict could endanger neighbors, relatives, or yourself. Parents taught children selective silence (Pettigrew 2007, 2013). Nepalis were cautious in talking about the situation to curious tourists, who came for beauty or adventure and seeing no evidence of conflict asked, "I guess there's no war influence here?" Nepalis generally answered "That's right. It's fine here." For tourists, on the whole, it was. Nonetheless, the war permeated Pokhara, including the lakeside area of tourist hotels and restaurants.

In January 2002 violence escalated in the state of emergency. This back stage of fear and caution, to which tourists were not privy, is an example of what can happen on the ground when global and local geopolitical forces intersect. In the wake of coordinated attacks by Al Qaeda upon the United States of America on September 11, 2001, security concerns and awareness of the United States' "war on terror" contributed to tourism's decline worldwide. Nepal's case is interesting in that this external political event coincided with internal political struggles—namely a civil war and the massacre of most of the royal family—exacerbating the local effects of a worldwide phenomenon. In Nepal, arrivals dropped from about 464,000 in 2000 to fewer than 216,000 in 2002 (MTCA 2003).

A half-century of political experiments and change culminated in the People's War in Nepal. From 1846 to 1951 a dominant elite, the Rana Dynasty, enforced an isolationist policy. Ruling Nepal like a vast feudal estate, they enacted a legal code that allowed them to extract labor and resources from a rural peasantry. Political movements elsewhere inspired dissent and when the Rana regime fell in 1951, political experimentation began. In 1960 King Mahendra implemented a one-party system of government. Many felt this perpetuated the inequities of the Rana period under a different guise. After three decades, catching the wave of democracy movements worldwide around 1990, a popular movement to estab-lish a multiparty democracy under a constitutional monarch succeeded. Citizens could once again form political parties, freely debate, and contest in elections. Variously inspired left-wing parties with close links to India became vocal after decades of enforced silence. After a few years of the new order, Maoist members of the Communist Party of Nepal-Maoist found the pace of structural change too slow and the persistence of inequality still encoded in law unacceptable. When the Nepal Maoists launched their People's War in 1996, they intended to replace a multiparty democracy with a communist republic. In five years the conflict grew to a guerilla force in the offensive position against the RNA. By the time they signed a peace accord in 2006, the Maoists had displaced the elected government throughout most of the country, and nearly a half-million people had been forced from their homes or land. The economy was in shambles, 13,000 people had died as a direct result of the insurgency, thousands more were maimed, and countless others missing (Bhattarai, Conway, & Shrestha 2005; Hutt 2004; Lawoti and Pahari 2010; Shah 2008; Thapa and Sijapati 2003).

In January 2002 casualties were rising dramatically. Before this, the world media did not widely report on the conflict, and tourism steadily grew (Bhattarai et al. 2005). But after the events of 2001, both inside and outside Nepal, arrivals declined rapidly. Inside Nepal in June 2001, King Birendra and most of his family (the royal lineage) were massacred in Kathmandu. In the midst of the national mood of shock, suspicion, and uncertainty which followed, the Maoists expanded their campaign.

Outside Nepal, the events of September 11 unfolded in the United States, precipitating a decline in tourism worldwide and a growth of discourses on terror and international relations. On November 26, 2001, after only six months on the throne, the new king, Gyanendra, declared a national state of emergency (noted above). Echoing post-9/11 global refrains of the "war on terrorism," the Nepali government promulgated the TADO (Terrorist and Disruptive Activities [Control and Punishment] Ordinance), identified the Maoists as terrorists, and for the first time deployed the RNA to help stop Maoist expansion. King Gyanendra suspended rights to freedom of expres-sion, peaceful assembly, privacy, and information, and rights against preventative detention (Hutt 2004). In the post-9/11 world campaign to name and eradicate "terrorists," the United States and Britain gave military aid to help Nepal overcome their recently named "terrorists." Thus as the result of policies spawned by events half a world away, the recently engaged RNA was well armed and casualties mounted dramatically. As mentioned above, an Amnesty International (2002) report documenting this period described the widespread use of arbitrary arrest, illegal detention, disappearance, torture, and extra-judicial killing by the RNA. It also noted widespread killing and maiming by Maoists of people not cooperating with their cause. The report expressed great concern about the overall deteriorating human rights situation, and abuses by the army, the police, and the Maoists.

Maoist leaders issued statements asserting that tourists were safe. Still, by the close of 2001, Indian visitors had decreased by 24 percent, American by 60 percent, British by 45 percent, and Japanese by 63 percent (MTCA 2003). Lisle (2018), Butler and Suntikul (2013), Hall and O'Sullivan (1996), and Richter (1992) have shown how tourism can be affected by unpredictable internal and external influences, such as political instability and international conflict. Likewise, Bhattarai describes the effects on the economy:

> Regardless of one's views and interpretations of the ongoing cycle of political turmoil and violence, there is little doubt they have engendered a profound sense of public fear, thereby greatly worsening the woes of Nepal's tourism …. Life revolving around tourism, has, in essence, taken a heavy toll.
>
> (Bhattarai et al. 2005, 684)

Fear and uncertainty in difficult times

Like Bhattarai, others have noted the pervasive sense of fear felt by Nepalis in conflict-affected areas. In my five research periods during the war, friends told me of innumerable specific incidents: an elderly woman who had been my neighbor in the early 1990s was alarmed by RNA soldiers coming to the door at night, "just coming in, with no respect" to look for Maoists; a friend and his family received threats from the Maoists and paid "donations" because their son was in the army; a man I taught school with in 1985 had his hand amputated because he questioned Maoists in the village he taught in and refused to pay a punitive "donation."

The Maoists used violence and its threat to displace the state in wide swathes of rural Nepal, but they also used violence against civilians to quell opposition, punish people who informed on them, collect resources, and enact their policies. People suspected of being "class enemies" received threatening visits, often involving beatings, maiming, or death. The Maoist militia took "actions" unannounced and often in public, ranging from public humiliation or torture to death. These actions successfully deterred resistance. Fear for civilians was not continuous and unmitigated. Nonetheless Maoists spreading fear through the threat of violence, paired with openly conducted atrocities, effectively established their power and control (Amnesty International 1999, 2000, 2002; Fujikura 2003; Graham 2007, 238; Lawoti & Pahari 2010; Lecomte-Tilouine 2013; Pettigrew 2003, 2013).

Many non-aligned (non-Maoist, non-military) civilians felt like "a yam between two rocks" (Pettigrew 2003, 2013), that is, something soft and breakable between two hard forces. Non-aligned civilians had to negotiate interactions with Maoists so as to not seem a "class enemy"; these yams were also careful to avoid drawing the attention of the police and armed forces.

Silence and suspicion in the back stage(s)

The troubles were hidden from view and hidden by silence. Nepali reticence with tourists formed part of the wider culture of silence (Gautam 2004) that grew with the insurgency in the atmosphere described above. Maya, a 60-year-old woman whose family had owned a restaurant and hotel (where I first stayed in 1986), told me, "Of course we don't talk to tourists about such things. We want them to come. It is safe for them here, and we need them to come. But we also don't talk because we don't know who is listening." She lowered her voice and subtly glanced around to see who might be nearby, behavior I saw repeatedly with others. Pettigrew describes how caregivers raising children in a rural area during the war taught them to be silent and cautious, and rehearsed them in how to answer questions from all soldiers, whether Maoist or RNA, as it "could be a matter of life and death" (2007, 324). Commenting on this emerging practice of verbal restraint, a Nepali friend told me that he was shocked and disturbed by the changes he saw in his native village when he visited in 1998: "We used to sit outside and talk in the afternoon. Now that is gone, that nice part of village life. Now people stay inside." His father admonished him not to "walk around just talking about things." Deepak needed no persuading as he knew that recently a village man, the one person in the area who had a phone and "heard every-thing," was accused of being an informant and killed by Maoists.

Silence protects when trust can be dangerous. Lodge owner Maya's com-ments (and Jack's below) echo what Pettigrew and Adhikari conclude, that "people knew that the Maoist surveillance-society was perpetuated by local collusion .... Villagers ... betrayed each other. .... There was increasing uncertainty about ... the allegiances and motivations of even the most trusted confidantes" (2009, 404). People were even more fearful of the army and their informers. In her ethnographic work in a village under Maoist control, Lecomte-Tilouine describes what she calls "paralyzing fright," and explains that "one of the first things that was explained to me was that fright left vil-lagers feeling constrained in their freedom of speech and action" (2009, 388). She found that the

> new complicated communication strategy was ... often based on lies ....
> It was as if the revolution had entirely blurred communications .... It was

only at night, or in the forest, that people started to open up, to express their deepest anguish about the two opposing dangers hanging over them.

People would even fear that "their close relations would pass on 'reports' to the Maoists and denounce them as 'informants'" (2009, 399).

The unsaid and unseen along Pokhara's lakeside

When I arrived in December 2001 the lakeside area was very quiet, with many stores and stalls closed. Certainly the Pokhara area escaped the full impact and brutality of the war, but in 2002 on the Pokhara lakeshore, behind the appearance that "everything looks fine here," it was not. Here are some brief portraits of people a tourist might see as they looked around and thought everything looked fine. These portraits are all of people I had known before my 2002 visit.

A guesthouse family

I was surprised at the number of young people working or living at the Surya Guesthouse when I arrived. This family enterprise usually had a few children and youths around, but now there were over a dozen. These were all family members, sent from villages by parents who feared for their safety, or feared that Maoists might abduct them, or inspire them to join up. The rural to urban migration propelled by the conflict was already well underway.

A long-time expatriate restaurant owner

Jack came to Nepal in the 1960s to serve in the United States Peace Corps. He stayed, working in development, and eventually settled in Pokhara to open a hotel near the lakeside. I saw Jack in 2002 at his hotel's restaurant. I mentioned that my project this time was to write about tourism during the insurgency. He acknowledged it was a "good topic," and "resourceful, given the situation," and then wavered. "You're not writing about me are you?" with a "you'd better not be" look. I said, no, and he finished "not until it's long over anyway."

Noting the clear presence of police and army, I asked Jack if Maoists were active around the lakeside. "Of course, the place is crawling with them," he said, and then described how their presence affects daily life. For example, he raised pigs to supply meat to the restaurant. He lamented the need to butcher "the old way" by slitting the animal's throat. He preferred a quicker and less painful gunshot, but he knew the sound of a shot would alert everyone that someone had a gun. Jack explained that "the police or soldiers would come figuring I might be a Maoist, and the Maoists would come to get the gun." He said this was just an example. "Everyone is watching everyone." Jack paid money to both sides. Like other businesses he gave Maoists a regular "donation." To the police and army personnel, some of whom were restaurant customers, he gave what amounts to "protection money." "Not that they'd necessarily protect you, but at least they'd be less likely to bother you or your staff," he explained. Jack saw these payments as ways to keep people from harming his staff. Some likely had family and friends directly hurt by or involved in the war. Some were trying to avoid involvement. His staff all knew not to talk about the conflict with tourists, as "we don't know who is listening," or who the tourist might repeat things to. Jack noted the excitement of some tourists enjoying their very safe visit to a "boutique war." He also saw the potential risks of tourists relating what they had learnt about "people at such and such lodge," or "the guy who talked to us at such and such restaurant." He saw the danger of their Loose Lips if they talked freely about people they encountered as part of their experience of "finding out about the war." Jack did not want police coming to question his staff, and did not want Maoists coming because "someone said something" negative, positive, or ambiguous about either side to a tourist.

Like so many others, Jack was a yam between two rocks, trying to keep business going enough to pay his staff, trying to steer straight down the middle of the minefield of social relations and factions. His situation was different only in that he was there at all because of a previous geopolitical configuration, that of the political economy and idealism of the 1960s which inspired the Peace Corps. And even though he was a fair-skinned American, he was part of the situation to which most tourists were curious, yet blind. He was very much in the back stage, managing the production (of silence) for foreign and Nepali audiences of all kinds.

A dishwasher from the Dhorpatan Valley

Ram was born in a remote village in the Dhorpatan Valley, and in 2002 the 22-year-old washed dishes and cleaned at a restaurant close to Jack's. Dhorpatan is just to the east of Rukum and Rolpa, the heartland of the insurgency. Ram's brother joined the Maoists voluntarily having seen since childhood the violence that those with power can exert without cause or consequence. Ram's brother joined the Maoists in 1996, early in the conflict. Like many people in the Dhorpatan Valley area, since their early teen years Ram and his brother had traveled south in the winter looking for work, and had found it in the tourism industry. I first met Ram in 1997 in the kitchen of a trekking lodge north of Pokhara. He was portering for an Italian woman, and did not mention his brother. When I saw him in 2002 he told me about his brother. Ram's family had not seen the brother for over three years. Ram asked me where they could find out if he was dead or arrested, without risk to himself. He was glad to be away from his village, as the police (and the RNA) came through looking for Maoists; the Maoists would come through looking for recruits and wanting to know if anyone was passing information to or helping the army. The RNA soldiers and police intimidated by simply asking his parents about their sons and pressing for information. Both parents knew they could be arrested and tortured if the police had any real suspicion, or were given a tip that their son was a Maoist. So Ram washed dishes and cleaned in a restaurant along the lakeside, in return for food, a very minimal stipend, and a place to sleep in the restaurant kitchen at night. These conditions of work are not unusual for Nepal, and employment in any capacity lessened the chance that he would be thought a Maoist. He was one of the thousands already effectively displaced by the war.

Mani Tamang working at a restaurant

In the early 1990s I researched the production of religious art for the tourist market, and during that pre-insurgency time I talked to the handful of painters and dealers who had settled in Pokhara. One small shop stall I visited was about ten minutes' walk along the lakeshore from Jack's. It was a bamboo construction with an open front, exhibiting a few dozen paintings for sale. The couple who ran the stall in 1992 had a young son, who in 2002 would have been 20. He had kept company with Maoists and active sympathizers in the bazaar area of Pokhara, and then left in 2000, planning to train in the Maoist heartland of eastern Nepal. Like Ram's brother, the son had not been heard from since. When he joined the Maoists his parents were partly relieved as they felt it was dangerous for him to associate with the people he did. At least with the Maoists cadres he was out of sight much of the time. The parents feared that police could come any time for questioning, or worse if their son was captured and betrayed his origins and his family. The couple also had a 13-year-old daughter and prayed she did not choose to join. I am not sure what happened; the stall was gone the next year.

***

In presenting the situations of the Surya family, Jack, Ram, and Mani, I depict myself as in the back stage, a place where intimacies were shared. "We're frightened," they said, "and we don't know what will happen," and "I'm worried about my brother." It is significant that these conversations were with people I had known from before. It is significant that I spoke Nepali well, and obviously knew something of the situation. It is also significant that most revelations were accompanied by requests for help of some kind with troubles relating to the conflict.

In these portraits we see people who worked along the lakeshore where tourists thought that "everything seems fine." There were thousands with similar stories, and certainly many more to be heard along the lakeshore. There were the stories of the non-aligned people (the non-Maoists, non-military, the "yams") in the back stage of tourist–Nepali encounters. Tourist restaurants and the people who work in them are by their nature "for the tourist," but are not in any usual sense the kind of authentic Nepali life some tourists might want to encounter. Yet they contained the stories the tourists implicitly asked about when they said "Is everything fine here?" And Nepalis carried the pervading norms of how to live with fear into tourist interactions. "Of course it's OK here, no problems here, we're safe here, no Maoists here…" and "I know nothing about it," reflecting back the image the tourist already believed. In general, tourists believed that the Maoists were off in the hills far from Pokhara, and they believed they encountered the only real, local manifestation of the war while they were on the trails, paid their Maoist donation, and got a receipt. The Surya Guesthouse family, Jack, Ram, and Mani all told tourists "everything's fine here." And Nepalis would say "everything's fine here" within earshot even of the Surya Guesthouse family, Jack, Ram, and Mani, people who were in view of the tourist, but who were vulnerable and definitely not "fine." They knew they were also speaking in potential earshot of Maoists, army, police, and any number of people who might use information to target any person on any side of the conflict. The authentic war was all around the tourist. The authentic war was unseen and silent. Yet the tourist focused on the cultural performance on the trail as the "real encounter."

When a lie is the authentic

Goffman (1956) used dramaturgy to think about role performances that can be relaxed back stage. In these, people present themselves following norms and roles, and a successful interaction is one in which the audience believes the presentation. Taken up in the study of tourism by MacCannell (1973), these ideas have figured largely in discussions of authenticity and cultural performance for tourists. In these, the assumption is (after MacCannell) that the tourist wants an authentic experience to escape from some aspect of modern life, or have a particular kind of experience. This could be found, for example, in the "real Nepalis," or the "real Nepal." Given the growth of the industry, much has developed specifically for tourists, including all the businesses along the lakeside of Pokhara. Even in times of peace these were cultural productions. Nepalis are taught to and act in ways that meet tourists' expectations. They perform as waiters, as store clerks, as hoteliers, or as salespeople. Tourists generally recognize that this labor and these roles are "for the tourists," especially at restaurants with menus printed in English and hotels renting only to Western tourists. But as described above, it was the encounter with the Maoist on the trail, where money was asked for under implicit threat, that the tourist found their significant authentic encounter. They used phrases like "real Maoist," or "actual insurgent" to talk about the interactions. The war offered the thrill of a brush with danger and "part of history" to those who had safe homes to return to, resources to spend on leisure, and the nominal protection of their embassies. The encounter was a flourish to the trip and a back stage experience. After all, the Maoists were hiding from the government's security forces. Yet they were inviting them into dialogue about their struggles (as scripted by the total institution of the Maoist organization). But that was real, right?

Although Nepali tourist industry workers avoided all questions about the conflict and gave no answer aside from "that problem's somewhere else," they would usually, if asked, look at the Maoist visas when tourists had them out to look at and compare. Nepalis could communicate with tourists without indicating they had any knowledge of the conflict other than what was on the receipts, which they generally translated when asked by tourists. Then they left the interaction. The reading and translation, with no commentary, was, in my view, a collective authentication of the tourist experience. It was also a performance as a person removed from the conflict, untouched by war, and a "person who knows nothing" except for what was on the receipts.

Bruner explicitly moves away from the authentic/inauthentic, true/false, back/front, real/show oppositions developed by MacCannell and Goffman and the work they inspired. Bruner advocates that instead we look at tourist productions in their larger historical, economic, and political contexts and the particular local settings in which they take place (2004, 5). He also advocates that studies of total "tourist experiences" require ethnographies of both the tourist and the toured. In this war, presented in its historical, economic, and political context, the earlier terms of analysis remain useful and salient. In these local settings, it was the climate of fear, suspicion, and insecurity and the culture of silence they engendered that was the authentic, the true, the back, and the real. This fear permeated the country, most of the places tourists visited, and encounters between Nepalis. By the same logic it also shaped encounters between Nepalis and tourists. The collective cultural production of the tourism industry was to say "no problem here" despite who might have been right next door, or sitting at the table next to the speaker.

Ironically given the tourists' enjoyment of a real encounter, the trailside Maoist encounter was far more of a staged production and a performance than were encounters in town. The waiters' nodding at and reading the Maoist visas, the only time they spoke of the situation, confirmed it was Out There, away from here. The war was on another back stage. It was in the silences of Nepalis and in their presentation to tourists as "a person who knows nothing" that the tourists unknowingly had their authentic encounter and touched the real life of many Nepalis, even as the Nepalis concealed it. It is that concealment that was, in fact, authentic. This was all far from the "intimacy" (MacCannell 1973) that encounters back stage are thought to entail. But those were not intimate times. And this case asks us to consider that even though we can (as Bruner suggests) go beyond authentic/inauthentic, real/fake, and see productions simply as culture in their own terms, sometimes lies—or evasions, half-truths, and credible denials—could be at the heart of something integral to a toured place at a particular time. In Nepal during wartime, a lie was at the heart of an authentic encounter; the truth required that people lie.

References

Amnesty International (1999). *Nepal: Human rights at a turning point?*London: Amnesty International.

Amnesty International (2000). *Nepal: Human rights and security.* London: Amnesty International.

Amnesty International (2002). *Nepal. A Deepening Human Rights Crisis: Time for international action.* London: Amnesty International.

Baral, N. (2013). Evaluation and resilience of ecotourism in the Annapurna Conservation Area, Nepal. *Environmental Conservation.* 41(1), 84–92.

Bhattarai, K., Conway, D., & Shrestha, N. (2005). Tourism, terrorism and turmoil in Nepal. *Annals of Tourism Research.* 32(3), 669–688.

Bruner, E.M. (2004). *Culture on Tour: Ethnographies of travel.* Chicago: University of Chicago Press.

Butler, R., & Suntikul, W., eds. (2013). *Tourism and War.* London: Routledge.

Fujikura, T. (2003). The role of collective imagination in the Maoist conflict in Nepal. *Himalaya.* 23(1), 21–30.

Gautam, N. (2004). Maoist movement and development of silence culture: A case study of Dang District in mid-western Nepal, Master's, Tribhuvan University, Kirtipur.

Goffman, E. (1956). *The Presentation of Self in Everyday Life.* New York: Penguin Random House.

Graham, G. (2007). People's war? Self-interest, coercion and ideology in Nepal's Maoist insurgency. *Small Wars and Insurgencies.* 18(2), 231–248.

Hall, C., & O'Sullivan, V. (1996). Tourism, political stability and violence. In Pizam, A., & Mansfeld, Y. (eds.), *Tourism, Crime and International Security Issues* (pp. 105–121). New York: Wiley.

Hutt, M. (2004). Introduction: Monarchy, democracy and Maoism in Nepal. In Hutt, M. (ed.), *Himalayan People's War* (pp. 1–20). Bloomington: Indiana University Press.

Lawoti, M., & Pahari, A.K., eds. (2010). *The Maoist Insurgency in Nepal: Revolution in the twenty-first century.* Abingdon, UK: Routledge.

Lecomte-Tilouine, M. (2009). Terror in a Maoist model village, mid-western Nepal. *Dialectical Anthropology.* 33, 383–401.

Lecomte-Tilouine, M. (2013). *Revolution in Nepal: An anthropological and historical approach to the People's War.* Oxford: Oxford University Press.

Lisle, D. (2018). *Holidays in the Danger Zone: Entanglements of war and tourism.* Minneapolis: University of Minnesota Press.

MacCannell, D. (1973). Staged authenticity: Arrangements of social space in tourist settings. *American Journal of Sociology.* 79(3), 589–603.

MacCannell, D. (1976). *The Tourist: A new theory of the leisure class.* London: University of California Press.

MTCA (2003). *Nepal Tourism Statistics.* Kathmandu: Ministry of Tourism and Civil Aviation.

Nepal Tourism Board (2001). Press-Release on Emergency Declaration. Retrieved from www.welcomenepal.com.

Pettigrew, J. (2003). Living between the Maoists and the army in rural Nepal. *Himalaya.* 23(1), 9–20.

Pettigrew, J. (2007). Learning to be silent: Change, childhood and mental health in the Maoist insurgency in Nepal. In Ishii, H., Gellner, D.N., & Nawa, K. (eds.), *Nepalis Inside and Outside Nepal: Political and social transformations (pp. 307-348)*. Delhi: Manohar.

Pettigrew, J. (2013). *Maoists at the Hearth: Everyday life in Nepal's civil war*. Philadelphia: University of Pennsylvania Press.

Pettigrew, J., & Adhikari, K. (2009). Fear and everyday life in rural Nepal. *Dialectical Anthropology*. 33, 403–422.

Richter, L. (1992). Political instability and tourism in the third world. In Harrison, D. (ed.), *Tourism and the Less Developed Countries* (pp. 35–46). New York: Wiley.

Shah, S. (2008). Revolution and reaction in the Himalayas: Cultural resistance and the Maoist "new regime" in western Nepal. *American Ethnologist*. 35(3), 481–499.

Smith, V.L., ed. (1987). *Hosts and Guests: The anthropology of tourism*. Philadelphia: University of Pennsylvania Press.

Thapa, D., & Sijapati, B. (2003). *A Kingdom Under Siege: Nepal's Maoist insurgency, 1996 to 2003*. Kathmandu: The Printhouse.

2 From tourism to terrorism

Timbuktu and the traffic in global imaginaries

Angela Montague

Described as Burning Man meets *One Thousand and One Arabian Nights*, the Festival in the Desert (Anglicized) is a globally recognized gathering held annually outside the city of Timbuktu in Mali, West Africa. Conceived by members of the Grammy Award winning Tuareg rock band Tinariwen, it is described as a melding of "modernity and tradition"—essentially a world music festival grafted onto nomadic gatherings of Malian Tuareg (Kel Tamashek). Organizers of the festival had many hopes and, until recently, it had many positive outcomes for Tuareg, the state of Mali, and tourists. But from the start the festival was a fragile enterprise fraught with contradictions. Being born out of a rebellion in the 1990s, it was envisioned as a way to bring peace to the region yet was thrown into exile when a separatist movement was co-opted by supporters of Al Qaeda of the Islamic Maghreb (AQIM) in 2013. Festivals provide a site for investigating the spatial-temporal aspects of tourism mobilities and highlighting the interconnectivity of hosts and guests within global frameworks. In the case of the Festival in the Desert, it also provides a window onto how hosts manage tourism in times of conflict.

In this chapter, I address how different "imaginaries" are mobilized within the festival and tourism marketing (see e.g. Salazar 2012) and analyze how the various front and back stage regions of the festival provide a rich case for analyzing how festival participants understand and utilize festival space. What is revealed is a complex interplay of competing global discourses and imaginaries. My analysis of the Festival in the Desert shows that Malians, especially in the North, are aware of how they are romanticized by tourists, as well as how they are vilified as Muslims by Western media. Navigating somewhere between these various half-truths and stereotypes, tourism workers in Mali and organizers of the festival sought to maximize their appeal in order to bring in much needed economic development. At times this meant working to emphasize the exotic aspects of Malian culture as quintessentially African, and to romanticize the lives of nomads, while deemphasizing the poverty under which they live and which the festival seeks to ameliorate. After several Western governments issued travel warnings for Mali, organizers shifted tactics and began highlighting Mali as a safe place to travel, stressing that Islam is a religion of hospitality and peace in an attempt to combat diminishing tourist arrivals.

In order to understand the mobility of tourism imaginaries, I suggest that we view tourism as part of a discursive practice between those places sending and those receiving tourists, whereby the social relations between the two are constituted in a set of hierarchical, and historical, relations stemming from colonial and Orientalist imaginaries produced in the Global North (Said 1979). I view these discourses as part of a complex matrix of overlapping *scapes* (Appadurai 1990), where global flows are not unidirectional, but are part of a shifting world navigated by multiple actors and articulated within "contact zones" (Pratt 1992). Tourism marketing is a prime example of Western discourse about the "Other," where the so-called "West" has historically created a rather narrow image of Africa that has been hard to shake for those who live on the continent. In this way, tourists go in search of an Africa already constructed in and through their own social histories in what has been called the "tourism imaginary," a sort of social practice that renders a tourist destination as "credible" by appealing to preconceived notions of a destination and its people (Urry 1990; see also Salazar 2012). When the image is positive, it is adopted by Africans through a practice of self-exotification that they then "perform" for contemporary tourists by branding themselves as exotic.

The concepts of *back stage* and *front stage* are likewise instructive for understanding tourism. They were first articulated by Goffman (1959) as a way of distinguishing between the "front regions" where performances are made for the consumers/customers of a social establishment and the "back regions" where performers relax and recuperate before performing again. Dean MacCannell (1973) later applied these concepts to tourism by noting a series of stages that accommodate tourists (front stage), and those that are supposedly off limits (back stage). The notion is that the back stage preserves the authenticity by hiding the stage props. To penetrate the back regions is the way to break down the processes of mystification and take part in the "real" and intimate lives of locals (MacCannell 1973). I argue that festivals are actually *intended* to bring the supposed back stage into the front regions. Festivals are enjoyed by tourists because they represent a distillation of local culture, and often make visible the social life of foreign places in ways that a tourist could not see or participate in on any given day. As Kirshenblatt-Gimblett points out, "The foreign vacationer at a local festival achieves perfect synchrony: everyone is on holiday, or so it seems" (1998, 62). Festivals also blend and blur the distinctions between hosts and guests as both are there to make a holiday. But festivals also conceal as much as they reveal. To "festivalize" culture relies on the trafficking in the imaginaries of global discourse while also glossing over conflict and politics, in spaces I call the "nether regions."

Background

Mali is one of the world's poorest nations (as defined by GNP), and inhabitants in its northern regions, many nomadic, are considered the most impoverished. Timbuktu, which lies in the north of Mali (and is both a city and a region), was once fabled to have streets paved with gold. Although this was never true, it is further from such myths now. For this reason, the festival had hoped to become a factor in job creation in the region, promoting local development as well as "bringing together the people of the earth" (History: Festival au Désert 2013). The festival also aimed to reinvigorate a tradition of nomadic gatherings held after seasons of migration, but which had largely been abandoned. Tuareg, a stratified group of nomadic pastoralists, have never felt fully integrated into the nation of Mali. National borders, drought and desertification, forced sedentarization policies, and political unrest have severely altered the ability of many pastoralists to make a living, and development continues to be centralized in the more southern regions of the nation around the capital, Bamako, which is largely agricultural. Beginning in 1960 with Mali's independence from French colonial rule, Tuareg hoped for their own independent nation. In fact, separatists have risen up and demanded it on several occasions.

Figure 2.1 Map of Mali
Source: United Nations, Mali Map No. 4231 Rev. 3, March 2013.

The Festival in the Desert was opened to non-Tuareg Malians and foreign tourists on the first full moon of 2001. This was only a few years after an armed rebellion by Tuareg separatists (including members of Tinariwen) took place against the state of Mali from 1990 to 1995. The festival's significance grows in light of the history of this region, where civil unrest has been an ongoing fixture. The festival was a way in which members of a specific clan (*tewsit*) of Malian Tuareg, the Kel Ansar (Kel Antessar alternately), attempted to use the globalized space provided by tourism to promote peace and intercultural dialogue, and, as I argue, to stake a claim to their place within the Malian nation. The festival was born out of the 1990s rebellion, and under the direction of Manny Ansar, positioned itself within the goals of peace, promoting Malian music broadly in an attempt to bring economic development to the North of Mali through performance.

Methods

My analysis of the festival and tourism in Mali is based on ethnographic fieldwork conducted in Mali between 2004 and 2011. I learned of the Festival in the Desert while working on a development project with a Tuareg woman from the Ministry of Education in Bamako. In 2005, I acted as a tour guide for a group of US Americans who traveled to the Festival in the Desert while I was analyzing tourist experiences (including my own) through participant observation. I was later hired by a Malian friend who runs a small tour-operating business based in Mali, which enabled me to understand expectations and hesitations tourists have when traveling in Africa. I returned to Mali to conduct research on tourism and development from 2010 to 2011. During this time, I lived with a Tuareg family in Timbuktu for the months surrounding the three-day festival, and spent my days interviewing those with whom I was staying and visiting restaurants and hotels in order to interview tourists and tour guides in the city.

During the festival in 2011, I went back and forth between several tourist camps where I interviewed dozens of festivalgoers who were from the UK, USA, Denmark, and Norway, predominantly. I spoke with vendors and security guards who were working the festival, and I attended press conferences, where I was able to interview performers and festival organizers. The family I stayed with in Timbuktu, and later in Bamako, are closely related to the festival director, Manny Ansar, whom I had the opportunity to formally interview and interact with on several occasions. Most interviews were semi-structured and informal, and conducted in either French or English.

Blending front and back stage

The Festival in the Desert, as with other festivals, was a hybrid front stage/ back stage venue, as it had events meant for both locals and tourists to simultaneously enjoy (whether or not the latter understand all of it), and visitors were encouraged to put on a "cheche" (a traditional Tuareg headscarf worn by men) and become Tuareg for a day. The festival was conceived after Tinariwen performed at Les Nuits Toucouleurs festival in Europe in the late 1990s. Inspired, they came up with the idea of taking the traditional nomadic gatherings of Tuareg and overlaying a global music festival template on top of that, inviting musicians and tourists from the Global North to expose Malian music and Tuareg culture to the world and hopefully generate economic opportunities in the area. Although the festival was marketed as an exotic gathering of nomads, it was in fact neither fully a local nor global event, disrupting the notion that tourism is done by global travelers to local places where people are relatively immobile. Malian musicians may have come from Bamako in the South of Mali or the North, but all traveled to be there. Malians, other Africans, Europeans, North and South Americans all made the journey to the temporary space of the festival.

The Festival in the Desert literally had two stages with which we can analyze some of its front and back stage elements. In fact, the two stages highlight the way that "traditional" and "modern" aspects of the festival are articulated and negotiated. The *Scène Traditionnelle* (also called the small stage; see Figures 2.2 and 2.3) was dedicated to Tuareg traditional music known as *tendé*.[1] Here competitive performances of poetry, dance, and music by Tuareg participants took place using a simple amplification system. This "stage" had no clear demarcations; it was simply a flat area with rugs laid out and speakers pointing in one direction, though not directed toward a fixed audience. Likewise, there was no actual "back stage"; crowds of people standing or sitting on camels gathered behind groups of seated (Tuareg) families, who sit behind groups of women, some of whom were singing, clapping, ululating, and/or playing instruments. In the front men may be performing a type of martial arts utilizing swords in rhythmic fashion.

Tourists were able to watch these performances, yet they were introduced and discussed over a PA in Tamasheq, and were largely intended for Tuareg festivalgoers who were often simultaneously performers/contestants in these events. They were not advertised on a program of any sort, aside from a time of day when the performances occur. Word-of-mouth told the performers when their group was up. As stated above, these performances were competitive, but a non-Tuareg tourist would neither be aware of nor included in the judgement of the performances. In this way, the small stage was nearly entirely back stage to foreigners, while simultaneously being open for the tourist gaze (see Figure 2.4).

Performances on the main stage, or *Grande Scène* (Figure 2.5), were dominated by musicians from Mali who had reached some sort of international acclaim, such as Ali Farka Touré, his son Viex Farka Touré, Tinariwen, and Tartit (from the North), and Salif Keita, Oumou Sangaré, and Bassekou Kouyaté (from the South). Each year there were also musicians from various countries in the Global North who came to play (but were not paid), including such names as Robert Plant (2003) and Bono (2012). This stage was set up in a standard concert format with a massive amplification system, soundboard, and lights, and an MC announced each performance in French. While watching these performances, one might forget that they were on the edge of the Sahara Desert, as the feel was similar to many outdoor concerts and festivals that one might attend anywhere in the world. As one of my informants

1 The tendé describes not only the instrument, a mortar drum, but it also is a genre of music and a social event. The tendé events, characterized by poetry contests, camel races, and festive gatherings, are what the Festival in the Desert was modeled after.

Figures 2.2 and 2.3 Scène traditionnelle. Photo by author, 2005

Figure 2.4 The tourist gaze. Photo by author 2005

Figure 2.5 Tartit on "Big Stage." Photo by author 2011

from the US said, "this feels like Coachella or Burning Man," a sentiment that was also echoed by a travel blogger who stated that the event could be described as "'Burning Man' meets 'One Thousand and One Nights,' an otherworldly experience that captured the Tamashek tradition of nomadic clans meeting to celebrate in the middle of the desert" (Conley 2013, n.p.).

In between sets, this stage was also used for promoting social development projects to Malians in attendance. For instance, between two sets in 2011, there was a comedic dramatization of an obstinate grandfather being convinced to allow his granddaughter to go to school for the good it would do the family. Because the play was in Tamasheq, outsiders did not necessarily understand it, but I spoke with several tourists afterward who said they enjoyed the little skits between the music as "cultural displays," without worrying about not understanding them.

There was an official back stage area, beneath the rear part of the big stage, where you found performers mingling, relaxing, jamming, and getting ready for their performances. In 2005, I visited this area, and it felt a bit like a tomb. The ceiling was low, and the lighting came from lanterns sparsely placed. The "green rooms" were more like cubbies than dressing rooms, with curtains providing minimal privacy. There were a few tents behind the stage, mostly in the Tuareg nomad style, where more high-profile performers, such as Ali Farka Touré in 2005, spent their pre- and post-performance time. Tourists and outsiders technically do not have access to this literal back stage.

In various other back stage regions of the festival there were still more layers that were not intended for touristic display. For instance, many nomadic Tuareg made use of the space as they would have historically. Traditional nomadic festivals were a venue for political maneuvering, negotiating marriages, and settling disputes, in addition to being light-hearted cultural celebrations that organizers want to safeguard (History: Festival au Désert, 2013). In 2011, one of the organizers was married on the Saturday of the festival and, according to Manny, at least ten other families were having their wedding celebrations during the three-day event, albeit in the "back stage" space beyond the gaze of foreign tourists.

Interestingly, in a true mash-up of local and global, front stage and back stage, one of my consultants, a traveler called "Dancing Dave," shared with me a story that resulted in him being married at the festival as well. Dave and his wife were traveling through Mali and other African destinations as they celebrated their 30th wedding anniversary. During their stay in Dogon Country (a popular destination in central Mali) Dave asked one of his tour guides, Hamma, about the possibilities of having a "recommitment" ceremony to mark the occasion. Hamma mentioned that many weddings did take place at the festival and said he'd talk to the other guide. What transpired, Dave said, was the highlight of his trip, which he chronicled in a blog titled "Our Tuareg wedding" (Hooper 2011). He was awakened early on the second day of the festival and told to go meet with the chief to arrange the marriage. A ceremony followed in which he and his wife, in fine Tuareg attire, exchanged vows. But the wedding did not go off without a hitch. For instance, at one point, his wife was taken to a tent and held until he made an offer that was acceptable for her release, a process similar to Tuareg traditional weddings.

Dave was finally able to retrieve his wife, after several negotiations, but, as he relayed to me, he could not tell at which points the ceremony was supposed to be taken seriously, and at which points it was in jest. Most tourists are unaware of how locals participate in festival activities, nor are they aware of the conferences, discussions, and weddings that are taking place, beyond the dunes, so to speak. In fact, one tourist, a doctor from the UK, asked me at one point if everyone was just dressed up for tourists. He assumed that it was all a performance to make money. This skepticism by postmodern tourists, what Bruner has called the "questioning gaze" (Bruner 2001), is underscored by the belief at some level that the festival was staged and therefore not "authentic."

But the festival is first and foremost a local event, at least according to organizers; they set it up as a way to bring back the tradition of nomadic gatherings, while also sharing their cultural heritage with outsiders. Manny told me that they wanted to simultaneously "grow the festival while maintaining intimacy." They did this by only having around 1000 tickets available for foreign visitors and by showcasing a majority of Tuareg musicians over international acts at the festival. Some Tuareg I spoke to lamented that there were too many outsiders, while others complained that there were not enough (particularly paying attendees) to bring economic opportunity to more people. Manny said that the festival never made a profit, but it had been able to fund various development initiatives. For instance, festival revenue was able to pay for a teacher for one year at a nomadic school in Essakane, and paid the tuition, room, and board for several Tuareg students to study at schools in Bamako and Algeria. Development was a back stage goal of the festival, something that was not forefront in the way the festival presented itself as a world music event to tourists. Instead, I found festival press and marketing relied heavily on stereotypical tropes found in popular discourse on Africa and the Middle East.

According to Salazar, it would be hard to imagine tourism without the seductive force of imaginaries (2012). The festival makes use of extensive exotifying descriptors to draw out the appeal of difference. Because of a long history of regarding Tuareg as "noble savages" and romanticizing the life of nomads, especially in Europe, most festival press centered on those aspects most associated with nomadism: camels, caravans, and tents. Likewise, men that I encountered selling jewelry and other trinkets at the festival frequently greeted tourists with "Je suis Tuareg, je suis nomade." Ironically, Tuareg society is hierarchical, and historically artisans were not nomadic, as only nobility took part in caravans. But the sales pitch worked, according to one of my informants who said he was well aware of how Europeans romanticized the Tuareg and he used it to sell jewelry. A former festival organizer who had helped initiate the festival, Issa Dicko, left the team to run the development agency EFES. He pondered that "Perhaps the Europeans romanticize the Tuaregs too much and their clichés could actually be harmful to us as a community" (Brouet 2004, n.p.). MacCannell theorizes that leisure tourism originated from the alienation felt in modern industrial society and that what tourists are after is the authenticity they lack in their own lives, a situation likened to the traditional quest for the sacred. He argues that tourists are searching for some perceived lack, which can only be found in more "traditional" societies. Thus, perhaps if a destination can highlight its traditional aspects, it can further its brand appeal. But as Dicko feared, images of sand dunes, men on camels in turbans with swords, and references to "the middle of the desert" perhaps overshadow the economic and political goals of the festival.

In an analysis of text on several websites offering tours to the festival, I noted that few had any mention of the development goals or cultural significance of the festival, aside from reference to "ancient traditions." The images on 13 different websites were dominated by pictures of camels, Tuareg men with veils, and vast expanses of white sand dunes (see websites for operators such as Saga Tours, Touareg Tours, From Here 2 Timbuktu, Fulani Travel, and Guerba). These are not false images; they do capture reality, but I argue that they do not capture the development goals that many with whom I spoke stated were the impetus behind inviting outsiders. But as one of my consultants asked: "Would tourists still come to see us if we are sitting at desks?" Image is everything in advertising, and tourism is a product for sale. As Watson and Kopachevsky state:

> Tourism, by its very nature, is shaped by a very complex pattern of symbolic valuation; and this takes place in a structured social context over which tourists themselves have no immediate control. The essence of modern capitalism is the remanufacture of images, many of which effectively obscure the injuries of class, race, and sex.
>
> (1994, 656)

Not only does tourism obscure these differences but it also obscures history. When it comes to the non-Western world, most Western media regurgitate the same stereotypes that have been circulating for centuries. In looking at imagery and descriptions of tours highlighting the festival, I found that most mentioned that the festival was a way to preserve Tuareg culture. This goal was highlighted, I believe, because it aligns well with the notion that Tuareg are a "traditional" culture that should remain static, unchanged, primordial. It also continues a tradition in the West where Africa is assumed to be outside modernity. Media amplify the supposed ancient, unchanged, aspects of the culture with such phrases as: "For centuries, the Tuareg nomads have gathered at oases to make music and race camels" (Newberry 2004, n.p.) and "For centuries, the Tuareg had held these desert gatherings" (Denselow 2004, n.p.).

Other media highlight the otherness of the location, for instance: "The Festival of the Desert in Mali might not have the name recognition of Newport, New Orleans, or Montreux, but on the 'Exotic' and 'Remote' scales, it has all music festivals beat" (Carberry 2004). "Timbuktu seemed absolutely remote—dusty, drab and extremely exotic" (Sattin 2004, n.p.). "Remote" is perhaps a function of being in "Timbuktu" and "exotic" by virtue of being African. Exotic is the quintessential marker for all that is "Other." A *New York Times* multimedia piece on the festival has very little text besides stating that the festival is a "time-shifting experience" that takes place in a remote Malian city (Moloney 2008, 15). The author ends his piece with the statement that his eyes, in seeing turbaned men leaving on camels, and his ears, in hearing rock bands performing on a brightly lit stage, were "separated by hundreds of years" (15).

The "mystery of Timbuktu" was a major part of the appeal of making the long and arduous trip to the festival (and the city). Once in the city, lines formed in order to get one's passport stamped with the seal of Timbuktu. In my interviews with tourists, every single one (out of more than 30) stated that going to Timbuktu was a highlight of the trip. The thought of going to Timbuktu most assuredly carries with it a wide array of predetermined mental imagery. Timbuktu is the quintessential out-of-the-way place, colloquially equivalent to "the middle of nowhere." It represents a challenge and holds an aura of escape. In the 18th century, colonial powers raced against each other to try to enter this fabled city. Tales of Timbuktu's wealth no doubt prompted much of this fascination, and indeed is said to have encouraged European exploration of West Africa. It was the most popular city in Africa for centuries, but was so difficult for Europeans to reach that in 1824, the Paris-based Société de Géographie offered a 10,000 franc prize to the first non-Muslim to reach the town and return with information about it. Today it is perhaps more often conceived of as a non-place, for by definition it could be "any distant or outlandish place."[2]

Tourism officials in Mali were quite aware of the draw of Timbuktu and actively worked to promote it on tourist agendas. Inscribed in 1988 as a UNESCO World Heritage Site, there was an inherent understanding of its interest and importance on account of its "Outstanding Universal Value" (http://whc.unesco.org/en/list/119/). But besides its material heritage of historic libraries, universities, and ancient manuscripts, Timbuktu's mayor believed it mostly held intangible appeal as a "place to escape from the world." "Our asset is our name," he is quoted as saying (Boukhari 2000, 44). "The word 'Timbuktu' says something to everybody, even people who don't know where Mali is," said Aminata Traoré, the Minister for Culture and Tourism, when the city was declared a UNESCO World Heritage Site (Boukhari 2000, 45). "These days, people in the West have a great urge to get away

---

2   "Collins English Dictionary," Complete & Unabridged 11th edition. Retrieved December 6, 2012 from CollinsDictionary.com.

from it all. Timbuktu hasn't got much to sell, but it can sell dreams," she adds. This quote perfectly exemplifies MacCannell's use of Marx's theory of alienation.

Branding is an essential practice in tourism marketing today. Neoliberal policies encourage niche markets, and, in the case of cultural tourism, this necessitates making distinct and recognizable a destination's culture for sale. Branding is the context by which any given destination—a nation, for example—makes itself stand out against contenders, which means presenting your destination as unique, and in many cases exotic. Thus, if any given destination wants to attract a would-be tourist, they must create intrigue; marketers often do this by drawing on preconceived, stereotypical imagery and language in order to appeal to tourists' fantasies. John Urry argued that the touristic gaze focuses on particular signs when traveling (such as the "typical" German beer garden, or the "typical" French café), and these signs create the template for a tourist's agenda. The people, places, and things that make it onto the itinerary show "how tourists are in a way semioticians, reading the landscape for signifiers of certain pre-established notions or signs derived from various discourses of travel and tourism" (Urry 1990). Thus branding, one could argue, is a process whereby the destination must create sign-value that appeals to these pre-established notions.

Although some of these descriptors may appear to be innocuous, and as briefly touched on above, locals make use of their appeal as the Other, relying on one-dimensional stereotypes and tropes of Africa and Africans can backfire when the other side are imaginaries of disorder, chaos, and danger.

The "nether regions:" Beyond the back stage

In 2008, France issued a travel advisory against traveling to the North of Mali. The US and many other countries followed suit. Beginning in 2008, the US Embassy stated that it recommends against travel to the North "due to kidnapping threats against Westerners," and that "U.S. citizens are specifically reminded that the restricted areas include Essakane, site of the popular 'Festival au Desert'" (US Embassy 2009). Travelers I spoke to regularly asked about these warnings. During the 2011 year, I set up several tours to Mali, some of which were specifically to the Festival in the Desert for 2012. Because of travel warnings against visiting the North of Mali by many powerful states (United Kingdom, United States, Sweden, Germany, France, Australia, for example), travelers from these countries wanted to understand what safety measures would be taken by the operators. Of the 21 individuals that I assisted with travel to Mali, eight decided not to go to Timbuktu because of concerns they had related to an advisory by their government.

On the other hand, many felt that the warnings were overblown. A well-traveled man in his fifties whom I interviewed at the festival in 2011, said: "As for the safety warnings … they are simply absurd … given that no

American has ever been harmed in Mali. In fact, I have been to over 25 countries and have never seen such a remarkable love for Americans." Another traveler to the 2011 festival stated: "Before I went, I was a bit worried about the security alerts but I have to say I couldn't see what all the fuss was about. I don't remember one police stop." Another tourist I interviewed said:

> There's certainly a propaganda campaign under way to dissuade people from visiting parts of Mali that in every sense are completely safe and secure. I'm personally not convinced by the level of threat implied in recent travel advisories from the UK and US.

One afternoon in 2011, as I crossed a dune, I was greeted by Salim, a young Tuareg vendor at the festival. I sat down in the sand to look at what he had to offer, and we struck up a conversation about the travel warnings. He said, "France does not care about Mali and that is why they exaggerated the threat of Al Qaeda ... Al Qaeda is everywhere; it is in New York and Paris, but no one is giving warnings against travel there." Salim felt that even if Al Qaeda did threaten to kidnap Westerners in Mali (which they had done), a Tuareg would never let that happen because they pride themselves on being hospitable to outsiders. Of course, there were a few specific events that did make Mali look increasingly unsafe. In December of 2008 two Canadian nationals who worked for the United Nations were kidnapped in Niger. In June of 2009 four European tourists were kidnapped along the Mali–Niger border, and one British hostage was killed. A US citizen was killed in Mauritania in June as well. In November of 2009 a French citizen living in the Malian city of Ménaka (about 500 miles from Timbuktu) was kidnapped. Al Qaeda took responsibility for all of these. But locals in Timbuktu and at the festival felt that the travel warnings were an overreaction to the problem. At the time of my fieldwork in Mali, I felt that those reporting on kidnappings that had happened on the borders of Niger or Mauritania lacked an understanding of the geography of Mali, because many of the incidents mentioned above happened hundreds of miles from where the festival took place. As one Tuareg consultant put it: "They are confusing these remote regions with tourist spots, and these are not places most tourists would go to. They are on the edges of civilization, out in the bush, not even nomads go there; they know it is dangerous."

Regardless, organizers did move the festival site from its location in Essakane, a small village, to just outside the city of Timbuktu beginning in 2010 to ease some of the fears that tourists and governments had. The Malian government also provided military security and throughout the day armed military patrolled the perimeter of the main site and were speckled throughout the crowds as well. In 2011, to show that the area was indeed safe, the (then) president of Mali, Amadou Toumani Touré, even attended for the first time. In his address at the camel races, he thanked tourists for having the "courage" to come despite the travel warnings. He took time to explain that

Islam is a peaceful religion, a tolerant religion that is not about violence or aggression. It is a religion of brotherly love and peace. "Here in Mali," he said, "it is a symbol of faith and trust in God and the good of all people." Mali welcomed all people, he said (Touré 2011).

The impression management that went on at the 2011 edition of the festival was overt and forceful at times. Every press conference that I attended made mention of the travel warnings and how they were erroneous or harmful. The event was continually described as a "bridge between cultures," an example of "intercultural dialogue." These comments seemed to be in response to representations of Muslims as a whole. "Occidental cultures," Manny said, "misunderstand Islam and think that we are all terrorists." Tamnana, a traditional Tuareg band who spoke at a press conference, said: "Please share the message that the Tuareg region is not a place of terrorism or violence but a place of peace and solidarity with the world." They thanked everyone for coming to Timbuktu despite the travel warnings. "The festival helps the lives of so many people here and is very important to so many people to have tourists putting their money into the economy. Many people make a living this way."

However... barely 24 hours after the conclusion of the 2012 edition of the festival, on January 17, the Mouvement National pour la Libération de l'Azawad (MNLA)[3] staged an insurrection against the state of Mali. Their first attack against the Malian army occurred at Ménaka, a town in the eastern region of Gao, and the next day they attacked Tessalit, hometown of members of Tinariwen. This time the separatists were far better equipped than in earlier attempts (in 1990 for instance); clashes with Malian forces proved that this time Tuareg fighters, who numbered as many as 3000, had a decided edge. Some have attributed this to the Arab Spring in Libya, as many Tuareg were in Gaddafi's armies and left with heavy armory as his regime crumbled (Morgan 2013, 10). Because of the defeats that Malian forces were experiencing, contempt grew as the MNLA pushed further south, aiming to take over Timbuktu and areas around Mopti. With these defeats and advances, military discontent began to fester around the capital of Mali, and by March of 2012 a military junta staged a coup and ousted President Touré.

With chaos in the South and without an official head of state, the insurgency coursed on in the North, gaining its own momentum and taking over Timbuktu by the end of March. But it also gained its own chaos. In May of 2012, the MNLA signed a pact with Ansar al Dine (defined as a militant Islamist group), and together declared an *Islamic* State of Azawad. Soon afterwards one member, Iyad Ag Ghaly, purportedly broke ranks with the MNLA and partnered with the North African faction of Al Qaeda known as AQIM as well as the movement for Jihad in West Africa, MUJAO.[4] On August 22, 2012, insurgents

---

3   National Movement for the Liberation of Azawad in English, generally referred to as Tuareg rebels from the North of Mali and thought to have been trained and fought in the Libyan army under Gaddafi.
4   Mouvement pour le Tawhîd et du Jihad en Afrique de l'Ouest (Movement for Jihad in West Africa).

declared Shari'a law in Timbuktu, which effectively outlawed all forms of secular music and instituted strict interpretations of Islamic legal codes. Militants confiscated tapes and equipment as they made attacks on radio stations and musicians' homes in Timbuktu and other northern cities. On one end of the spectrum are stories of people having property damaged. One young man whose phone rang playing a Tinariwen tune had it taken from him and smashed, for instance. But on the other side of the extreme, violent personal punishments were beginning to be carried out.

While occupying Timbuktu, Ansar al Dine also targeted World Heritage sites, burning thousands of priceless medieval manuscripts, one library, and dozens of mausoleums and shrines of Sufi saints. "The destruction is a divine order," said a spokesman from Ansar al Dine. Timbuktu is known as the City of 333 Saints. Islam came into Mali in the 9th century with Muslim Berbers and Tuareg merchants, the latter had been converted by the founders of Sufi brotherhoods. Veneration of Sufi saints counts as idolatry, a heretical practice that cannot be tolerated by Salafists (who follow Sunni Islam). All of this in a town that is known for being a crossroads and a meeting place of people from all walks of life. At present, however, Timbuktu is not welcoming many outsiders except those who are part of the United Nations Multidimensional Integrated Stabilization Mission in Mali (MINUMSA), which was established in April of 2013. A peace deal between the government and Tuareg rebels was signed in 2013, but ended later that year as Malian soldiers fired on unarmed protesters. In 2015 a ceasefire was signed, but low-level fighting continues. In 2017, Mali was dubbed "The World's Most Dangerous U.N. Mission" as 118 peacekeeping forces have been killed in just four years (Sieff 2017).

In interviews with Manny in 2011, he emphasized that Essakane and the festival were absolutely safe. It was not until after the takeover that he admitted that Salafist groups had been threatening the festival since its earliest years. As a Kel Ansar, a clan known to be defenders of Islam, he had the backing of powerful chiefs and elders who had been negotiating to keep the festival open because it brought money to the area. However, in 2011, Western donors refused to fund the event due to the warnings, Manny said, leaving the festival without any European or American donors. As already mentioned, the move to Timbuktu was due to threats by AQIM that they would target Westerners, and it turned out the threats were more real than any of us could have imagined. Manny and other Tuareg I spoke to in 2011 said that most Malians are not sympathetic to Salafism or Wahhabism.[5] In fact, most said that true Islam is not extremist, seeing it as "naturally a tolerant religion," as one consultant put it. But in an interview with Andy Morgan, a journalist and former producer for Tinariwen, Manny stated that

5   Wahhabism is an offshoot of radical or orthodox Islam named for the 18th century preacher from Saudi Arabia Muhammad Ibn Abd al-Wahhab. The term is sometimes used interchangeably with Salafism, which is actually an offshoot of Wahhabism.

2007 was actually when things began to change. This is when the "red lines were first drawn," Manny told Morgan.

> The Al Qaida [sic] people were wandering around the desert at that time ... But they weren't aggressive. They visited the camps near Essakane and said, "don't worry, we're Muslims like you." But then later, their argument began to change. The first alert was when they said, "we've got nothing against you. We just have the same enemy, which is the West, the non-believers." That's when I understood that things were going to get difficult, because our festival was based on people coming from all over the world, without distinction.
>
> (Morgan 2013)

Conclusions

Tourism is described as the "largest peaceful movement of people across cultural boundaries in the history of the world" (Lett 1989, 275). I argue that the festival was an attempt at democratic peace brokering and diplomacy in a multicultural context, and, as such, fits well within the rubric of other "World Music Festivals" that see in music the "weapon of peace." In his memoirs from the festival, Intagrist el Ansari, a Tuareg journalist, says:

> One can cross both ministers, ambassadors, Princess Caroline of Monaco, a billionaire owner of the famous MTV, and a shepherd who supports his eight children with five goats, or a craftsman who offers his crafts; all so different and so similar, taking place on the same large white dune, of fine and pristine sand.
>
> (El Ansari 2010)

In these contact zones, diverse people grapple with each other, negotiate understanding, and potentially leave with greater cultural awareness. This is one way in which I see cultural tourism as a literal and figurative dialogue between different groups who are seeking common ground. I am reminded here of Victor Turner's description of *communitas*—that point when all distinctions of difference are stripped down and a sort of unity is achieved (Turner 1969). Those with whom I spoke in Mali felt that intercultural dialogue was made possible by tourism and was helping to break down barriers of difference.

But are the differences really stripped down when so much of cultural tourism is about exotification? Positive and negative imaginaries are sides of the same coin that flatten the experiences, histories, and politics of the cultures and the conflicts on the African continent. Tourists want to go to a primitive, exotic, remote destination with romantic appeal, and the news of terrorist takeovers, kidnappings, and exile falls in line with and confirms the fears of would-be travelers. In order for tourists to return to Mali it will take more than the conflict being over. The nation will have to drastically rebrand itself. The impression management at the festival was effective, according to many whom I interviewed in 2011. But according to the number of arrivals, there was a steady decline beginning in 2008 when the first travel warnings were issued. What I found particularly interesting, when I was actively working with tourists organizing travel, is that when the warnings were issued, tourists simply changed their itineraries to other African destinations. For instance, when travelers decided that Mali looked too dangerous to visit, they booked tours to Ghana or Senegal.

The interchangeability of Mali for another African destination highlights the way that many Westerners conceptualize Africa, and it reveals another global imaginary—Africa is full of all the same people: "Africans." In their book, *Mistaking Africa*, Curtis Keim and Carolyn Somerville (2018) describe and analyze the prevailing misconceptions about the continent and its people, the first of which is "Africa is one big country" (3). They note how most adults in the United States know very little about Africa at all and conceive of the continent as being relatively homogeneous, rather than a vast continent comprising over 50 countries, with more than 1.2 billion inhabitants who speak over 2000 languages (3). In fact, when I was organizing a tour for friends of mine to go to the Festival in the Desert, discourse around travel preparations included talk about a trip to "Africa," not Mali.

The current tagline on the official website for Mali tourism is "Le Mali: Une Afrique Authentique" (http://officetourismemali.com/), evidence that they understand their market (even if it is at a standstill). Accompanying the tagline are shifting images of mud huts, masked dancers, turbaned men on camels, people singing, clapping, and drumming, and men dancing in red grass skirts, with cowry shell straps over bare chests, swinging their heads in a blurred frenzy. What could be more African? However, at present (2019), Mali's economic plan is to continue to diversify agriculture and avoid tourism—which had made up close to one-third of all foreign revenue prior to the conflict—until the region is more adequately stabilized. Manny continues to hold hope that the festival will return to Mali in the near future. In the meantime, he has been producing performances of Malian music throughout the world under the moniker "Cultural Caravan for Peace," until the day Timbuktu can once again be a crossroads of cultures sharing its hospitality with travelers from around the globe.

References

Appadurai, A. (1990). Disjuncture and difference in the global cultural economy. *Theory, Culture & Society.* 7(2), 295–310. doi:10.1177/026327690007002017.

Boukhari, S. (2000). Timbuktu online. *UNESCO Courier* [print magazine]. 53(3), 44–45.

Brouet, L. (producer) (2004). *Festival in the Desert* [*motion picture*]. World Village USA.

Bruner, E.M. (1991). Transformation of self in tourism. *Annals of Tourism Research.* 18(2), 238–250. doi:10.1016/0160-7383(91)90007-X.

Carberry, S. (2004). Festival in the Desert [press release]. Rock Paper Scissors [webpage]. Retrieved from http://www.rockpaperscissors.biz/index.cfm/fuseaction/current.alt_press_release/project_id/108/alt_release/50.cfm.

Conley, C. (2013). Timbuktu is calling... To Mali or not to Mali? Fest300 [blog]. Retrieved from http://www.fest300.com/blog/timbuktu-is-calling-to-mali-or-not-to-mali/.

Denselow, R. (2004, January 7). How the desert festival began. *The Guardian*. Retrieved from http://www.theguardian.com/music/2004/jan/08/popandrock1.

El Ansari, I. (2010). Memoir: 'Le Festival au Désert.' Africultures.com [webpage]. Retrieved from http://www.africultures.com/php/?nav=article&no=9796. [Translated from French by author.]

Goffman, E. (1959). *The Presentation of Self in Everyday Life*. Garden City, NY: Doubleday.

History: Festival au Désert (2013). Festival au Desert [webpage]. Retrieved from http://www.festival-au-desert.org/index.cfm?m=0&s=2.

Hooper, D. (2011). Our Tuareg wedding... Festival au Desert... Timbuktu, Mali. TravelBlog.com [blog]. Retrieved from https://www.travelblog.org/Africa/Mali/North-West/Timbuktu/blog-610326.html.

Keim, C., & Sommerville, C. (2018). *Mistaking Africa: Curiosities and inventions of the American mind*. New York: Westview Press.

Kirshenblatt-Gimblett, B. (1998). *Destination Culture: Tourism, museums, and heritage*. Berkeley: University of California Press.

Lett, J. (1989). Epilogue. In *Hosts and Guests: The anthropology of tourism* (pp. 275–279). Philadelphia: University of Pennsylvania Press.

MacCannell, D. (1973). Staged authenticity: Arrangements of social space in tourist settings. *American Journal of Sociology*. 79(3), 589–603. http://www.jstor.org/stable/2776259.

Moloney, K. (2008, May 11). Mali, S.U.V.'s and camels deliver the fans. *The New York Times*. Retrieved from: https://www.nytimes.com/2008/05/11/travel/11why.html.

Morgan, A. (2013). Music, culture and conflict in Mali: A report for Freemuse. Copenhagen: Freemuse.

Newberry, B. (2004). The remotest festival in the world. *Geographical*. 76(6), 53–58.

Pratt, M.L. (1992/2006). *Imperial Eyes: Travel writing and transculturation*. 2nd edition. New York: Routledge.

Said, E.W. (1979). *Orientalism*. 1st Vintage Books edition. New York: Vintage.

Salazar, N.B. (2012). Tourism imaginaries: A conceptual approach. *Annals of Tourism Research*. 39(2), 863–882.

Sattin, A. (2004, November 28). Hurry, we'll be late for the party: Mali's celebration of Tuareg culture has become a world party. *The Sunday Times*. Retrieved from https://www.thetimes.co.uk/article/hurry-well-be-late-for-the-party-in-mali-nqfxt2pbltv.

Sieff, K. (2017, February 17). The world's most dangerous U.N. mission. *The Washington Post*. Retrieved from https://www.washingtonpost.com/sf/world/2017/02/17/the-worlds-deadliest-u-n-peacekeeping-mission/?noredirect=on&utm_term=.4a30a104926b.

Touré, A.T. (2011, January 8) Address at camel races, Festival au Désert. Timbuktu: Mali.[Translated from French by author.]

US Embassy (2009, November 28). Warden messages 2009. US Embassy in Mali [webpage]. Retrieved from http://mali.usembassy.gov/travel-warning-for-mali.html.

Turner, V. (1969). Liminality and communitas. In *The Ritual Process: Structure and anti-structure* (pp. 94–113). Chicago: Aldine Publishing.

Urry, J. (1990). *The Tourist Gaze: Leisure and travel in contemporary societies*. London: SAGE.

Watson L., & Kopachevsky, J.P. (1994). Interpretations of tourism as commodity. *Annals of Tourism Research*. 21(3), 643–660. doi:10.1016/0160-7383(94)90125-2.

Part 2

Staging Tourism as Identity Performance and Structural Critique

3 The presentation of collective self in touristic life

Dancing and painting for touristic consumption in highland Ecuador

Joe Quick

In cultural tourism, there often exists a separation between the culture that is performed or portrayed for touristic consumption on the one hand and the culture that is lived by hosts through their everyday experience on the other. As John Urry (2002) observes, tourists know the destinations they visit long before they leave home, and they encounter those destinations through the expectations and stereotypes that they carry with them. Hosts respond pragmatically by studying the desires of touristic visitors and offering up enactments of culture that engage those visitors' expectations. Thus, as Blanca Muratorio writes of tourist-oriented artisans in highland Ecuador, "the indigenous people of the Sierra have mastered the subtleties of the competitive scene and fully understand that they should wear 'typical clothing' and assume the 'appropriate bodily attitudes' if they want to legitimize, authenticate, and increase their sales" (2000, 56, my translation). Moreover, hosts learn to engage tourists through genres of cultural performance and representation that communicate local distinctiveness in non-local registers by adhering to globally circulating discourses of cultural difference. Consequently, it has been common among scholars and travelers alike to bemoan the perceived inauthenticity of tourist-oriented mobilizations of culture that do not reflect the cultural realities of hosts, particularly when the hosts are indigenous people.

However, ethnographers such as Laura Peers (2007) have found "that while there are many difficulties with cultural tourism, it can also renew indigenous cultures" (2007: 65). Peers conducts her research among Native American interpreters who perform a version of their own ancestors' daily lives at historic sites. Their audience of mostly non-Native visitors often frustrate and even insult the performers through an unthinking adherence to preconceptions about indigenous peoples and their cultures. The performers spend much time and great effort to confront and correct the misperceptions of visitors to the sites where they work. Yet even when their audiences fail to appreciate their efforts to communicate historical indigenous lifeways, Native historical interpreters learn through their performances to think in critical, self-conscious ways about their own cultural identities in the present.

In this chapter, I argue that such critical collective self-reflection may also be prompted by cultural performances and representations that adhere to global structures of cultural difference and touristic preconceptions about indigenous people. Indeed, I go a step further to argue that through outsider-oriented genres of dance and painting, the indigenous Kichwa people of Quilotoa, Ecuador *simultaneously* cater to touristic expectations *and* engage in a critical collective effort to construct a vision of indigenous community life that unfolds multiple temporalities. This is possible because there exists a form of what, drawing on Eduardo Viveiros de Castro (2004), might be called "partially controlled equivocation" in the genres of performance and representation through which Quilotoans engage tourists. That is, Quilotoans enact collective self through genres that communicate different things to Kichwa people and to non-Kichwa outsiders, but this multivocality is recognized only by Kichwa people. To anchor my discussion, I focus on events related to the festive inauguration of the community-managed Princesa Toa Hostel in November 2014.

Following a brief theoretical and methodological orientation, I divide my analysis of the inaugural festivities into two parts. The first of these parts discusses styles of dance that enacted community in distinct modes throughout the day of the celebration. One genre of dance captured the spirit of the community through its connection to the religious-agrarian festival calendar. The other genre of dance has its origins in a traditional festival dance that communicates community to Kichwa people in a way that goes unrecognized by tourists, but it was deployed in a skit that explicitly reenacted Quilotoa's origin story for visitors. The second part of my discussion focuses on a series of paintings that was prepared in advance of the inauguration by Klever Latacunga, a Quilotoan painter. The composition of Klever's paintings helps to clarify how multiple storylines and temporalities characterize the artistic genre which Quilotoans and their neighbors in nearby Tigua have developed for touristic consumption, as well as the multiple storylines and temporalities that were communicated through the dances discussed in the first section. Finally, I conclude with a discussion of how the innovation of these expressive genres provide Quilotoans opportunities to reflect critically on the past, present, and future of their community.

Orientation

In the scholarly literature on tourism, performances and representations of culture have been critiqued on the grounds that exoticization, folklorization, heritage-ization, commodification, and other forms of objectification alienate cultural traditions from their communities of practice. A primary concern of critics is that economically or politically powerful outside forces take control of cultural expression such that performances are not only oriented toward a non-participant audience, but they are wholly determined by the desires or dispositions of that audience. For instance, in an early contribution to the anthropology of tourism, Davydd Greenwood (1989) critiqued changes to the Alarde, an annual event held in the Spanish town of Fuenterrabia. Greenwood characterized the traditional Alarde as "a ritual whose importance and meaning lies in the entire town's participation and in the intimacy with which its major symbols are understood by all the participants and onlookers" (176). He wrote that the tradition "was not a performance for pay, but an affirmation of their belief in their own culture" (178). However, when the local council of Fuenterrabia resolved to market the Alarde to tourists, the structure of the event was transformed. Greenwood wrote, "In service of simple pecuniary motives, [the council] defined the Alarde as a *public show to be performed for outsiders* who, because of their economic importance in the town, had the *right* to see it" (178, emphasis in original).

Another line of critique has revolved around the notion of authenticity in cultural performance. This body of scholarship has been heavily influenced by Dean MacCannell (1973), whose theory of performance in tourism was rooted in Erving Goffman's (1959) theatrical metaphor for social interaction. Goffman showed that all social interactions are performative inasmuch as each participant in a given interaction enacts a self that is loosely scripted: "To be a given kind of person, then, is not merely to possess the required attributes, but also to sustain the standards of conduct and appearance that one's social grouping attaches thereto" (75). A typical social actor will be prepared to enact any number of distinct selves, each of which is shaped by the standards of conduct that are sustained within a distinct shared "definition of the situation."

Extending the theatrical metaphor, Goffman referred to the space in which a social presentation of individual or collective self is sustained as the "front" region of the performance, whereas "A back region or backstage may be defined as a place, relative to a given performance, where the impression fostered by the performance is knowingly contradicted as a matter of course" (112). MacCannell (1973) theorized that the touristic search for authenticity drives a desire to access the back stage of hosts' lives, yet this desire is perpetually frustrated by hosts who present tourists with a "false back," a front region that has been made to seem like a back region. Some tourists do not mind; the false back "does not shock, trick, or anger them, and they do not express any feelings of having been made less pure by their discovery" (601). Yet for other tourists, the discovery of a false back can be deeply upsetting.

Such critiques are not unfounded. It is undoubtedly the case that many tourist-oriented performances of culture do not faithfully reflect the traditions and experiences of culture that give meaning to the everyday lives of local people, because what is enacted is constrained by what is palatable to touristic audiences. These performances may even do symbolic violence to the cultural practices that they represent. Yet, as Goffman wrote, "the performance is something the team members can stand back from, back far enough to imagine or play out simultaneously other kinds of performances attesting to other realities" (1959, 207). Such distance allows tourist-oriented cultural performers to push back against the definition of the situation that tourists assert, to control what is revealed and what remains hidden, and to think critically about their collective presentation of self. As Peers documents among Native American historical interpreters,

> Cultural performers have always been perfectly capable of distinguishing between overtly constructed cultural representations for tourists and the culture of everyday lived experience. Native performers and their communities engage in serious and often heated discussion of these issues: performances are deliberately choreographed, and the selection of cultural elements to be shown to the non-Native public is debated.
>
> (2007, 65)

In this chapter, I discuss examples of tourist-oriented cultural performance and representation that take place in the Centro de Turismo Comunitario Laguna Verde Quilotoa (CTC Quilotoa—the Green Lake Quilotoa Center of Community-Based Tourism) in the highlands of central Ecuador. I show that Quilotoans present a version of their culture that appeals to tourists even as they undertake critical reflections on indigenous society that tourists do not witness. While it is true that Quilotoans engage in many of their most heated discussions about the past, present, and future of their community in back stage regions that are off limits to tourists, many of their deepest commentaries are included in the very performances and representations that they offer up to tourists. That tourists do not recognize these commentaries for what they are is a consequence of what Eduardo Viveiros de Castro calls "equivocations."

In Viveiros de Castro's words, equivocation is "the referential alterity between homonymic concepts" (2004, 3). That is, an equivocation occurs when interlocutors use the same or very similar words to refer to different things. In a case of uncontrolled equivocation, there occurs "a failure to understand that understandings are necessarily not the same" (11). On the other hand, controlled equivocation is "a type of communicative disjuncture where the interlocutors are not talking about the same thing, and know this" (9). The case of tourist-oriented cultural performances and representations in Quilotoa falls into an intermediate category, because Quilotoans are well aware that tourists do not understand Quilotoan portrayals of Kichwa culture in the same way that Quilotoans themselves understand those portrayals. But tourists do not demonstrate an awareness that their own interpretations do not match those of the Quilotoans. I call this situation "partially controlled equivocation."

The research on which the present analysis is based was conducted during a seven-week period of ethnographic research in Quilotoa in 2012 and a year-long period of fieldwork in 2014–2015. In this chapter, I focus my attention on examples of dancing that took place during festivities that marked the inauguration of the community-managed Princesa Toa Hostel and on a series of paintings prepared in anticipation of the inauguration by Klever Latacunga.

Dancing community

It is November 10, 2014. Soon after breakfast, the community is aroused by the lilting sound of two *pifanos* (cane flutes), which are accompanied by a bass drum and a snare drum. The music, which emanates from the large parking lot at the center of the community-run tourism complex, is an unmistakable sign that a fiesta is getting started. Today is the grand opening of the new community-run hostel, the Hostal Princesa Toa.

The fiesta gets started following the standard pattern for the observance of the Catholic feast days in indigenous communities of the Ecuadorian Andes. Several loosely coordinated teams of costumed dancers cavort to the music of the flute and drum ensemble. The teams weave among one another, but each set of characters sticks to its own storyline. The cowboy and *vaca loca* (crazy cow) play at bullfighting. The cowboy deftly avoids most of the vaca loca's charges, but from time to time he is bowled over and onlookers must rush in to rescue the cowboy from the animal's horns. The *payaso* (a clown that is said to represent the foremen and owners of the haciendas of past genera-tions) and his retinue of wild animals play follow-the-leader games. The payaso waves a large Ecuadorian flag attached to a staff as foxes, monkeys, and tigers run and skip in a line behind him. From time to time, they stop, clasp hands, and play at weaving themselves together into geometric arrangements.

These teams of dancers belong to the religious-agrarian festivals that punctuate the year in Ecuador's rural highlands. Each major fiesta in the religious-agrarian calendar has its own set of costumed characters. For example, during Corpus Christi, dancers with towering headdresses and col-orful capes adorned with mirrors accompany the sponsors of the daily bull-fights. Similarly, during the Christmastime celebration of Three Kings, *yumbos* (wild men) dressed in white frocks and colorful aprons cavort with flags attached to mock spears. However, such fiesta-specific dancers have not turned up for the inaugural celebrations for the Hostal Princesa Toa, nor do they appear in the festivities held in honor of other holidays. This is only logical, since the storylines that these characters enact are closely associated with particular holidays. The teams that dance in celebration of the new hostel are those that one is likely to encounter in all of the festivals distributed throughout the annual festival cycle.

A little later in the morning, the brass band hired for the celebration arrives and begins to play near the entrance to the parking lot. The music of the two ensem-bles clashes from time to time, but no one minds. This is normal during a fiesta. In the meantime, delegations have arrived from the two agencies that funded con-struction of the new facility: Maquita Cushunchic—Comercializando como

Figure 3.1 Costumed dancers cavort in the main parking lot of the CTC Quilotoa. The Hostal Princesa Toa appears in the background

Hermanos (MCCH; Lending a Hand—Marketing as Brothers), a Quito-based Catholic assistance agency; and Cooperación Española (Spanish Cooperation), a partnership among governmental and civil society institutions in Spain that funds a wide variety of international development projects. More and more Quilotoans also gather. Locals, visiting dignitaries, and ethnographer alike, we all take out our smart phones to commemorate the day in photos and videos. Once everyone has gathered, the elected leaders of the CTC Quilotoa and the visitors from MCCH and Cooperación Española lead a procession a short distance up the road to the new hostel.

As the procession takes shape, another troupe of dancers joins the celebration. This group stands out in several respects. Whereas the other dancers are all adult men, this group is composed of preteens and teenagers. There are ten young women dressed in white blouses, long black or navy blue skirts, pink shawls, and *alpargatas* (sandal slippers). Each wears a dark felt fedora and has wrapped her ponytail tightly with a woven band. Some carry spindles and small bundles of wool, symbolizing the traditional shepherding livelihoods of indigenous people in the highest reaches of the Ecuadorian Andes. Others carry small trays that have been painted in bright colors by local artists, indexing modern tourist-oriented livelihoods in Quilotoa. Another young woman wears nearly the same costume except for a white straw hat. She is accompanied by a young man dressed as a condor: he wears a white shirt and long white pants, a red poncho tied tight about his waist with a rope, a white scarf around his neck, a condor mask, large wings that cover his back and arms, and a tail that hangs down toward his feet. Two smaller boys wearing sheepskins on their backs are also associated with this group. Unlike the other costumed dancers, this group has choreographed its movements: the dancers sway from side to side as they move forward with a shuffled walk in two parallel lines along the route of the procession.

The choreographed shuffle of the young dancers is related to the *serpenteado* (snake-like) dance that Michelle Wibbelsman (2005) has documented during the celebration of Inti Raymi in the Otavalo area of northern Ecuador. Like the young Quilotoan dancers, the participants in the Otavalo serpenteado move in a shuffled walk and often arrange themselves into two lines. However, in the Otavalo version the dancers do not coordinate their costumes. Instead,

> the costumes of the line dancers reflect contemporary themes and depict corrupt politicians, popular television and movie characters, and international political figures, or reveal local social dynamics such as the presence of evangelicals, regional vendors, hippies, tourists, reporters, and researchers in the Otavalo area.
>
> (207–208)

The Otavalo dancers' movements are interfered with by the *Aya Uma* (spirit head), a trickster character who wears a double devil-faced knit mask. Wibbelsman writes:

> It is significant that this trickster spirit head, who enacts both order and chaos, dances in the main plaza separate from the winding lines of

Figure 3.2 Young dancers in matching costumes participate in the procession

dancers and tries to interrupt the intertwining double-helix. The Aya Uma lies down in front of the dance troupes, blocking their passage. He mimics the troupe leader and tries to lead the dancers in the wrong direction. Much to the amusement of the crowd, the dancers wind around and over him without missing a beat. They ignore his leadership and remain indifferent to his efforts to sabotage the choreography .... My interpretation is that the inevitable progression of the serpenteado is an enactment of the moral fabric of society that the Aya Uma unsuccessfully tries to undo.

(208)

In Zumbahua Parish where Quilotoa is located, the serpenteado dance is performed by numerous groups of youth during the grand civic parade that marks the final day of the Corpus Christi festivities in the parish center. In this context, each troupe represents a particular school or other community-level institution. These groups usually wear matching costumes reflecting the everyday styles that were popular in the area during past decades, and they typically dance to prerecorded folkloric Andean music played on a stereo in the bed of a pickup truck. Many—but not all—of these groups include an aya uma character. I have also seen the children of Quilotoa perform a version of the serpenteado during a school fieldtrip to another school in the tropical cloud forests to the west of Zumbahua Parish. The school children danced to prerecorded music in coordinated costumes representing highland styles of the past, but their performance did not include an aya uma. Each of these dances is intended as a public display of community to a group of non-community members: in the parade, the audience consists of people from other communities in Zumbahua and neighboring parishes; in the case of the school field-trip, the audience consisted of students and teachers from a more distant community.

In the early afternoon, following several hours of speeches by the leaders of the CTC Quilotoa, MCCH, and Cooperación Española regarding their work together to make the new Hostal Princesa Toa a reality, the young choreographed dancers gather in front of a temporary stage that has been set up for the inaugural festivities. An emcee climbs onto the temporary stage and puts on a CD of commercial folkloric music. He calls out to locals and visitors who are milling about nearby, exhorting them to turn their attention to the group of young dancers.

As the music starts, two lines of young women enter the performance area from opposite directions, dancing toward one another in a quick shuffled step. One line curls around to form a parallel line with the other as they dance in place and two other characters dance in meandering lines around the performance area. One of these meandering characters is the young woman in the straw hat from earlier in the day. She tends a pair of sheep, played by young boys, who are pestered by another pair of young boys dressed as foxes. The second meandering character is the young man dressed as a condor. As the parallel lines of dancers sway in one direction and then another, a story unfolds: the condor finds the young woman, woos her, and finally carries her away on his back. As the story concludes, the serpenteado dancers take turns at weaving one line through the other and then dance off stage in different directions.

The story enacted by the young dancers is a version of Quilotoa's foundational myth of the condor who fell in love with Princesa Toa, the namesake of the new hostel. In the story, the condor saw Princesa Toa from afar and decided to woo her. Cunningly, he disguised himself as an attractive young man in order to draw her attention, and approached her as she was tending her sheep. After a period of courtship, he eloped with her to his home in the far upper reaches of the highest Andean peaks. Naturally, the young woman's parents were upset by her disappearance, and gathered a group of neighbors to bring her back to live among her human relatives. However, Princesa Toa soon became despondent without her husband, and her parents allowed her to return to her husband the condor.

Like the aya uma in the more traditional serpenteado dance, the condor and Princesa Toa weave their story among the lines of dancers representing community in this skit. Unlike the aya uma, they do not attempt to interrupt the fabric of that community. If anything, they strengthen that fabric by weaving the foundational myth of the community into an instance of its enactment. In this sense, their performance is similar to that of the skits performed during the *Sumak Ñusta* (beautiful princess) competition held on the first night of the Corpus Christi celebrations in Zumbahua. In both contexts, the actors attempt to embody the community itself by adopting the shuffling dance of the serpenteado, carrying symbols of traditional rural culture such

Figure 3.3 Still from a video recording of the Princesa Toa folkloric skit

as bundles of wool and barley, and reenacting stylized stories about the very origins of life in the highlands.

What are we to make of the distinct styles of dance performed during this event? Each enacts a story of community, but they do so in quite distinct modes that communicate community according to distinct temporalities. The characters drawn from the traditional religious-agrarian calendar act out a collection of storylines that appear in festival dancing throughout the year, but are not tied to any fiesta in particular. Their dance captures community through a broad reference to the annual cycle of rural life in the Andean highlands. In the morning, the younger choreographed dancers enact community by coordinating their costumes and movements in an expression of collective identity rooted in an older form of expression through dance. In the afternoon, the young dancers present a highly stylized version of Quilotoa's origin myth, drawing on the same style they performed earlier in the day, but replacing the meddling aya uma that traditionally seeks to disrupt community cohesion with the figures at the core of Quilotoa's mythical origin story.

Each of these stories of community weaves among the others, but they do not interact directly. Such a dynamic is typical of Andean storytelling conventions, which weave together the storylines of many characters that each has its own trajectory (Allen 2011). It is also typical of the scenes painted by the artists of Quilotoa and nearby Tigua. Thus, I now turn to a painting prepared by Klever Latacunga in advance of the inauguration of the new Hostal Princesa Toa. The painting rehearses similar stories to those that were danced during the inaugural festivities, and it allows for a deeper understanding of how such stories weave together in Kichwa visions of storytelling.

Painting community

The artists of Quilotoa depict agrarian life in their communities in a brightly colorful, baroque style. This was initially developed in the 1970s by Kichwa artist-entrepreneurs from the nearby communities of Tigua in direct response to the interest that international tourists and foreign folk art dealers had begun to show in the decorated drums that Kichwa musicians have traditionally played during Corpus Christi celebrations. Indeed, the material traces of this adaptation are evident in the paintings themselves, which are composed on pieces of uncured sheepskin stretched tightly across wooden frames. Few tourists stop along the road that passes through Tigua, so many of the early innovators of the genre ultimately moved away from their rural homes in order to gain more direct access to urban tourist-oriented craft markets. However, tourists soon began flock to Quilotoa to visit the emerald-green lake that shines serenely within the caldera of the volcano for which the community is named, so the Quilotoans who adopted their Tiguan neighbors' art form have been able to rededicate themselves to their rural community through tourism.

The artists of Tigua and Quilotoa are subject to the "tourist gaze" (Urry 2002) and have learned to anticipate what international tourists expect of indigenous culture. Consequently, painters have learned to avoid contentious political themes and they minimize the presence of overtly non-indigenous or non-traditional material culture in the scenes they illustrate. Yet the artists do not simply paint what the tourists want to see. To the contrary, Dorothea Whitten argues that they "paint the nation as they see and experience it" (2003, 247) and that their paintings "reflect a clear sense of alternative modernities" (2011, 146). As Colloredo-Mansfeld learned in Tigua, painters compose their paintings so as to selectively include only those themes and "objects that partake in the flow of indigenous work within communities" (2011, 19).

Colloredo-Mansfeld (2011) also found that Tiguan artists judge the expertise with which a scene has been brought to life based on the storylines that compose the action of the scene. Each painting tends to illustrate multiple storylines, and each storyline must be depicted in such a way that it is allowed to play out fully. For instance, a path might be necessary so that the characters may traverse it. Or a woman might be necessary in order accompany her husband. Like the episodes that are stitched together in Andean storytelling (Allen 2011), the storylines that compose these paintings intersect at various points, but each is also complete in itself. Colloredo-Mansfeld writes, "The lines perceived in a Tiguan painting become the lines of interpretation, the literal guiding lines for a viewer to tell what the picture is about" (2011, 21).

Here, I discuss a series of paintings that Quilotoan artist Klever Latacunga prepared following the announcement that MCCH would sponsor a competition to create the artworks with which the public areas of the new Princesa Toa Hostel would be decorated. Each of the paintings in the series explores several intersecting stories about Quilotoa as a community. All of them include at least three themes in common: traditional rural livelihoods, the tourism infrastructure managed by the CTC Quilotoa, and the story of the condor and Princesa Toa. The painting pictured in Figure 3.4 also depicts the celebration of Corpus Christi. In one mode or another, each of these themes captures Quilotoa as a community.

The central theme of this series is Quilotoa's history of institution-building, as illustrated by the inclusion of the newly constructed Hostal Princesa Toa and the Kirutwa Restaurant in all of the paintings in the series. In this painting, one also finds the scenic overlook, the thatch-roofed information booth, and the small building that houses the pumps that supply water to the community. It is notable that the private homes and businesses that crowd around these community buildings in real life do not appear in this series of paintings. Individuals and families in Quilotoa have much to be proud of, but this is a depiction of the literal construction of community where there existed only muddy pastures a generation ago.

Figure 3.4 Painting depicting community-managed tourism infrastructure, mythical origins, and other stories of community in Quilotoa. Painting by Klever Latacunga, 2014

Klever depicted various scenes from the story of Princesa Toa and the condor in the series. In this example, Princesa Toa tends her sheep in the middle foreground while the condor prepares to don the poncho of an attractive young man as he soars in the sky above the scene. In other paintings from the series, he approaches her on the ground or carries her on his back in the sky. Taken together, they rehearse the major events of the same foundational myth that the young dancers acted out in their skit on the afternoon of the inauguration.

In all paintings from the series, as in virtually all tourist-oriented paintings and most paintings that are not destined for sale to tourists, the central themes are depicted within the context of agrarian livelihood pursuits. Due to the ubiquity of this agrarian frame, it might be easily overlooked, but its significance should not be ignored. Many Quilotoans do not participate in agrarian activities as their parents and grandparents did. To depict the tourism infrastructure managed by the CTC Quilotoa and the mythical origins of the community as existing within the frame of agrarian pursuits is to establish the mythical origins of the community and the collective pursuit of the future in the context of lived history. This is reinforced by the Corpus Christi dancers in the lower right foreground of this painting (see Figure 3.4). Their presence serves as a reminder of the historical and material origins of the genre as well as the culminating moment in the annual religious-agrarian festival cycle through which Quilotoans and their neighbors celebrate their rural indigenous identities.

In short, Klever's series of paintings interweaves the history of the tourism complex managed by the CTC Quilotoa, the chartering myth of the community, the ritual-agrarian festival cycle, and the everyday livelihoods of the past, present, and future. As in the dances performed during the inauguration of the Hostal Princesa Toa and in Quilotoans' lived experience more generally, each of these storylines stands alone, but each must be understood in relation to the others.

Discussion

In the context of tourism, Quilotoans' collective presentation of self is both multistranded and multivocal. On one hand, the multistrandedness of Quilotoan dance performance and artistic representation has its roots in narrative conventions that are widely shared by indigenous people throughout the Andean region. Just as no one minded on the morning of the inauguration of the Hostal Princesa Toa when two bands simultaneously played distinct styles of music with different tempos, Quilotoans do not mind that their enactments and depictions of community interweave storylines that unfold according to distinct temporalities. Indeed, such interweaving is expected; it is a defining characteristic of Andean narrative convention (Allen 2011).

On the other hand, the multivocality of these collective presentations of self originates outside of the local setting in the circulation of globally hegemonic codes for the expression of cultural distinctiveness. As Richard Wilk (1995) writes, this hegemony does not entail the homogenization of cultural diversity; rather, it "is to be found in *structures of common difference*, which celebrate particular kinds of diversity while submerging, deflating or suppressing others" (118, emphasis in original). In the beauty pageants that Wilk discusses, as in the pageantry and artistry of tourism in Quilotoa, "very real and 'authentic' differences in experience and culture continue to exist, but are being expressed and communicated in a limited and narrow range of images, channels and contests" (118).

According to Wilk's (1995) account, there occurs in Belizean beauty pageants a "collision between local standards of beauty, deeply embedded in cultural constructs of gender and sexuality, and international standards which are widely believed to be those of the dominant white nations in the north" (127). In other words, beauty is a site of what Viveiros de Castro (2004) calls "equivocation." That is, beauty is a concept that may appear to be shared by people of different backgrounds when they agree that a particular pageant participant is beautiful, but it actually means something distinct to different groups of interlocutors. Wilk shows that behind the scenes, organizers and contestants make creative use of beauty pageants as tools for expressing collective identities and communicating a range of social and political messages.

Yet when the beauty of Belizean women is displayed on the global stage, it is expressed according to global structures of difference.

In Ecuador and elsewhere, "indigenous culture" is another site of equivocation within global structures of difference. Nor is tourism the only context for this equivocation. In international development and transnational environmentalism, indigenous people find it necessary to present themselves according to particular visual and physical codes (Conklin 1997), speak in particular ways (Graham 2002), and generally engage a field of symbolic politics in which their culture is mobilized as a resource within communicative frames that are appealing to non-indigenous outsiders but do not reflect the lived realities of indigenous experience (Conklin and Graham 1995). In short, it is common in many spheres of engagement between indigenous and non-indigenous social actors that interlocutors mean quite different things when they invoke indigenous culture. Inasmuch as indigenous people are usually aware of this difference while their non-indigenous interlocutors are often unaware, this phenomenon may be termed "partially controlled equivocation."

Such partially controlled equivocation undoubtedly occurs when Quilotoans dance or paint for touristic consumption. As Goffman (1959) anticipated, these presentations of collective self prompt critical reflection on social life, but they are not constrained to the back stage area of tourist-oriented performance as MacCannell (1973) theorized. Quilotoans are able to explore themes of culture and community openly in their tourist-oriented presentations of collective self because tourists simply do not recognize that these critical discourses are taking place. My ethnography has not generated any evidence that most tourists recognize the significance of many of the themes I have discussed in this chapter. Certainly, the typical touristic visitor to Quilotoa is not prepared to appreciate how storylines mix without blending in Kichwa representations of community life.

References

Allen, C.J. (2011). *Foxboy: Intimacy and aesthetics in Andean stories*. Austin: University of Texas Press.
Colloredo-Mansfeld, R. (2011). Space, line and story in the invention of an Andean aesthetic. *Journal of Material Culture*. 16(1), 3–23.
Conklin, B.A. (1997). Body paint, feathers, and VCRs: Aesthetics and authenticity in Amazonian activism. *American Ethnologist*. 24(4): 711–737.
Conklin, B.A., and Graham, L.R. (1995). The shifting middle ground: Amazonian Indians and eco-politics. *American Anthropologist* 97(4), 695–710.
Goffman, E. (1959). *The Presentation of the Self in Everyday Life*. Garden City, NY: Anchor Books.
Graham, L.R. (2002). How should an Indian speak? Amazonian Indians and the symbolic politics of language in the global public sphere. In Warren, K.B., & Jackson, J.E. (eds.), *Indigenous Movements, Self-Representation, and the State in Latin America* (pp. 181–228). Austin: University of Texas Press.

Greenwood, D.J. (1989). Culture by the pound: An anthropological perspective on tourism as cultural commoditization. In Smith, V.L. (ed.), *Hosts and Guests: The anthropology of tourism* (pp. 171–185). Philadelphia: University of Pennsylvania Press.

MacCannell, D. (1973). Staged authenticity: Arrangements of social space in tourist settings. *American Journal of Sociology.* 79(3), 589–603.

Muratorio, B. (2000). Etnografía e historia visual de una etnicidad emergente: El caso de las pinturas de Tigua. In Carrión, F. (ed.), *Desarrollo cultural y gestión en centros históricos* (pp. 47–74). Quito: FLACSO.

Peers, L. (2007). *Playing Ourselves: Interpreting Native histories at historic reconstructions.* Lanham, MD: AltaMira Press.

Urry, J. (2002). *The Tourist Gaze.* London: SAGE.

Viveiros de Castro, E. (2004). Perspectival anthropology and the method of controlled equivocation. *Tipití.* 2(1), 1–20.

Whitten, D.S. (2003). Actors and artists from Amazonia and the Andes. In Whitten, Jr., N.E. (Ed.), *Millennial Ecuador: Critical essays on cultural transformation and social dynamics* (pp. 242–274). Iowa City: University of Iowa Press.

Whitten, D.S. (2011). Indigenous ethnographers portray their world. In Whitten, Jr., N.E., & Whitten, D.S. (eds.), *Histories of the Present: People and power in Ecuador* (pp. 143–161). Champaign: University of Illinois Press.

Wibbelsman, M. (2005). Encuentros: Dances of the Inti Raymi in Cotacachi, Ecuador. *Latin American Music Review.* 26(2), 195–226.

Wilk, R. (1995). Learning to be local in Belize: Global systems of common difference. In Miller, D. (ed.), *Worlds Apart: Modernity through the prism of the local* (pp. 110–133). London: Routledge.

4 Violence as tourist spectacle in eastern Indonesia

Exploring the imaginaries of pain, identity, and power in Manggaraian tourism encounters

Maribeth Erb

World-making, imaginaries, and emotions: Contemplating the power of tourism

> ...tourism does not just axiomatically reproduce some given realm of being (be it a projected "people," a promoted "place" or a propelled "past"), but commonly makes, de-makes or re-makes those very populations, destinations and heritages.
>
> (Hollinshead, Ateljevic, & Ali 2009, 428)

The power of tourism to shape the world, this world-making ability, has been extensively commented upon over the past decade and a half by many researchers in critical tourism studies (Hall & Tucker 2004; Hollinshead 2004, 2007, 2009; Hollinshead et al. 2009; Meethan 2001). Imaginaries about exotic places and peoples circulate across the globe. They spur tourists, but also engage varying local actors to remake and reshape, to fulfill or extend these touristic fantasies (Salazar 2010, 2012). In contrast to an approach that saw tourism as a part of the "outside" that "impacted" local cultures like "billiard balls," a more nuanced way to understand the relationship between tourism and local culture was argued for long ago by people such as Wood (1980, 1993), Picard (1990), and Errington and Gewertz (1989), who asserted that tourism is instead something that is an integral part of local culture; there is thus no clear "back stage" and "front stage" boundary between local and touristic culture but instead a tight integration. Touristic imaginaries are thus imbibed and remade within local cultural contexts. However, this remaking is always a struggle that is potentially contested by various actors, with their own agendas formed by local, national, and international cultural and identity politics. Although critical tourism scholars have focused on this aspect of power in tourism, there has been less attention paid, Raoul Bianchi argues (2009), to the structural inequalities produced by tourism and the spread of global capitalism. He lamented a lack of understanding about the "relationship between discourses and the diverse forms of capitalist development and territorial logics of state power of which tourism constitutes a key part" (493).

An attention to power necessarily must include, he argues, a recognition of the material bases of the inequality that tourism can foster. In the pursuit of exploring the intersection between these different threads of a critical tourism approach, I want to include in this chapter an analysis of an aspect of tourism encounters that has only recently been explored, that is, the question of emotion. What I do in this chapter is incorporate into these theoretical deliberations about culture, identity, power, and inequality a consideration of how emotions are promoted, reshaped, and remade within tourism, against the background of material struggles and potentially latent hostilities that are fomented due to these material inequalities. I do this through contemplating violent spectacles as tourist attractions and how they are presented to play on emotions. I consider at the same time what is the role of cultural displays in tourism on the local inhabitants' lives. Are cultural displays "staged" and is there a distinctive touristic "space," a so-called "front stage" that is clearly separated from a quotidian "back stage" for people on Flores island, in eastern Indonesia? I pay attention to these issues through thinking about the more recent attention in tourism studies to the question of emotion, and how emotions of both tourists and locals become involved in world-making processes and the material struggles that this world-making engenders.

Picard and Robinson (2012) open up the issue of the encounter of different emotional cultures that takes place within tourism (Picard 2012, 14). Their discussion underscores how important emotions are to tourism. People expect to be subjected to very different experiences that will elicit sometimes strong emotional reactions. Awe, wonder, happiness, grief, shame, horror, anger, envy, desire, and fear are all emotional reactions that play out in the spaces of tourism in ways that are sometimes overwhelming to the participants (Picard 2012, 1–3). What helps to create these feelings are the strangeness of the encounter, the expectation of meeting with something that has not been seen before, something that is not a typical part of one's cultural script. The encounter of different emotional cultures means that what is expressed, however, may not be understood within these "contact zones." Experiencing strong emotions is an expected part of the tourist adventure; similarly tourists and locals often recognize that these emotions may bring into relief cultural difference. There are also actors who attempt to manipulate the emotions that are felt and displayed within tourism-oriented spaces. Service industry managers coax and educate tourism workers to always display emotions that relay friendliness and helpfulness, assumed to be desired by tourists. Tourists are also instructed on appropriate reactions to particular places by advertisements, guide books, and other means of relaying information about particular locales, such as various types of travel writing. As Picard suggests, what people actually feel and the emotions they are told they will feel are often at odds with one another. Emotions are notoriously difficult to express and communicate in language (2012, 13).

In this chapter, I explore the world of emotions and cultural expression in a tourist locale in eastern Indonesia by examining the presentation of violence in the display of an important cultural performance on western Flores. I look at the accounts of the meaning of these performances found in promotional material, and compare these with those of tourism workers from the local community as well as performance group members in a region that is the main gateway to the Komodo National Park. I analyze how these explanations construct a particular image of the culture of the region which is complementary to the natural attraction that has become so famous, that of the Komodo Dragon (*Varanus komodensis*). Various actors promoting cultural display, I suggest, manipulate the presentation and understanding of these displays in order to create certain understandings of the people and their culture. At the same time these cultural displays are emotionally very important events for people in west Flores, and they fight for the ability to present a way of understanding this culture that is more appropriate to their own feelings and philosophy. There are struggles over these understandings and depictions, which are created within the context of dramatic changes to the material bases of life in this rapidly growing tourist area. Instead of seeing these various dissonant understandings as evidence of a "front stage"/"back stage" binary of tourist–local understanding and action which prioritizes an idea of what is "authentic," I prefer to examine how these stages of action play out for different audiences, and how audience understanding and participant action can be mutually transformative and represent the struggles over identity, culture, and inequality in tourism spaces.

Wonderful Indonesia and enchanting Labuan Bajo

The district government in western Flores, in the eastern Indonesian province of East Nusa Tenggara, has been hoping, since at least the early 1980s, for tourism to develop and bring both benefits to the local communities and revenue to the local government. The increased interest in tourism dated to the creation, in 1980, of the Komodo National Park, a territory consisting of several islands and the surrounding seas, just west of the island of Flores (Erb 2000; Walpole & Goodman 2000). The fame of this park is due to the unique Komodo "dragon" (*Varanus komodensis*), the largest land lizard in the world, that is found only on a few islands in the park and on the western part of Flores island. In 1991, the Komodo Park was named a UNESCO World Heritage Site and in the 1990s started to receive attention from international conservation organizations that began to monitor and promote the unique marine life of the park, sometimes clashing with the fishing communities which had been living off the wealth of the sea for centuries. These international organizations, particularly the Nature Conservancy, worked hard to promote the park, and co-managed it for a time with the park authorities (Erb 2012). They provoked the resentment of many local people, however, with their draconian and, to the locals, "neocolonial" style of managing the park, and eventually were forced to retreat from their managerial role in the mid 2000s.

Although a trickle of outsiders had also begun to establish small hotels and diving operations in Labuan Bajo, a small town in western Flores and the main gateway to the park, the greater increase in investment and hotel development began only after another international NGO, Swiss Contact, started organizing and providing assistance for tourism enterprises in 2005. Their efforts to organize and standardize tourism-oriented activities and businesses in Labuan Bajo inspired confidence in larger investors. Around the same time, political changes in Indonesia, spurred by the fall of the long-time dictator Suharto in the late 1990s, had led in the early 21st century to widespread administrative changes and the divisions of districts across Flores. Labuan Bajo become the capital of a new district, that of West Manggarai, in 2003 (see Figure 4.1),[1] which led to a major population increase, both due to the hoped-for employment potential of tourism and the wave of new civil servant jobs that the division created.

A small number of big chain hotels opened in the late 2000s, but the "gold rush" in west Flores tourism only began after Komodo was chosen in 2011 as one of the "New Seven Wonders" of the natural world, a competition started by a Swiss organization in 2007.[2] After Komodo was chosen, the numbers of domestic tourists rose dramatically, as did the amount of attention and investment in tourism developments from national-level tourism players (Erb 2013, 2015). At the same time more and more foreigners started to buy up land and set up a variety of establishments in and around the town of Labuan Bajo, both extremely cheap backpacker places and increasingly high-end boutique and villa tourism options. In a short time, all the land along the west coast of Flores had been bought up, and the price of land in and around Labuan Bajo and the surrounding peninsula of northwest Flores skyrocketed. With soaring land prices it become difficult for Florenese who wanted to move to Labuan Bajo to afford land, and the cost of living rose dramatically. Food was increasingly imported into Labuan Bajo from other islands, with local farmers reaping little benefit from tourism because of the higher land transportation costs. The growing numbers of hotels and restaurants willing to pay higher prices for fruits, vegetables, and meat drove up the costs of food. The most dramatic inequality in resource competition, however, as Stroma Cole has recently documented (2017), is the problem of water. The coastal areas of Flores are drier than the interior, and water has always been a problem. With the rising population and increasing numbers of hotels using huge amounts of water,

1   West Manggarai was split from Manggarai district in 2003, and in 2007 East Manggarai was also created. These Manggarai districts have a certain amount of cultural unity; however, there is considerable linguistic and cultural variation across this large area, especially in the far western part, where Labuan Bajo and the focus of major tourism developments are found, and the far eastern part, bordering on Ngada district.

2   The New Seven Wonders Foundation was started in 2001 to allow people across the globe to vote for the New Seven Wonders of the World (finalized in 2007), and the New Seven Natural Wonders (finalized in 2011), via digital communications media. See New Seven Wonders (n.d.).

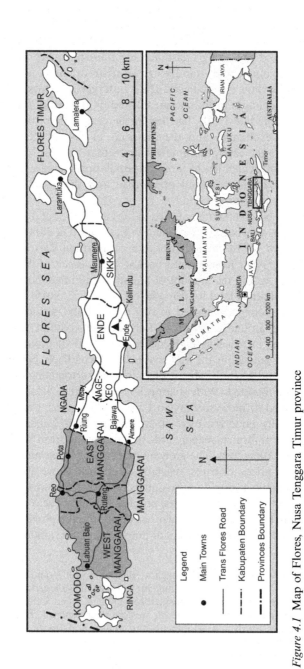

Figure 4.1 Map of Flores, Nusa Tenggara Timur province

the poor of the town struggle to meet their daily needs, and pay a much higher rate than those with steady suppliers (19). Tourists and the wealthier immigrant owners of tourism businesses are often unaware of these difficulties to access water and the struggles the indigenous communities face on a daily basis. Material inequalities produced by tourism growth and investment continue to expand.

Not long after Komodo won the title of a "New7Wonder," the central government began playing a more active role in promoting the park, and over the past half-decade a number of "mega-events" have contributed to an even more dramatic change in the tourism landscape and character of tourism developments in and around Labuan Bajo and the Komodo park. An Indonesian "Sail" was planned for Komodo for 2013, 11th in a series of "yacht rallies" starting from Darwin which were initiated to make remote parts of Indonesia better known. Increasingly the central government coupled these Sails with huge infrastructural improvement programs, investing trillions of rupiah into the chosen destinations (Erb 2015).[3] The final, spectacular ceremony of "Sail Komodo," complete with military ships and attended by the president of Indonesia, was held in Labuan Bajo in September 2013. The idea of these promotional niche events caught on, and in early 2016 a number of Florenese living in the national capital, Jakarta, initiated the first "Tour de Flores," an international bicycle race crossing the island of Flores from east to west, with the intention of making Flores better known. Funds were solicited from each of the district governments on Flores, and again the closing ceremony was held in Labuan Bajo. All of these major events (the Tour de Flores being repeated again in 2017 and 2018) have garnered a considerable amount of criticism from activists who argue the monies used to hold these events, and the lavish ceremonies that accompany them, could be better used to bring more needed programs to the peoples of Flores. The elites who attend these events are treated to amenities beyond the imaginings of most of the population of the island, underscoring the poverty of the Florenese people. At the same time the promotional aspect of these events, critics argue, is wholly unnecessary, since Flores and the Komodo Park are already very well known, and need no promotion to the small numbers of participants who are involved in these specialized types of tourism (sailing and cycling).

Another media event also had a defining effect for Labuan Bajo and the Komodo Park. In around 2015 or 2016, a photo went viral of the island of Padar in the Komodo National Park which, according to many posters on TripAdvisor and other blog sites, is the most spectacular view in all of Indonesia. Capturing the island of Padar, with a black sand beach on one side and a white sand beach on the other (with Komodo Island and its famed Pink Beach in the background), the photo inspired visitors to trek up the hill to

---

3   Accusations of corruption of the vast money that was allocated continue, and in July 2018 in Labuan Bajo, the head of the Government Tourism Board was detained to investigate reported misuse of funds to promote and organize cultural events during the huge festival held in Labuan Bajo at the end of the Sail, in September, 2013. See Floresa (2018).

take a "selfie," causing a huge upsurge in the numbers of tourists interested in visiting the park.[4] One dive shop owner in Labuan Bajo indicated that this was a defining moment, and since then, he argued, the character of tourists visiting Labuan Bajo and the park has begun to change; instead of the hardy backpacker type predominating, a more demanding type of tourist is becoming more predominant.

In 2016 the central government identified Labuan Bajo as one of the ten "priority destinations" that were to become "New Balis" (Adiakurnia 2018; Soegiarto 2016). Their goal in accelerating the development of those ten priority destinations was 20 million tourists visiting Indonesia.[5] Labuan Bajo is, in fact, one of the four "extra-ordinary" priority destinations that is getting the earliest attention. In order to accelerate this process, Labuan Bajo tourism developments are to be managed specially by a central government Tourism Authority, and will become a "special economic tourism zone," bringing together under one umbrella the efforts of several ministries to stimulate the rapid development and investment in tourism (Valenta 2018). Under this new Tourism Authority (formed in April, 2018, see Wonderful Indonesia 2018), the central government will be turning the Komodo Airport of Labuan Bajo into an international airport (slated for 2020), and has begun work on reconstructing the ferry terminal so as to turn it into a luxury-class marina, complete with a hotel, restaurants, and shopping mall reputedly to be of "international standard" that can cater to a higher class of tourist seeking facilities for their yachts. This marina was projected to open in August 2018 in time for the ASEAN games held in Jakarta and Palembang, with side trips planned for the participants to Komodo and for the IMF meetings in Bali in October, 2018.[6] In anticipation of the high-level events planned, when I last visited Labuan Bajo in July 2018, a luxury hotel resort was being built, carved into the hillside on a beach not far outside of Labuan Bajo town. While driving by the site, a friend commented that this feat of building such a hotel, in such a location, was previously beyond the imaginings of any members of the local community.

4   This was especially the case with domestic tourists, with the numbers almost doubling between 2015 and 2016 from over 15,000 to just under 30,000 (Dinas Pariwisata dan Budaya 2017, 55).

5   Indonesia, despite its size and vast cultural and natural diversity, has lagged far behind other ASEAN nations in terms of tourism arrivals, something the Indonesian government is resolved to change. In 2015, Thailand had nearly 30 million visitors, Malaysia over 25 million, and tiny Singapore over 15 million. Indonesia had reached over ten million for the first time (ASEAN Secretariat 2017, 181). Those are the most recent figures available.

6   The original plans to bring the 3000 IMF delegates to Flores to visit the park resulted in a flurry of speculation as to where they would stay, when I visited Labuan Bajo in July 2018. At that time the number of five-star hotel rooms built to cater to the projected elite visitors fell far short of the expected numbers. In the end, only 50 IMF delegates went to Labuan Bajo after the October meetings. See Kewa Ama (2018).

Indeed, the differences in material existence that these projects underscore is becoming more and more dissonant to local sensibilities. A security guard at the construction site of the new marina hotel commented about the accompanying shopping mall which will connect to the new hotel: "These shops will be clean, they will be according to the taste of foreigners, very clean." His comment and the various other structures that are being built conjure a vision of a parallel world being constructed, entirely apart from the dusty, dirty, garbage-strewn streets, gutters, and streams of Labuan Bajo. This construction, this separation, is mirrored across the landscape, where in the more remote corners of the dry and secluded north Flores peninsula, on steep hillsides near beaches, myriad types of accommodation have been and are continuing to be constructed for wealthy, elite tourists, who prefer to shun the town of Labuan Bajo and are whisked from the airport to these enclaves, with minimal interaction with the local peoples. Sally Ann Ness calls these types of developments a "darker side of place" (2005), querying the innocence of the tourist paradise, and suggesting that tourism begets violence. It is not surprising that acts of real violence have started to creep into the everyday interactions in Labuan Bajo between locals and foreigners, with a few isolated incidents of tourists being attacked by locals (Erb 2018). The most recent was the rape of two tourists, one French and one Italian, in June 2018 (Coconuts Bali 2018; Siregar 2018). One friend related his veiled threat to a foreign hotel owner who had revealed her plans to buy a boat so she could also ferry tourists to Komodo and Rinca islands in the park: "You can do this, sure," he said, "but do not be surprised if your boat sinks one night." Fishing people who were displaced from their fishing activities by the early conservation efforts in the Komodo park and forced into the alternative livelihood of "fishing for tourists" would not appreciate the "tourists" (meaning foreigners) starting to push them out of these livelihood activities as well. The increasing marginality of local populations, especially the coastal fishing communities, is, as mentioned above, particularly felt in terms of inequality to access of important resources such as water (Cole 2017). The irony is that while Labuan Bajo developed as a tourist town, with spaces that have become more segregated and access to resources increasingly differentiated, it has been "branded" by the Minister of Tourism as "Enchanting Labuan Bajo" (Dinas Pariwisata dan Budaya 2017, 27). "Enchanting" is not a word most people would use to describe the streets of the town itself. Views from the sea or from hotels and restaurants to islands in the distance may be "enchanting," but a close-up experience of the town is dusty, dirty, and pungent. The vistas of the tourist experience and the realities of living in the town are extremely dissonant, leading to what might be called the "ambiguous gift of capitalist modernity" (Hall & Tucker 2004). These inequalities and frustrations may someday become more acutely felt in interactions; however, for the most part, the specter of violence in west Flores is currently a symbolic one. The way that these symbols of violence have been wielded and adapted to the changing circumstances of Labuan Bajo and Komodo tourism is what I turn to now.

Tourist spectacles: The violence of man and beast

The Komodo dragon has long been a source of imagining the violence and adventure of the remote world of nature outside of "civilization." Timothy Barnard argues that these imaginaries of the violence of an "antediluvian" place like Komodo originated mainly from the early documentary films about Komodo dragons (2009, 2017). Naming them "dragons" already had a romantic, mystical ring, and was initiated, Barnard tells us, by William Douglas Burden, the first person to have filmed these lizards in the 1920s (Barnard 2009, 45–49). Films are a particularly important way of creating "imaginaries" and, as Barnard says, filmmakers who accompanied various early expeditions "sought not only scientific information but also cultural narratives in which common tropes could be conveyed to the public" (2017, 225). These tropes are part of the bases of tourism imaginaries, created and circulated at least since the time of colonialism. In order to produce interesting films, these filmmakers started to stage their productions, and, as Barnard suggests, "Such introductions reveal broader cultural tensions and anxieties about the perceived savagery and violence outside of Western civilisation" (225). The original footage of these animals was in fact very tame and unexciting. The "dragons" themselves are extremely lethargic and do not usually pose any threat to human beings. In order to create "dramatic interest," the Komodo dragon needed help, and as Barnard shows, the image of the violent Komodo dragon became the stimulus for King Kong and other more fantastic imaginary creatures of early cinema. The "dramatic interest" and imaginary violence of the Komodo have become even more exaggerated in recent decades, with *Komodo* (1999) and *The Curse of the Komodo* (2004), horror science fiction movies depicting rampaging Komodos. These films help to stimulate tourist imaginations and to reconfirm imaginaries about the "perceived savagery and violence outside of Western civilisation" (Barnard 2017, 225).

Cultural displays and violent imaginaries

> Even though there is an element of violence in caci this art form possesses a message of peace, sportsmanship, mutual respect, and intimate friendship.
> (Dinas Pariwisata dan Budaya 2017, 23, translation by author)

Consistent with these tropes of violence and savagery are the various performances that have become icons of west Florenese culture: the knuckle boxing of Ngada district (Florestourism.com 2018b), and the whip games of the Manggarai districts (Florestourism.com 2018a, see also Erb 2001, 2008). My focus here are these whip games, known as *caci*, played throughout the three Manggarai districts of the most westerly part of Flores (see Figure 4.1). Similar to the exaggerated dramatization of the Komodo dragon as exceptionally violent and savage, the promotional depictions of the *caci* whip

Figure 4.2 Promotional poster for a cultural festival in Labuan Bajo, July 2017, depicting dramatic leaps

Figure 4.3 Playing caci, cultural festival, Labuan Bajo, July 2017

games have also been dramatically exaggerated in recent years so as to fore-front an acrobatic and exciting imagery of the game (see Figure 4.2), with leaps and bounds that rarely appear in the actual contests (see Figure 4.3). In May, 2017, *caci* was formally identified as the "cultural tourism icon" of West Manggarai, complementing Komodo as the "nature tourism icon" (and one of the icons of all of Indonesian tourism).

Caci is an interesting contradictory performance to contemplate. *Caci* appears to be an exotic display, because the men who hit one another alter-nately with whips dress up as animals with buffalo horns and goat tails adorning their headdresses, creating a kind of masked spectacle of hybrid man and beast. While violent, it is also most often performed to welcome highly honored guests to western Flores and is considered the height of Manggaraian cultural integrity, sportsmanship, and respect. *Caci* is an important symbol of Manggaraian hospitality, since across the districts of Manggarai, one village will invite another to send a team to play *caci* for one to three days, depending on the size of the ritual event and the ability of the village hosts to kill enough animals to feed the many guests. One might say the ultimate "guests" in Manggaraian culture are the *caci* players (referred to as *meka landang*—"the traveling guest"); they are males who arrive, are greeted with wine and sacrifice, show off their virility to all the young women in the village, and seek the blood of their opponents. Jacques Derrida's theo-rization about hospitality as an inevitably contradictory act, always infused with elements of hostility, is well illustrated by the role of *caci* in Manggar-aian culture (Derrida 2000; Erb 2013). *Caci* as an important activity of tour-ism performance is also apt, given the contradictory nature of hospitality associated with tourism: the struggles over who is in control, the incoming investors masquerading as tourist guests; or locals, who are becoming increasingly uncertain of their identity as the "master" or "hosts" in the local situation (Cole 2017, 21; Erb 2013).

There is much discussion in the tourism literature about how tourism creates different spaces of action: front stages where culture is performed for tourists and people interact with them, versus the back stages, where the "real" world continues. The argument as originally presented by MacCan-nell (1973) has been debated and reargued in many interesting and subtle ways (e.g. "touristic borderzones" [Bruner 1996], "utopic spaces" [Causey 2003], "empty meeting grounds" [MacCannell 1992]). In west Flores there has never been a clear division between what is done for tourists and what is done in a local context. There has always been a desire to include foreigners in any major event and to do so with considerable eagerness. A major event is when food is offered that people would not be embarrassed to serve honored guests (always a concern when receiving visitors in Manggarai). An increasing number of people deemed important are attending various cere-monies and events, meaning that standards are being raised to cater to spe-cial guests. These guests are often associated in some way with the government and, interestingly, in Flores no division is made between events put on for "tourism" and those put on in the presence of government offi-cials. Government officials often outnumber tourists, and the demands for lavishness grow with the level of government official. This was particularly evident in the, to my mind, rather ill-conceived Sail Komodo event, where government extravagance and pomp ended up marginalizing tourists to Labuan Bajo, because government visitors from Jakarta and the provincial capital, Kupang, crowded into the hotels, leaving little space for tourists during September 2013. The military pomp of the extravagant escort for the president, who attended the closing ceremony, frightened many of the remaining tourists—ironically, including the sailors from around the world who the event was supposedly meant to honor (Erb 2015). A similar lack of differentiation between tourists and other special guests occurs in villages, where tourists are especially welcome to an already planned event, the more the merrier, and there is no concern if they are unexpected. It is when tour-ists show up unexpectedly in a more quotidian setting that people get uncomfortable and do not know exactly how to deal with them. In this way, tourist spectacle and spectacles in general are not conceptualized as being in any way separate or distinct, and the audience desires are also not specifi-cally differentiated.

In this context, the *sanggar*, officially recognized art and cultural groups, fulfill a certain need in west Florenese tourism, in addition to their stated purpose of preserving culture and tradition. *Sanggar* groups tend to be invited to cultural festivals, whether the main purpose is specifically a display for tourism or any other event—opening ceremonies, welcoming ceremonies, national ceremonies—where traditional cultural performances are desired. In this way they have become professional culture experts, who are ready to put on cultural displays upon request. The village of Melo is particularly famous for this. Located less than 20 km. east of Labuan Bajo, it is officially pro-moted via the Swiss Contact website.[7] Visitors can go to Melo and pay to have a "traditional welcome," plus watch a cultural display of *caci* and other dances for less than $100US. The site is also advertised and well known for its panoramic view of the seas of the Komodo park. Manggaraian people have mixed feelings about these specifically touristic performances that are "made to order," so to speak. Although, for example, tourism board officials praise the "entrepreneurship" of Melo villagers in selling culture to tourists, they are also clear that this is not "real" *caci*, when it is done as a "display," and not part of a major event. Some are critical of this, and suggest that it has been on the whole a bad thing for the unity of this village. How can people who are related, who are part of one village play *caci* against one another? It is forbidden to play *caci* against relatives, and hence it is not surprising that sometimes bad signs occur during the playing of *caci* in that village, with

7 See http://florestourism.com/districts/melo/; it is also mentioned by some other blogger/promotional sites (Adventoro 2018; Rossiter 2016; Tanzil 2011).

people getting serious wounds that are understood as an "ancestral curse" (see more below).

Questions about *caci*, how it is portrayed, what it means, and how it is played preoccupy many in the tourism business. Culture is an asset that people recognize as something to sell, but at the moment, there is still a considerable amount of concern that it be presented in a "genuine" way for visitors. This, however, is not only so tourists will see "real *caci*," but also for the next generation to know how it is played, so they can learn to play it properly, and appreciate its important role in Manggaraian culture. Thus positing a "back stage" and "front stage" of Manggaraian life is meaningless since things that are done for tourists are always still considered part of genuine culture, even if they are just a "display." But displays are also mildly frowned upon, since there is a greater chance of them being done incorrectly; even if only as display, *caci* is always potentially dangerous (see below). Thus *caci* being performed merely as an "attraction," instead of included in a cultural event, is thought of with considerable ambivalence.

Caci as war, *caci* as fear: The origins and emotions of *caci*

Although *caci* is said to be the height of Manggaraian culture and civilized behavior, many people, when talking about *caci*, emphasize how it is "warfare." "*Caci* is serious business, it is war. People go in to the *caci* arena searching for blood" is a typical comment about *caci*. "If a person is hit, he desires revenge," said Henry, an organizer of a *sanggar* in Labuan Bajo that specializes in playing *caci* at cultural festivals. Henry rejects the idea of putting on a display of *caci* specifically for tourist groups, since his main aim is making sure the younger generation know how to *play caci* properly. Even though his group is an "art" group, they readily accept invitations to play in villages, in ritual competitions. A player will not forget a person who has drawn his blood, he told me, and will always hope to meet them again on the field of *caci*. People will also remember those they have hit, and are aware that they will want to hit back. Henry mused about his own experience as a *caci* player. He had played since high school, and was a clever dodger of his opponents' whips. Before a person is hit, he said, he is curious to know what it would be like. This is part of the ambiguity of *caci*; one may dread being hit, but at the same time wants to be hit, to know what it is like to be hit, and thus be a "real" *caci* player. Ironically, the more he is hit, the more scars he has, the more of a *caci* "expert" the player is seen to be. Those who manage to dodge the whip and have no scars to show are considered greenhorns, and will be discounted by the *caci* committee unless younger inexperienced players are offered by the other side. Also, it is believed that being hit increases the desire to play, since he will want revenge. The committee will always want to pick a player that has scars, therefore, knowing his desire to play is stronger, thinking that his enthusiasm is greater. Henry said a person becomes proud of his wounds, since they are a mark of a credible player who knows what he is doing, even though, ironically, the person with many wounds might be a poor player. At the same time, Henry commented, though one may wish to be hit and to gain more "status" as a player, it is also considered "good luck" if he is not hit. Hence we can see many ambivalent feelings associated with the playing of *caci*.

The insistence that *caci* is war is, on reflection, a rather unusual claim; actual conflicts waged between people in Manggarai are conducted with makeshift "cannons" and machetes, not with whips, which are actually very awkward as serious weapons. The use of buffalo skin whips in the past, according to Antonius, a ritual expert, was not for warfare but to discipline slaves. The *caci* contest itself, according to Antonius, originated in the competition between a wealthy man and a poor man for the hand in marriage of the beautiful daughter of a rich man. When the players met to fight, one wore a pair of buffalo horns, while the other a pair of ram horns. They each fought with their own masculine "bestial" style, imitating a different animal. The contest was set according to specific rules; each opponent was given three turns to hit, while the other attempted to shield himself from the blows. The matches in the present continue to follow these rules: one fighter hits, while the other protects himself with a buffalo skin shield. They also evoke that original contest, Antonius said, as men continue to wear a headdress of buffalo skin made to

Figure 4.4 Caci player displaying buffalo horn headdress

Figure 4.5 Caci player displaying goat tail ornament

look like horns (see Figure 4.4) and the tail of a goat (see Figure 4.5) as part of their *caci* adornment.

To this day when there is a wedding feast for the final stage of a marital union, there must be *caci*. *Caci* is a very expensive affair: many animals are killed, both in sacrifice and to feed the guests, costs not every family can afford. *Caci* is also played, however, at various other village-level ritual affairs. *Caci* is meant to make things very "*rame*" (lively), but this in itself, Antonius explained, is part of its sacred quality. *Caci* should be performed during a major ritual to bring people together, so they will be witnesses for the events that are to take place. The sacred quality of the *caci* affair derives from the sociality and hospitality, not any particular sacrificial prayer associated with the contest. Every major ritual must be done with the knowledge of the ancestors and their invited presence; they must be informed, with drums and gongs and sacrifices, that a large ritual is to be carried out. *Caci* is part of this "liveliness," part of the hospitality; the liveliness itself helps to create the "sacredness," since both the living and the dead will attend, "consecrate," and bless the affair.

Although *caci* is not a sacred activity per se, it is always described as having mystical qualities. This is because the players, as representatives of their village and their ancestral community, are accompanied by the spirits who are invited to the ritual where *caci* is to be played. Since the ancestors attend, they will watch over the players and protect them from serious wounds. A team who goes to play *caci* must be sure that all players who want to participate have committed no offenses or wrongdoing, since this is *nangki*—a transgression against ancestral rules, and will result in *beke*—a serious wound (which is a sign of transgression). They meet in the village ritual house the night before they leave to play, and are advised by elders not to go if they have any faults. On the journey the next morning, various stops are made, especially at rivers, where any inadvertent faults are left behind so as not to endanger the players in their contests. The procession into the host village is always led by an elder, steeped in magical knowledge, who seeks out the place where the earth spirits of the host village are located, to prevent them from inflicting wounds on the *meka landang* (visiting guest) team.

A serious wound is always a sign that a player has committed a major transgression. The word *beke'* refers to a hit on the face, especially the eye, or being hit on a vein where the blood flow will not stop. These serious wounds are not only an admission of the player's transgression of customary rules but also a loss for the entire team. *Caci* contests between players are not judged in terms of winning or losing, and most contests have no winner. The only time there is a loser is when there is a *beke'*. Interestingly, one possible reason for a player being inflicted with a *beke'* is if he unknowingly plays against a relative. Normally people who know that someone on the opposing team is related to them will bow out of contesting that person. Some commentators on the *caci* displays in the village of Melo related that the members of the village, who are all related, play against each other, pretending to be opponents. This, however, is forbidden. Although one tour guide told me they secretly signal one another to show where they will hit, so as not to draw blood from their relative-opponent in these displays, many tour guides who bring groups will encourage the *caci* players to "really play" *caci* to make the contests more authentic. The tour guides even ply the contestants with palm gin to boost their courage. Thus commentators say it is not surprising that there have been some grave cases of *beke'* in the Melo *caci* displays. Not only is it forbidden to play with relatives, but it is also much more exciting to play against people from far away. Henry, the organizer of a Labuan Bajo *sanggar* mentioned above, was eager to play against a team from the far eastern part of Manggarai in the next government tourism festival in which his group was scheduled to play. This was a part of Manggarai where he knew no one. It is always better, he said, if one's "enemies" in *caci* were opponents you did not know and from as far away as possible.

Caci is more than just hitting and defending, however. The term *lomes* encapsulates the movements, the style, and the songs of the *caci* player. Players aspire to be admired for their *lomes*, obviously part of their desire is to attract the attention of young women, especially for young players. After one defends, the player always shouts out and then sings to the audience as part of his display of *lomes*, calling out the special name he has taken on as a *caci* player. When a player has been hit, even if the wound is visible, he will always yell out to his team, "Was I hit?" and they will answer, "No!" ("*Kena?*" "*Toe!*"). Especially if he has not been hit, he will tend to taunt his opponent through song; for example, Henry often taunts "Lando nao daeng, eh!" ("You think you play well, but I could read your movements!") Although it is not always obvious if the player has been hit, the songs he sings offer a clue. If he is hit, a player may sing an *embong larik*—a "lullaby to the whip," said to be the tears of the player that cannot be shed in any other way. These songs are the opportunity for a player to express sadness about some misery in his life—unrequited love, the death of parents—coupling the bad fortune with the blood of *caci*. In this way, *caci* expresses the discipline of the male Manggaraian, who can overcome his grievances and his difficulties in life through engaging in the contest of the whip.

Caci as performance has different meanings depending on the audience. Local commentaries on *caci* often claim it shows the highly civilized culture of the Manggaraian people; many rules surround the game, indicating cultural control and self-restraint. The *caci* player must show discipline and patience; he is not allowed to act in a vengeful way if he is hit by an opponent. *Caci* players who are most praised can sing and move in aesthetic ways, and can entertain the audience with their art, skill, and wit—their *lomes*. Despite this emphasis on *caci* as the pinnacle of Manggaraian culture, politeness, and discipline, one man who works for the tourism board scoffed at these explanations: "What kind of 'civilized' behavior is this? ... People hit each other! Is this 'civilized?'" Thus, not all Manggaraians accept the explanation of *caci* as a refined, civilized activity. Foreign audiences watch the performances with bemusement and confusion, not really understanding the purpose of the movement, the fighting, and the singing. They often seek an understanding in the metaphors of "win" and "lose,"[8] which are irrelevant in *caci*.

A purely touristic display of *caci* is different from *caci* played at a ritual feast or even at a national or regional festival where the whole village participates as active audience members, singers, players of instruments, and cheering team members. One foreign NGO manager described her own experience watching *caci* in the village as lively, colorful, and cheerful. Although the players hit one another, there was amusement and laughter; the overall atmosphere was not one of violence. However, when *caci* is played at a hotel or on a beach, what is left, she felt, was mostly the violence. The tourist displays of *caci* underscore an underlying savage picture of Manggaraian culture, which she felt was not accurate. However, even when visitors have the opportunity to observe *caci* played in a village setting, not all recognize the gaiety, the liveliness, and the humor of the *caci* games. Recognizing this predicates some knowledge of local people and local culture, which the NGO

---

8   For example, one Dutch visitor posted many impressive pictures of *caci* on his blog, with the last one proclaiming "The winner!": https://www.roelburgler.nl/en/p ortfolio/flores-warrior-dance.

coordinator had, but which the average tourist does not. When they know about the occurrence of a ritual where *caci* will be played, guides will endeavor to bring tourists who are interested in seeing a cultural performance to that village. But guides cannot easily convey the local logics or environment of *caci* to a visitor. One guide commented that the tourists he had taken to a village ritual performance of *caci* were very frightened when they saw the players hit one another and draw blood. However, he managed to calm them with this explanation, "Blood is the norm for a *caci* player. The players themselves are not afraid; they know being hit is a consequence of playing *caci*. As the expression goes," he said, "if you go to a river to bathe, you will get wet. If you go to play *caci*, you will bleed." There is no ambiguity in the playing of *caci*. People set out to hit one another, and people will be hit and bleed in the course of a day's contest. The meaning of *caci*, its emotional power, and the imaginaries about it both in the tourist and the village ritual context are, however, highly ambiguous.

Many tourists comment on the openness and warmth of the Manggaraians. Yet *caci*, with its aggression and fierceness, has become the main cultural attraction of West Manggarai tourism in the midst of this friendliness. I suggest this ambiguity is emphasized as inequities that accompany tourism developments in Labuan Bajo and the surrounding areas become starker. Might the promotion of *caci* as "war" be a response to this material inequality? An attempt to generate fear among tourists? Antonius, the ritual expert, raised another point to ponder: "Who won the contest and married the wealthy man's daughter?" I asked as an afterthought to our discussions. "The rich man or the poor one?" His answer indicated a shift in Manggaraian moral sentiment about wealth. In past stories, the poor and the orphaned were assisted by the spiritual world, and became victorious. But now, "it was the wealthy man," he responded. In this corner of western Flores, Indonesia, people who have come to increasingly rely on tourism have begun to expect that the wealthy will always win.

Concluding thoughts

Tourism has helped to usher in many "ambiguous gifts of capitalist modernity" (Hall & Tucker 2004, 6). Although many aspire to the fruits of tourism, not everyone can afford and some are increasingly hard hit by the costs. The increased population that has come with political/administrative changes and rapid tourism growth has exacerbated frictions around water and waste, access to land, and the rising cost of living. It is unclear whether the central government's recently appointed Tourism Authority will be able to manage the challenges. With the central government's target of 500,000 tourists by 2019 (a five-fold increase over 2017), the town's development is increasingly detached from local sensibilities, local realities, and local control. Frustration with the growing gap between the hopes and the unfolding reality around tourism is expressed in culture and tradition, perhaps the only arena still under local control.

References

Adiakurnia, M.I. (2018,January 19). Apa kabar 10 destinasi prioritas pariwisata "Bali Baru"? Retrieved from https://travel.kompas.com/read/2018/01/19/164355827/apa-ka bar-10-destinasi-prioritas-pariwisata-bali-baru.

Adventoro (2018). Manggaral cultural experience—Melo & Cecer Village. Retrieved from https://www.adventoro.com/products/manggaral-cultural-experience-melo-ce cer-village.

ASEAN Secretariat (2017). ASEAN Statistical Yearbook 2016/2017. Retrieved from https://asean.org/wp-content/uploads/2018/01/ASYB_2017-rev.pdf.

Barnard, T.P. (2009). Chasing the dragon: An early expedition to Komodo Island. In van der Putten, J., & Kicline Cody, M. (eds.), *Lost Times and Untold Tales from the Malay World* (pp. 41–53). Singapore: NUS Press.

Barnard, T.P. (2017). "Sufficient dramatic or adventure interest": Authenticity, reality and violence in pre-war animal documentaries from Southeast Asia. In Deprez, A. (ed.), *The Colonial Documentary Film in South and South-East Asia* (pp. 223–235). Edinburgh: Edinburgh University Press.

Bianchi, R. (2009). The "critical turn" in tourism studies: A radical critique. *Tourism Geographies.* 11(4), 484–504.

Bruner, E. (1996). Tourism in the Balinese borderzone. In Lavie, S., & Swedenburg, T. (eds.), *Displacement, Diaspora and Geographies of Identity* (pp. 157–179). Durham, NC: Duke University Press.

Causey, A. (2003). *Hard Bargaining in Sumatra: Western travelers and Toba Bataks in the marketplace of souvenirs.* Honolulu: University of Hawai'i Press.

Coconuts Bali (2018). Indonesian regent calls for parading rapist of French, Italian women through the streets of Labuan Bajo. Retrieved from https://coconuts.co/bali/news/indo nesian-regent-calls-for-parading-rapist-of-french-italian-women-through-the-streets-of-la buan-bajo/.

Cole, S. (2017). Water worries: An intersectional feminist political ecology of tourism and water in Labuan Bajo, Indonesia. *Annals of Tourism Research.* 67, 14–24.

Derrida, J. (2000). Hospitality. *Angelaki.* 5(3), 3–18.

Dinas Pariwisata dan Budaya (2017). Statistik wisata terpadu (Integrated tourism statistics), Pemerintah Kabupaten Manggarai Barat, Labuan Bajo.

Erb, M. (2000). Understanding tourists: Interpretations from Indonesia. *Annals of Tourism Research.* 27(3), 709–736.

Erb, M. (2001). Conceptualizing culture in a global age: Playing caci in Manggarai, Working Paper no. 160, Department of Sociology, National University of Singa-pore. [Originally published in French (2001), Le Tourisme et la Quête de la Culture à Manggarai (Tourism, and the search for culture in Manggarai), in Picard, M., & Michaud, J. (eds.), special issue on the "Anthropology of Tourism in Southeast Asia," *Anthropologie et Sociétés.* 25(2), 93–108.]

Erb, M. (2008). Darah, Keringat dan Air Mata Manggarai (Blood, and tears in Manggarai), National Geographic Indonesia Supplement, December edition, Ekologi dan Budaya Flores Barat (Ecology and Culture of West Flores), UNESCO.

Erb, M. (2012). The dissonance of conservation: Environmentalities and the envir-onmentalisms of the poor. *Raffles Bulletin of Zoology.* 25, 3–15.

Erb, M. (2013). Gifts from the other side: Tourism: Thresholds of hospitality and morality in an eastern Indonesian town. *Oceania.* 83(3), 295–315.

Erb, M. (2015). Sailing to Komodo: Contradictions of tourism and development in eastern Indonesia. *Austrian Journal of Southeast Asian Studies*. 8, 143–164.

Erb, M. (2018). Dying in a strange land: Tourism, hospitality and promises to the dead. In Kaul, A., & Skinner, J. (eds.), *Leisure and Death: Lively encounters with risk, death, and dying* (pp. 41–57). Louisville: University of Colorado Press.

Errington, F., & Gewertz, D. (1989). Tourism and anthropology in a post-modern world. *Oceania*. 60, 37–54.

Floresa (2018). Dua Pekan Usai Jadi Tersangka Korupsi, Kadis Pariwisata Mabar Ditahan. Retrieved from http://www.floresa.co/2018/07/09/dua-pekan-usai-jadi-tersa ngka-korupsi-kadis-pariwisata-mabar-ditahan/.

Florestourism.com (2018a). Caci whip fighting. Retrieved from http://florestourism. com/activities/caci-whip-fighting/.

Florestourism.com (2018b). Sagi, traditional boxing. Retrieved from http://florestour ism.com/activities/sagi-traditional-boxing/.

Hall, C.M., &Tucker, H., eds. (2004). *Tourism and Postcolonialism: Contested discourse, identities and representations*. London: Routledge.

Hollinshead, K. (2004). Tourism and new sense: Worldmaking and the enunciative value of tourism. In Hall, C.M., & Tucker, H. (eds.), *Tourism and Postcolonialism: Contested discourse, identities and representations* (pp. 25–42). London: Routledge.

Hollinshead, K. (2007). "Worldmaking" and the transformation of place and culture: The enlargement of Meethan's analysis of tourism and global change. In Ateljevic, I., Pritchard, A., & Morgan, N. (eds.), *The Critical Turn in Tourism Studies: Innovative research methodologies* (pp. 165–193). Amsterdam: Elsevier.

Hollinshead, K. (2009). The "worldmaking" prodigy of tourism: The reach and power of tourism in the dynamics of change and transformation. *Tourism Analysis*. 14(1), 139–152.

Hollinshead, K., Ateljevic, I., & Ali, N. (2009). Worldmaking agency—worldmaking authority: The sovereign constitutive role of tourism. *Tourism Geographies*. 11(4), 427–444.

Kewa Ama, K. (2018).Peserta IMF-Bank Dunia Nikmati Komodo di Labuan Bajo. Retrieved fromhttps://kompas.id/baca/utama/2018/10/15/peserta-imf-bw-nikma ti-komodo-di-labuan-bajo/.

MacCannell, D. (1973). Staged authenticity: Arrangement of social space in touristic settings. *American Journal of Sociology*. 79(3): 589–603.

MacCannell, D. (1992). *Empty Meeting Grounds: The tourist papers*. London & New York: Routledge.

Meethan, K. (2001). *Tourism in Global Society: Place, culture, consumption*. Basingstoke, UK: Palgrave.

Ness, S.A. (2005). Tourism-terrorism: The landscaping of consumption and the darker side of place. *American Ethnologist*. 32(1), 118–140.

New Seven Wonders (n.d.) Project History. Retrieved fromhttps://about.new7wonders. com/new7wonders-project-history/.

Picard, D. (2012). Tourism, awe and inner journeys. In Picard, D., & Robinson, M. (eds.), *Emotion in Motion: Tourism, affect and transformation* (pp. 1–19). London & New York: Routledge.

Picard, D., & Robinson, M., eds. (2012). *Emotion in Motion: Tourism, affect and transformation*. London & New York: Routledge.

Picard, M. (1990). "Cultural tourism" in Bali: Cultural performances as tourist attraction. *Indonesia*. 49, 37–74.

Rossiter, K. (2016). Wonderful Indonesia: Melo Village & Labuan Bajo, Flores. Retrieved from https://www.becomingyou.co.za/wonderful-indonesia-melo-village-la buan-bajo/.

Salazar, N. (2010). *Envisioning Eden: Mobilizing imaginaries in tourism and beyond.* Oxford: Berghahn.

Salazar, N. (2012). Tourism imaginaries: A conceptual approach. *Annals of Tourism Research.* 39(2), 863–882.

Siregar, P. (2018). A French tourist became the rape victim in Labuan Bajo. Retrieved from http://news24xx.com/read/news/8033/A-French-tourist-became-the-rape-victim -in-Labuan-Bajo.

Soegiarto, Y. (2016). Developing 10 priority tourism destinations 2016: Ambitious yet feasible. Retrieved from http://www.globeasia.com/special-reports/developing-10-p riority-tourism-destinations-2016-ambitious-yet-feasible/.

Tanzil, N. (2011). Enjoying "caci" dance in Melo Village, Flores. Retrieved from http s://www.nilatanzil.com/enjoying-caci-dance-in-melo-village-flores/.

Valenta, E. (2018). Pemerintah bentuk Badan Otorita Pariwisata Labuan Bajo Flores. Retrieved from https://beritagar.id/artikel/berita/pemerintah-bentuk-badan-otorita -pariwisata-labuan-bajo-flores.

Walpole, M.J., & Goodman, H.J. (2000). Local economic impacts of dragon tourism in Indonesia. *Annals of Tourism Research.* 27(3), 559–576.

Wonderful Indonesia (2018). Labuan Bajo, buffer zone to Komodo National Park is now under Tourism Authority. Retrieved from http://www.indonesia.travel/sg/en/news/ Labuan-bajo-buffer-zone-to-komodo-national-park-is-now-under-tourism-authority.

Wood, R. (1980). International tourism and cultural change in Southeast Asia. *Economic Development and Cultural Change.* 28(3), 561–581.

Wood, R. (1993). Tourism, culture and the sociology of development. In Hitchcock, M., King, V.T., and Parnwell, M.J.G. (eds.), *Tourism in Southeast Asia* (pp. 48–70). London & New York: Routledge.

Part 3

Mediating Tourism Transactions and Neoliberal Logics

5   *Waah Taj!* [1]

Mediating Agra's heritage and local tourism economy

Riddhi Bhandari

Agra, an historic, second-tier city in India, is distinguishable from others just like it because of the Taj Mahal, a Mughal monument intended as a mausoleum by the emperor Shah Jahan for his wife, Arjumand Bano alias Mumtaz Mahal. The monument, planned in 1631, took about 20–22 years to be completed and speaks to Shah Jahan's love for his wife and his political achievements, and attests to the Mughal emperor's global networks and cosmopolitanism that allowed him to procure raw materials and artisans from different parts of the world.

Despite being battered by pollution (Datta 2018), political controversies (Akins 2017; Safi 2017), and the passage of time, the graceful marble façade of the Taj Mahal frames, towers over, and defines the city, drawing tourists from across the world, shaping local livelihoods and aspirations, and bringing the city world recognition as well as notoriety. Tourism is central to Agra and its economy and the Taj Mahal is at its heart. Yet, quickly flipping through travel guide books, like the Lonely Planet, on Agra, one is struck by the warnings and safety, and nuisance-related issues that alert unsuspecting tourists to the city and its machinations. At the core of these complaints is commission: a practice of directing tourists to certain shops and restaurants in exchange for money. Mostly, tour guides or a loose and ambiguous category of "touts" are identified as likely culprits.

Elsewhere (Bhandari 2017), I have discussed how commission alliances are indeed crucial to tourism in Agra and are rooted in the acute uncertainty of getting clientele (henceforth, uncertainty) that tourism entrepreneurs experience, particularly those with newer, middle-rung, less popular and well-known establishments, like showrooms, restaurants, and hotels (I focus on showroom owners who sell marble merchandise, jewelry, and leather products). With substantial investments in the market but not enough popularity, they fear being overlooked by tourists, who prefer other, older showrooms that feature in travel guide books or cheaper ones that line the lanes leading up to the Taj

---

1   Literally, "Wow, Taj!," a phrase commonly used to index the beauty of the monument, made popular by the Brooke Bond Taj Mahal tea advertisement. See the advertisement here: https://www.youtube.com/watch?v=e9t9968NHZ8.

Figure 5.1 Taj Mahal: a 17th century Mughal-era marble mausoleum built during the reign of Emperor Shah Jahan, among India's famed heritage monuments. Recognized as a UNESCO world heritage site and among the seven wonders of the world, Taj Mahal is a popular tourism destination. Photo credit: author

Mahal. Clientelist relations, often mobilized to counter uncertainty, are also harder in tourism because of the nature of visits: usually short-term, one-time, and often mediated by travel agents, tour guides, and drivers (Alao & Batabyal 2013; Geertz 1978; Guo et al. 2013; see also Cohen 1972, 2004).

Commission alliances are rooted in these anxieties and look to inject order and a degree of predictability into this precarious, uncertain economic life. Showroom owners often forge alliances with travel agents, tour guides, and drivers—those economic actors who have first and/or prolonged contact with tourists—predicated on the understanding that they will bring tourists to their establishments in exchange for commission (see also Edensor 1998 on Agra; Crick 1994 on Sri Lanka).

As these commission alliances bring together Agra's tourism entrepreneurs with Delhi-based travel agents and agencies, they raise functional questions of how these relationships are forged, negotiated, and maintained, and how opportunistic economic practices, like cheating or double-dealing, are checked. Encoded within these are the everyday practices of competition and collaboration that shape Agra's tourism, mediated by its nodal but "invisible" actors, convincers.

Brokers in a market: Mediating collaborations and competition

A superficial inquiry into the figure of the convincer reveals that he[2] is an intermediary economic actor who offers his services to Agra's showroom owners and assists them in establishing commission-based business relations with tour guides, drivers, and the Delhi-based travel agencies. For these services, convincers are paid money and varying perks by the showroom owners that employ them.

In a nutshell then, convincers occupy a space of connections that is often associated with mediators, constituting a link between two or more communities or actors, previously unfamiliar with one another (Acheson 1994; Mahmoud 2008; Vidal 2000; see also Lindquist 2015; Stovel & Shaw 2012). In discharging this role of connections, mediators are the quintessential entrepreneurs; with an ear to the ground, they keep themselves well attuned to the processes of change in political and economic systems, identifying (or creating) gaps in information, resources, and access. They channel their previous social, cultural, and monetary capital toward expanding their networks to bridge these gaps and further enhance their own position and assets in return (Asad 1972; Bailey 1963, 1969; Barth 1965; Berenschot 2011; James 2011).

Risk and its navigation constitute an important register through which the everyday work of mediators gains clarity, form, and substance. In markets, mediators look to control access to reliable information and valuable resources and maintain contacts with different entrepreneurs, state agents, and potential consumers (Acheson 1994; Mahmoud 2008; Seligmann 2009). Managing these key components—resources, information, people—mediators link entrepreneurs with markets, with traders, with capital, and with potential consumers, positioning themselves as crucial actors without whom business is hard, risky, and less profitable, if not entirely impossible (Crona et al. 2010; Heslop 2016; Krishnamurthy 2012).

However, since their own relevance is often contingent on ensuring that a pervasive sense of uncertainty and riskiness prevails that can only be rectified

---

2 Convincing is a highly gendered economic activity. Not only did I not meet a single female convincer, I did not even hear of one existing. To reflect this gendered nature of convincing, I consciously and deliberately use the gendered pronoun "he" to refer to convincers.

Figure 5.2 Taj Mahal during Urs, 2013, a three-day festival to celebrate the death and sainthood of Emperor Shah Jahan. Photo credit: Siddhi Bhandari

with their intervention, mediators guard their connections closely, simultaneously embodying gaps and the bridges across them (Krishnamurthy 2012). It is little surprise then, that their liminal position, while an asset for brokering, also raises questions about their loyalties and their motivations, and the work that mediators do is mired in moral ambiguity, suspicion, mistrust, and, sometimes, ill-will, usually expressed by the very people who rely on them (Bailey 1963, 1969). Additionally, as brokers exploit and reinforce risks and insecurities even as they alleviate them, they are morally condemned for profiting off of other people's needs (Bailey 1963; Breman 2008; Krishnamurthy 2012; Moazam, Zaman, & Jafarey 2009; Scheper-Hughes 2003). Finally, sometimes the task of mediators is itself an impossible one, entangled in its own contradictions. Deborah James (2011), for instance, shows that when performing quasi-state like functions, as with post-Apartheid land redistribution in South Africa, mediators lose trust quickly when they fail to deliver on their promises, something that happens frequently when such a large and morally charged project is undertaken.

It is this uneasy position that mediators occupy by virtue of their entanglements with risk that I wish to explore further. Much of the current scholarship has stressed the role of mediators in forging collaborations and networks. But economic competition is an integral part of market life and mediators can play a crucial role in executing it, employing their control over information and resources to press the advantage of those in their patronage or those who have hired them. Agra's convincers make explicit the role of mediators in economic competition; often competition is enfolded in the work they do toward fostering market collaboration. The impacts of such competition on entrepreneurs who work together in a local, socially intimate market, like Agra, and are tied together through myriad relations of sociality, also begs further exploration. This chapter attempts to explore these aspects by tracing the work lives of Agra's tourism mediators: the convincers.

Encountering Agra's convincers

One December evening in 2012, I was wrapping up my fieldwork for the day with one last trip to the tourism market that flanks the east entrance gate of the Taj Mahal. Entry to the Taj Mahal had closed and tourists were slowly emerging from the monument, milling about accompanied by their tour guides. Contrary to the languid tourists, entrepreneurs exhibited heightened activity; salesmen from different shops and restaurants, vendors, and hawkers were in hot pursuit, hustling their wares, swarming tourists and their guides. As I ambled along, sharing quick nods of acknowledgement, rushed smiles and occasionally, a few words, I came across a young man whom I identified as a restaurant employee. We nodded briefly to another before he headed off to meet with another young man that I recognized as a tour guide.

Inquisitive about his presence in the market, away from his restaurant at this busy hour, I decided to visit the restaurant the next day and was greeted by the same young man at the front desk. As we exchanged pleasantries, I asked what he was doing at the gate. He responded, "I go there every evening to do convey-sing." I did not understand the activity he was alluding to but slowly pieced together the following information: Vinay, the young man, was a restaurant employee, who during the day and at night worked the front desk, and in the evenings visited the Taj Mahal to request tour guides and drivers bring their tourists to his restaurant for dinner. "That's it, and I tell them the commission rate that has been fixed by the employer," he finished.

Owing to how it was pronounced—convey-sing—I was unsure if the term was "convey-sing" as in conveying a verbal advertisement of a particular establishment or "canvassing" as in targeted advertising undertaken by political parties close to elections to get votes. Both seemed like related and plausible explanations from the description of the work that Vinay had offered. Slowly, I learned that the term was "convincing," the act of convincing (through the incentive of commission) economic actors, like travel agents, tour guides, and drivers, to bring their tourists to a particular establishment.

The practice of convincing is closely tied with commission and ground-level networking in Agra and is just as pervasive. Simply defined, convincing refers to the act of persuading clients to patronize a particular establishment. However, in Agra, convincing looks to bypass the clients—tourists—altogether and instead focuses its efforts on entrepreneurs who accompany them, primarily tour guides and travel agents. Despite a simple and shared objective—to get clients to showrooms—convincing takes different forms in Agra, as made explicit by the work lives of Agra's convincers.

Shahid: I met Shahid in March 2013 with Munna, a businessman who had recently opened a new marble showroom and was aiming to get it ready for the upcoming tourism season of August 2013–March 2014. Munna needed a convincer and Shahid was in contention.

At the time of our first meeting, Shahid had been a convincer for seven or eight years. Prior to this, he had worked as a tour guide outside the Taj Mahal and, intermittently, as a salesman in a jewelry showroom. Explaining how he came to be a convincer, Shahid said that his work as guide and salesman had brought him in contact with other tour guides, drivers, and showroom owners. As these relationships spread and strengthened over time, Shahid realized their economic potential. His employer often asked him, as he was a salesman, to call upon his fellow guides to bring in their clients, offering him a small commission on subsequent sales. Over the years, Shahid would travel to Delhi during the off-season and, on behalf of his employer, offer commission to the travel agencies in return for sending their tourists to the showroom. Shahid performed this task in his capacity as a salaried showroom employee. Additionally, the owner covered his travel expenses, paid him a per diem, and gave him a small commission for every sale made through his negotiations. "I was already doing the work of a convincer, so I quit my job as a salesman and became a full-time convincer. It pays better," Shahid concluded. Shahid claimed to have "really good relations" with 50 Delhi-based travel agencies and said he was familiar with another 10 to 15. "The best convincer in Agra is Anand Babu. He has 500 companies under him. I am so-so only; a middle-range convincer," he said with open admiration.

For working with Munna's showroom, Shahid wanted INR 80,000 (approximately, US$1322) as an advance and a commission of 20 percent on sale.[3] In addition, he would be reimbursed for gas spent on convincing-related activities; Shahid had his own motorcycle. Munna, on the other hand, wanted to pay Shahid an advance of INR 60,000 (approximately, US$992) and commission at 15 percent. This wrangle continued for a good few months until it was settled on Shahid's terms.

The scope of Shahid's work included networking with local tour guides and with the Delhi-based travel agencies (henceforth, travel agencies). Explaining his work, Shahid said that once employed by a showroom, his first task was to compile a list of guides who could work for the showroom. He took special care to stay in touch with some foreign-language tour guides to make the list attractive to travel agents with foreign clientele.

3 INR is the Indian Rupee. At the time of fieldwork, the exchange rate was approximately, US$1=INR 60.50. http://www.oanda.com/currency/converter/ (April 15, 2014).

With the tour guide list in order, Shahid traveled to Delhi to meet with travel agencies there: per him, "I first focus on the ones that I have worked with earlier and the ones that the showroom has already worked with previously." Introducing himself and the new showroom that he is working with, Shahid begins convincing travel agencies; without giving out too much information, he shares his list of guides with the travel agencies and tells them about the commission percentage as well as an advance amount that the showroom is willing to pay. Negotiations continue until a deal is made or falls through; "I try to get at least 20–30 companies on board for one season," Shahid concluded.

Once the tourism season begins, Shahid's sphere of operation shifts from networking to surveillance. The travel agencies that are in alliance with the showroom contact Shahid and give him daily details of their tourists who are scheduled to visit Agra. This includes details of their arrival and departure, the sights they want to see, their requirements for types of guides (usually language specifications but sometimes even their dressing and presentation), and so on. Shahid shares this information with the showroom owner and the two together decide on the appropriate tour guide, eventually passing on the "file"—information on the tourists, arrival, meeting point, time, etc.—to the selected guide. The guide is then responsible for meeting the tourists at the designated spot and conducting their tour. Shahid provides a strict specification of time that is to be spent sightseeing and the time to be spent in the showroom, where tourists can make a purchase.

On the day of the visit, Shahid reports to the showroom and waits there until the guide calls to inform him that he is with the tourist party and heading to a monument; Taj Mahal is usually the first, followed by Agra Fort. When the tour is supposed to be over, as per pre-decided time specifications, Shahid heads to the monument and looks out for the guide. Unknown to the tourists, he discreetly follows the party to the next monument and restaurant, whatever the plan may be. Once the party is headed to the showroom, Shahid calls the owner to inform him.

Convincers, like Shahid, are specialist economic actors, whose sole task is to facilitate commission alliances and monitor them. However, other economic actors, usually salesmen, undertake convincing in a part-time capacity.

Lokesh and Raghu: Lokesh and Raghu worked as salesmen in a marble and jewelry showroom. Lokesh worked the marble section and, like Vinay, in the mornings, before coming to the showroom, and in the evenings, when the Taj Mahal closed, he would head there to convince guides to bring their tourists to the showroom. According to him, all salesmen in the showroom were encouraged to undertake this part-time convincing; most worked in teams, sharing their work and earnings but Lokesh preferred to go solo.

Unlike Shahid, Lokesh's approach to convincing was indiscriminate and unplanned. According to him, he sought out all guides, without any concern for whether they had prior "setting"[4] with another showroom. Explaining his strategy, Lokesh said, "If it [prior commission alliance] exists, I try to break it. It is my job to cut such arrangements. Money is a big thing, madam, and everyone is susceptible to it." Upon zeroing in on guides who appeared interested, Lokesh would request them to bring their tourist clients to the showroom. He would quote them a commission amount and hand them the showroom card with his name on it. When they brought their clients to the showroom, the guides would hand this card to the manager to let him know which of their employees facilitated this arrangement and who should get commission if a sale is made. Lokesh would earn a 10 percent commission on such sales.

As the world of convincing opened up to me, I came to see that many of Agra's tourism entrepreneurs were engaged in convincing or working towards it. While to be a full-time and specialist convincer, like Shahid, was an aspirational model, it was relatively easier and low-risk to convince on the side, like Lokesh.

Raghu, one of Lokesh's older co-workers, also engaged in part-time convincing, albeit in a more formalized capacity than Lokesh. Raghu had worked in his current place of employment for nearly a decade (working the jewelry section) and had taken on the additional responsibility of convincing four years ago. According to Raghu, when he initially came to work in tourism, there were only a few big showrooms in Agra and the owner, Rudra, would himself travel to Delhi and negotiate directly with travel agencies. However, as tourism expanded, the number of travel agencies in Delhi and the number of showrooms in Agra have increased, necessitating a more professional and consistent approach to convincing.

Since Rudra's showroom is relatively well known and has been in business for over a decade, Raghu said that they mostly conduct their business with 12 to 15 travel agencies with whom they have enduring relations. Most of these relations are personal and direct, between the travel agents and the showroom owner, rather than being convincer-determined, as with Shahid. Raghu's job as a convincer, then, is to go as a representative of the showroom and renew these relations for the upcoming tourist season. In this capacity, Raghu is the "official face" of Rudra's showroom through whom commission arrangements can be negotiated and settled with the understanding that the terms of agreements that he brings to the table are approved by Rudra.

Raghu rarely facilitated new commission arrangements, terming them "risky business," and owing to a deal gone sour with one fly-by-night travel agent, which I will come to shortly, it seems unlikely that he will venture into this territory in a hurry. However, Raghu often utilized his personal relations with guides and drivers to urge them to bring their clients to his showroom, especially for jewelry shopping, the section he worked in the showroom.

---

4 "Setting" is used here to refer to commission-based arrangements.

Figure 5.3 Tourist at the Taj. Photo credit: Rachel Cantave, photo taken by her tour guide during her visit to the Taj Mahal, 2015

Convincing Agra's tourism economy

The underlying motive of convincing is to draw tourist clients into show-rooms and other establishments, thereby maintaining a steady flow of clients and mitigating the uncertainty of getting clientele. However, none of the convincers I spoke with ever interacted directly with tourists, requesting or urging them into their showroom. According to Lokesh, tourists are terrified and rude and treat anyone who approaches them with suspicion and anger:

> You go to the gates every day and must have seen how they [foreign tourists] behave with *lapkas.*[5] They just walk away quickly [laughs]. And then the police are there. If they [foreign tourists] complain to them, I'll get into trouble. Besides, all the rich tourists come with guides, so it serves our purpose to just speak to the guide. As if the guide will let us take his clients directly. He has to see his "setting" also.

5 *Lapka* is a local term used to refer to a wide variety of self-employed ambulant entrepreneurs such as guides, photographers, hawkers, and salesmen who work from outside the Taj Mahal. Colloquially, it invokes the image of jumping up to catch something, here, tourists.

Shahid simply deemed this unnecessary since tourists' itineraries are planned down to the detail by their travel agencies.

Convincing travel agencies is of primary importance to establish commission alliances that last for the duration of the season and may even be repeated over several seasons. International tourists, who are perceived by Agra's tourism entrepreneurs as having significant purchasing power, often hire these travel agencies to plan their tours. Since they plan their travel itineraries, arranging their accommodation, travel, driver, guide (which is now offered by Agra's shop owners as an added benefit to the agencies), and even the places where they will stop to eat, drink, and shop, these agencies have considerable influence in determining where the tourists go when they visit Agra. Consequently, it becomes essential for Agra's entrepreneurs to establish alliances with these travel agencies to ensure a regular supply of tourists to their establishments. Convincing such alliances establishes a complete consumer chain and assures an initial, predictable, and long-term flow of tourists that an entrepreneur can expect for the duration of the season. Mostly, such convincing requires specialists who can represent the showroom either full-time, like Shahid, or in some formal capacity, as Raghu did.

However, showroom owners often look to buttress specialized convincing with everyday localized convincing. This is undertaken by employees, like Lokesh and Vinay, in a part-time capacity and focuses exclusively on guides, looking to persuade them to bring their tourists to the showroom with inducements of commission. This form of convincing centers on poaching allies like tour guides from other alliances, by offering them an opportunity to make additional money by side-stepping preexisting commitments. Guides often use these opportunities to test a potential new alliance. Over a period of time, many guides and drivers approached this way may become a part of the new alliances but, usually, there is a period of overlap when guides are tied in one alliance but divert some of their tourists to another showroom. Localized convincing captures a facet of aggressive and opportunistic competition among Agra's tourism entrepreneurs, and is often a point of tension among them.

Convincers and the control over market information

A crucial difference between specialist and part-time convincers is their control over market information and their responsibility for ensuring the reliability of such information. Specialist convincers possess market information on travel agents that will allow a showroom owner to decide whether to approach them for an alliance and to arrive at appropriate terms for an offer. This includes a sense of their commission rate, an assessment of the type of tourists a showroom is likely to receive through them, particularly their purchasing power, and information on the market reputation of the travel agents that will indicate whether they will make reliable and worthy alliance partners or not. By virtue of being a repository of travel agencies–related knowledge, the convincer frees his employer from having to compile such information from scratch. With a specialist convincer in their hire, showroom owners do not have to expend their own time and resources in forging relations with travel agents, accumulating relevant information about them, and making quick assessments about the viability of an alliance with them. Since part-time official convincers work through the contacts of their employers, they are only responsible for renewing alliances. They do not facilitate new relations with travel agencies and only solicit additional guides and drivers to bring their tourists to the showroom.

Different types of showrooms need the services of specialist and part-time convincers. The newer, lesser-known, middle-range establishments, like Munna's, rely overwhelmingly on specialist convincers. Because they are new in the business, these entrepreneurs are not known to the travel agents, do not share any close business relations with them, and do not possess any intimate market information about them; all of these are essential in establishing commission alliances. The travel agents are not familiar with the new entrepreneur; they do not know if the showroom owner will be a reliable partner who will make commission payments on time and without cheating, and if the quality of his goods and his guides will meet the standards to satisfy their tourist clients. The territorial distance that separates Agra's entrepreneurs and the travel agents further reinforces this unfamiliarity. In this scenario of mutual unfamiliarity, it is likely that if a new showroom owner directly approached travel agents, they would be wary of entering into a business alliance with him. Here, the specialist convincer steps in so that the entrepreneur's newness in the business is not a severe handicap to his operations. The convincer fulfills twin roles here: he provides ready-made knowledge of the travel agencies to his employer and stands in as the showroom owner's security and guarantee with them. These convincers help facilitate the initial and important network arrangements with travel agents to ensure a steady flow of tourists, establishing complete consumer chains that will last for a season.

While the older and well-reputed establishments are frequently recommended to tourists in travel guide books, travel blogs, and third-party websites, attracting tourists without much mediation, they too have begun to feel the pressures of Agra's expanding and competitive tourism, especially from the new showroom owners, who, in a bid to make a place for themselves, undertake convincing aggressively and offer large sums of advance payments and bigger commission to travel agencies. As a result, the older establishments too need to continuously engage in renewing their commission relations with travel agencies. This may be done directly by the owner, using his own personal contacts, or through a part-time official convincer, like Raghu.

The "risky" entrepreneurs

Information and the ability to control it positions convincers in a constant engagement with risk that occurs at multiple levels. First, convincers use information to mitigate risks for their employers. Yet their everyday activities—from negotiations to surveillance and poaching—and control over information, pose risks to their allies and competitors. And finally, to be a convincer entails engaging with risks at a personal, individual level.

I have outlined above how convincers help mitigate uncertainty and its related risks (of running an unprofitable business, of not getting clients, of having non-reciprocal or cheating allies) for their employers. By virtue of possessing crucial market information, specialist convincers are powerful allies of showroom owners and important nodal actors in Agra's tourism. Yet, an undercurrent of resentment defines this relationship, primarily arising from the showroom owners' dependence on convincers. Mostly, this is articulated as popular moral condemnation of the work that convincers do—which earns money but not respect—and the money they earn as being easy and ill-deserved, stressing its inevitable karmic futility (see also, Huberman 2010; Parry 1989).

Tour guides were also harsh in their judgement of convincers, owing to their surveillance work and the associated risks it carried for tour guides. Convincers keep a close watch on the actions and movements of tour guides and report on any errant behavior on the part of guides that indicates potential cheating, double-dealing, or simple inefficiency to control tourists. The ambit of such "errant behavior," however, is contentious because of its ambiguity—it being easily subject to manipulation and misunderstandings. In an intimate local market like Agra, where entrepreneurs know each other as friends, neighbors, and kinsmen, a social call can easily be interpreted as an opportunity for cheating and double-dealing. Furthermore, while Agra's entrepreneurs may look to exclude tourists from decision-making, tourists frequently express their agency by overriding decisions made on their behalf. For instance, they may decide not to shop altogether or insist on visiting another showroom that they have heard and read about. These instances can easily be construed as evidence that the guide is not fully committed to his alliance, that he is directing tourists elsewhere or that he is unable to control his tourists. For these, the guide could be fired from his job and earn a reputation as being lax with tourists, thereby hindering his future employment options. Resentful over the close surveillance, tour guides often stressed that convincers have economic and occupational motivations to exaggerate the risks of cheating. They need to demonstrate their occupational relevance to showroom owners to be hired as full-time employees and not simply as off-season negotiators whose tasks end once alliances have been solidified.

Thus, while convincers' control over accurate and reliable market information is necessary to mitigate uncertainty in Agra's tourism market, their very value rests on ensuring that risks in the market are only kept at bay with their mediation. Convincers' risk-mitigating mediations are a constant reminder of potential risks that they pose to those who work with them. This ongoing churn of mitigating and maintaining risks manifests as resentment toward convincers by other entrepreneurs they help bring together into commission alliances.

Every entrepreneur who aspires to be a convincer also has to grapple with risks at a personal level, and his attitude toward entrepreneurial risk plays a big role in determining if he works as a specialist or part-time convincer. New specialist convincers may find it hard to establish themselves and secure initial employment. Commission alliances forged through such convincers could fall through, tarnishing their reputation and future work prospects; showroom owners may also demand that they make up the money lost in such alliances. Sometimes, ambitious young salesmen look to break out as specialist convincers but are promptly set back by other, similarly ambitious entrepreneurs. Raghu's encounter with a fly-by-night tour agency is illustrative and highlights some of the risks associated with entrepreneurialism. Raghu had taken initial steps toward becoming a specialist convincer by facilitating his first independent alliance with a new travel agency, forwarding an advance payment of close to INR 80,000 (US$1322). However, the travel agency did not send any clients to the showroom, and, after repeated protestations, gave him a check returning the advance money. This check bounced, and the travel agency soon shut shop and vanished. Although fortunately Raghu was able to trace the owners and recover the advance payment, he no longer pursued his efforts to be a specialist convincer.

But the opportunities and earnings for specialist convincers are attractive. Because they control market information about travel agencies and have personal contacts with them, specialist convincers enjoy mobility, freedom, and choice vis-à-vis their employment prospects, and, in fact, they do move around frequently and seasonally. Their remunerations are also higher than their part-time counterparts', who simply follow up on the employers' contacts.

However, control over market information comes with considerable responsibilities, posing risks for convincers. Convincers are responsible for ensuring that alliances are honored, upheld, and reciprocated, bringing the promised tourists to showrooms. As Agra's showroom owners increasingly forward an advance payment to the travel agencies in conclusion of negotiations to "seal the deal," non-reciprocity means a loss of capital, for which specialist convincers are liable. Recall Raghu's desperation to follow up with the travel agency, track them, and resort to verbal and physical threats to ultimately recover the money. The extensive surveillance undertaken by Shahid must also be read against this risk and culpability. Repeated bad deals pose reputational risks, tarnishing a convincer's credibility and possibly hindering his future employment prospects.

Conversely, convincers who work part-time and through their employers' contacts are relatively secure from having to bear the full brunt of any alliance that falls through. While they still have to conduct everyday surveillance to ensure reciprocity, they are not likely to be held solely accountable for any arrangements that do not work out. But the benefits that specialist convincers enjoy present themselves as risks, or at least hindrances, for the part-time convincers. Devoid of their own repertoire of contacts, these convincers' negotiating power regarding compensation is severely curtailed. New employment opportunities that open up for these convincers are those of employees—salesman, receptionist, manager—and not as convincers, until, like Shahid, they break away from their previous employment to become specialist convincers.

Guarding against social risks

These considerations of risk that convincers engage with everyday are contained within economic life, that is, they deal with how entrepreneurs' economic conduct is impacted for better or for worse by the intervention of convincers and how convincers themselves make choices regarding their economic conduct. Yet, as resentment and moral judgements toward convincers make evident, economic practices also engender affective responses and intersect with sociability among entrepreneurs.

In Agra, the circuits of commerce (Zelizer 2011, 2012) weave an intricate tapestry of intimacies and economic relations. Entrepreneurs are tied to one another through myriad relations of sociality; many are family members, extended kin, and tied through affinal relations, friendships, and shared neighborhood residence. While such embeddedness generally aids entrepreneurs in forging alliances and devising risk-mitigating strategies, in an intimate localized market, it always holds the possibilities of social strain (Hampton 2003). Entrepreneurs have to compete and outbid one another, poach each other's allies to secure their businesses, and sometimes they may not want to work with those they know or wish to discontinue working with those related to them. In such a scenario, ill-will and conflicts are commonplace that threaten existing relations of camaraderie, friendship, kinship, obligations, and cordiality. I refer to these as social risks that arise when convincers engage in three types of economic practices on behalf of their employers: negotiations (with travel agents and tour guides), poaching (travel agents and tour guides tied with other showrooms), and surveillance (tour guides). Convincers, I argue, intervene in these social risks, helping deflect tensions that can strain relations among entrepreneurs. They do so by embodying the separation between economic activities and social relations and absorbing the friction from competition, thereby allowing entrepreneurs to preserve their social relations while engaging in competitive business practices.

There are numerous points of tension where these social risks can emerge; I will discuss a few to stress the work that convincers do regarding them. The first such fault line emerges early on, when convincers woo the travel agencies. Since these relations are crucial to a productive season, the agencies are in high demand and each is contacted by several showroom owners from Agra. Before approaching travel agencies, convincers gather background information on the showrooms they worked with in previous seasons, their commission rates, and other perks that were offered to them as well as information on other showrooms who are assessed as competitors, also vying to work with the selected travel agencies.

Much of this information is, in Shahid's words, "dirty." For instance, Shahid would gather information on incidents when relations between travel agents and showroom owners had frayed. These included incidents when tourists had complained to the travel agency about the inferior quality of guides, aggressive marketing, or were unhappy with their shopping experience. He would stay abreast of the business conduct of different showroom owners, noting if they paid commission on time or if they underreported purchases to pay less commission. Such dirty information, according to Shahid, was easy to gather because Agra's tourism was small and business was conducted in the presence of many: guides, salesmen, and drivers. Invariably, such information found its way into the market's public realm, aided by competing entrepreneurs or unhappy employees and moving between friends and kinsmen. Tour guides were particularly eager to convey such information, aware that convincers were always looking to induct guides into new alliances. Armed with this information, convincers tailor their offers to promise marginally better payments, services, and perks, and to rectify the problems in previous alliances. Negative information on potential competitors is subtly disclosed to travel agencies, with the intention of undermining its fruition.

The continuous poaching of tour guides by convincers even after alliances had been forged was another sore point among showroom owners, and frequently generated ill-will. One time, Lokesh had successfully poached a well-known German-language guide from another showroom that lay in close proximity to Rudra's, and whose owner was also Rudra's affinal kin. When Rudra hired the guide and gave Lokesh a big commission, thus condoning his work, tensions between the two showroom owners became palpable: they would greet each other curtly but daily visits between them stopped for a while, before eventually resuming. When I asked Rudra about this, he bristled and said,

> I am not involved in this 'cutting', I never told Lokesh, 'go get me this guide.' You can ask him! He is my convincer; he is doing whatever he thinks is necessary. I just go with his decision. I do not control everything.

These forms of market competition through disseminating unfavorable information on one's competitors, with the intent of outbidding them or poaching their allies, were undertaken by convincers on behalf of their employers. Such aggressive market competition, while a normative feature of Agra's tourism, is nevertheless stressful for competing entrepreneurs (Lewis 2014). Outsourcing these competitive activities to a specialist economic actor allowed entrepreneurs to create a separation between their social relations and economic activities so that they could engage in aggressive market competition with their friends and family members without directly owning any responsibility for it; this helped preserve their social relations from the strains of economic life.

As entrepreneurs frequently mobilized their social relations to find work—tour guides lobbied their kinship, friendship, and *jaan pehchaan* (extended networks of acquaintances) when approaching showrooms for work, and showroom owners and salesmen too sought out guides based on their social networks. They also grappled with the obligatory pressures of sociality and had to find creative ways of conveying economic decisions that did not accommodate their social relations.

Before Shahid joined him, Munna expressed his frustration to me about his inability to get guides to work for him despite approaching many whom he knew fairly well. He lamented,

> I have shared my food with them and bought them tea. I have lent them money when they needed it and even helped some of them find jobs with showrooms and companies through my own connections. But now that I need their help, they turn their eyes away, they make excuses to not meet me and talk to me.

A moment later, he added, "they also cannot leave their jobs like this. It is all done through the convincer these days, so they are also helpless. Otherwise I'm sure many would have come."

Although it made economic sense that guides did not want to leave their existing jobs to join Munna's new business that was yet to take off, Munna himself believed that they owed him for the kindness and help that he had shown them. He thought to call in this debt, expecting reciprocity. When the reciprocity did not come, Munna was disappointed. But the presence of a mediating convincer provided him a means of rationalizing the guides' refusal and preserving relations with them for another day.

As these fault lines continuously threaten to unravel social intimacies, Agra's entrepreneurs look to preserve their competitive economic practices and their social relations by strategizing to disengage the two spheres as much as possible. The convincer is critical in working toward this disengagement. Tasked exclusively with discharging functions that embody competition, he keeps an ear open for "market talk" that is potentially damaging to the showroom's competitors, he negotiates new alliances and is responsible for breaking older ones, and he continues to poach allies even after alliances have been forged for the season. By discharging these functions, convincers, who in their risk-mitigating roles normally act as bridges between actors and information, also mark the separation between the economic and socio-moral spheres, between social obligation and economically sound decisions, and between competition and familiarity.

In turn, this frees the showroom owner from some degree of responsibility of being viewed as directly competing with his kith and kin or of not wanting to work with them. Obviously, this is not foolproof and absolute—everyone knows for whom the convincer works—but it helps maintain a façade of cordiality and prevents situations of direct confrontation, something that often happened among smaller shopkeepers who did not practice such a division of labor and where accusations of "stealing clients" often led to fights. How convincers retain their social intimacies while engaging in market competition is a question that deserves its own research. However, pervasive moral evaluations of their work as tainted and yielding "unproductive" money indicate that socialities are perhaps preserved because of a shared understanding that convincers suffer karmic retributions.

Concluding thoughts: Convincing through the lens of cultural contact

Exploring the role of mediators in markets, scholars have stressed their control over relevant and reliable information that positions them as critical nodal actors who mediate access to resources, buyers, and credit, mitigating risks of uncertainty and cheating (Acheson 1994; Mahmoud 2008; Vidal 2000; see also Stovel & Shaw 2012). In this framework, mediators are conceptualized as forging links and bridges that bring together previously unconnected actors in a series of collaborative relationships. As facilitators of Agra's commission alliances, convincers too enable collaborations among different entrepreneurs to shape and control tourist visits, but much of the work that they do rests on successfully conducting economic competition. Toward this end, specialist and full-time convincers gather intimate and detailed market information on showroom owners who may be potential competitors with the explicit intent of mobilizing this information to outbid them with travel agents should the need arise. In addition, they gather quotidian information on the activities of allies, especially tour guides, to check risks of cheating and opportunism. Part-time localized convincers, in willful ignorance of and disregarding market information on existing alliances, try to indiscriminately poach tour guides.

These activities of negotiation, poaching, and surveillance define the contours of economic competition in Agra. But competing entrepreneurs are also tied to one another through myriad social relations of intimacy and obligations. Consequently, economic competition also engenders social risks, threatening rifts in interpersonal relations. True to their paradoxical position, just as convincers foster social risks, they also engage in repair work. Specialist convincers, by being solely in charge of outbidding competitors, conducting surveillance, and hiring and firing allies, help their employers deflect strains that economic competition may cause to social relations. Similarly, by shouldering the responsibility to poach allies, localized convincers help their employers distance themselves from aggressive competition, again helping them deflect strains on their personal relationships.

While the role of mediators is often associated with forging connections and bridging gaps thus bringing together previously unrelated actors, my ethnography with Agra's convincers stresses their centrality in constituting the much needed boundaries that separate economic and social spheres. This role speaks to economic competition, a facet of market life alongside collaboration, the risks that it poses to the social life of the market, and the importance of convincers as mediators that simultaneously embody such risks and engage in repair work to deflect them.

In concluding this chapter, I want to consider the relationship of convincers to tourism. Cultural contact and the need to mediate it is at the heart of tourism. In studying cultural contact, scholars have long occupied themselves with deliberating on its implications. Early mediations on the question looked to understand how such cultural contact intertwined with the political economy of tourism and, following in the footsteps of colonialism (Bruner 2005; Smith 1989), impacted relations between the host communities and guests, sometimes engendering conflict while also fostering relations that sought to incorporate tourists into the existing social order (Pi-Sunyer 1973). But the implications of tourism's cultural contact are not limited to host–guest relations. Rather, social relations within local communities and their relations with private investors and the state have all been transfigured with tourism, often giving vent to economic anxieties and perceived exclusions from tourism's economic gains (Lewis 2014; Skoczen 2008; Stronza 2008; Waters 2003). This ethnography extends the scope of this inquiry to suggest that tourism markets gain form and substance in constant dialogue with global factors, such as changing tourism patterns, local political factors, especially the state-led promotion of tourism as a viable economic sector, and in anticipation of tourists' behaviors and practices. The resultant impact does not merely determine a particular tourism destination's popularity with tourists, but it also percolates downward, defining anxieties and shaping entrepreneurial strategies. Convincers mediate in this process, easing anxieties and even benefitting from them but never entirely succeeding in putting them to rest for good.

As this chapter argues, convincers mediate in economic competition and collaboration among tourism entrepreneurs, both facilitating and "cutting" commission alliances. Yet how do these conditions of work and the associated risks of uncertainty and opportunism gain salience? I have argued that they reflect the precarity of economic life that has, so far, proved inherent to tourism in Agra: international tourists visit irregularly and for short durations of time and mostly like to plan their travels through the travel agencies. In addition, tourists express "cultural" discomfort with bazaar-style soliciting, which is lent further validation through travel guide books and writings that warn against such practices and are freely circulated without a counter-narrative.

Convincers are a product of this economic precarity and look to ease it, both for entrepreneurs and, inadvertently, for visiting tourists. Since I have elaborated at length how convincers mediate with entrepreneurs' anxieties and economic precarity, I will turn to their role vis-à-vis tourists. In a tourism market, mediation has an added dimension of brokering cultural information and enabling a somewhat predictable experience of an unfamiliar place for tourists. Numerous agencies, like state-sponsored information centers and organizations dedicated to destination management, as well as actors, like travel agents and tour guides, work round the clock to provide tourists with information about history and place, as well as about places to shop, travel, and eat (Bruner 2005; Medina-Munoz & Garcia-Falcon 2000; Modlin Jr., Alderman, & Gentry 2011; Smith 1989; Strobl & Peters 2013; see also Geertz 1960). Through forging commission alliances, convincers also determine a near seamless flow of tourists from travel agencies to monument visits and places to shop and eat. In effect, these work to inject reliability into tourists' experiences, protecting them from the noise of persistent solicitations as well as the unpredictable quality of experience with food and shopping. But even as convincers look to ease anxieties for entrepreneurs and tourists, they do so by monetizing the former and bypassing the latter.

Furthermore, entrepreneurs' economic anxieties, momentarily held at bay with convincers' mediation, rear their head again, this time as social risks that threaten to unravel relations among competing entrepreneurs. The anxieties of tourists also return, now in the form of warnings about commission alliances and the surreptitious denial of consumer agency that they index. Convincers are always in the thick of these anxieties, in a way forever playing catch-up with the evolving tourism market, mediating to allay new and emerging anxieties of entrepreneurs and tourists. In this way, I see convincers standing in for and encapsulating Agra's tourism, a still emerging market that is in flux, filled with new opportunities but also beset with innumerable risks.

References

Acheson, J. (1994). Transaction costs and business strategies in a Mexican Indian pueblo. In Acheson, J. (ed.), *Anthropology and Institutional Economics* (pp. 143–166). Lanham, MD: University Press of America.

Akins, H. (2017, November 27). How Hindu nationalists politicized the Taj Mahal. *The Atlantic.* Retrieved from https://www.theatlantic.com/international/archive/2017/11/taj-mahal-india-hindu-nationalism/546374/.

Alao, O., & Batabyal A. (2013). Selling package tours to tourists: A contract theory perspective. *Annals of Tourism Research.* 42, 425–442.

Asad, T. (1972). Market model, class structure and consent: A reconsideration of Swat political organization. *Man.* 7, 74–94.

Bailey, F.G. (1963). *Politics and Social Change: Orissa in 1959.* Berkeley: University of California Press.

Bailey, F.G. (1969). *Stratagems and Spoils: A social anthropology of politics.* Oxford: Blackwell.

Barth, F. (1965). *Political Leadership among Swat Pathans.* London: Berg.

Berenschot, W. (2011). Political fixers and the rise of Hindu nationalism in Gujarat, India: Lubricating a patronage democracy. *South Asia: Journal of South Asian Studies.* 34(3), 382–401.

Bhandari, R. (2017). Debts and uncertainty: Circulation of advance money among tourism entrepreneurs in Agra, India. In Wood, D.C. (ed.) *Anthropological Considerations of Production, Exchange, Vending and Tourism: Research in economic anthropology*, 37, 233–256.

Breman, J. (2008). On labor bondage, old and new. *The Indian Journal of Labour Economics*. 51(1), 83–90.

Bruner, E. (2005). *Culture on Tour: Ethnographies of travel*. Chicago: University of Chicago Press.

Cohen, E. (1972). Toward a sociology of international tourism. *Social Research*. 39(1), 164–182.

Cohen, E. (2004). *Contemporary Tourism: Diversity and change*. New York: Elsevier.

Crick, M. (1994). *Resplendent Sites, Discordant Voices: Sri Lankans and international tourism*. Chur, Switzerland: Hardwood Academic Publishers.

Crona, B., Nyström, M., Folke, C., & Jiddawi, N. (2010). Middlemen: A critical socio-ecological link in coastal communities of Kenya and Zanzibar. *Marine Policy*. 34(4), 761–771.

Datta, D. (2018, July 21). Losing the Taj: Fighting a monumental neglect. *India Today Magazine*. Retrieved fromhttps://www.indiatoday.in/magazine/cover-story/story/20180730-losing-the-taj-1289803-2018-07-21.

Edensor, T. (1998). *Tourists at the Taj: Performance and meaning at a symbolic site*. London: Routledge.

Geertz, C. (1960). The Javanese kijaji: The changing role of a cultural broker. *Comparative Studies in Society and History*. 2(2), 228–249.

Geertz, C. (1978). The bazaar economy: Information and search in peasant marketing. *The American Economic Review*. 68(2), 28–32.

Guo, X., Ling, L., Dong, Y., & Liang, L. (2013). Cooperation contract in tourism supply chain: The optimal pricing strategy of hotels for cooperative third party strategic websites. *Annals of Tourism Research*. 41, 20–41.

Hampton, M.P. (2003). Entry points for local tourism in developing countries: Evidence from Yogyakarta, Indonesia. *Geografiska Annaler. Series B Human Geography*. 85(2), 85–101.

Heslop, L. (2016). Catching the pulse: Money and circulation in a Sri Lankan marketplace. *Journal of the Royal Anthropological Institute*. 22, 534–551.

Huberman, J. (2010). The dangers of dal⊠l⊠, the dangers of d⊠n. *South Asia: Journal of South Asian Studies*. 33(3), 399–420.

James, D. (2011). The return of the broker: Consensus, hierarchy, and choice in South African land reform. *Journal of the Royal Anthropological Institute*. 17, 318–338.

Krishnamurthy, M. (2012). States of wheat: The changing dynamics of public procurement in Madhya Pradesh. *Economic and Political Weekly*. 47(52), 72–83.

Lewis, J.S. (2014). A so black people stay: bad-mind, sufferation, and discourses of race and unity in a Jamaican craft market. *The Journal of Latin American and Caribbean Anthropology*. 20(2), 327–342.

Lindquist, J. (2015). Anthropology of brokers and brokerage. In Wright, James D. (ed.), *International Encyclopedia of Social and Behavioral Science*. 2nd edition (pp. 870–874). Amsterdam: Elsevier.

Mahmoud, H.A. (2008). Risky trade, resilient traders: Trust and livestock marketing in Northern Kenya. *Africa: The Journal of the International African Institute*. 78(4), 561–581.

Medina-Munoz, D., & Garcia-Falcon, J.R. (2000). Successful relationships between hotels and agencies. *Annals of Tourism Research.* 27(3), 737–762.

Moazam, F., Zaman, R.M., & Jafarey, A.M. (2009). Conversations with kidney vendors in Pakistan: An ethnographic study. *Hastings Center Report.* 39(3), 29–44.

Modlin Jr., E.A., Alderman, D., & Gentry, G.W. (2011). Tour guides as creators of empathy: The role of affective inequality in marginalizing the enslaved at plantation house museums. *Tourist Studies.* 11(1), 3–19.

Parry, J. (1989). On the moral perils of exchange. In Parry, J., & Bloch, M. (eds.), *Money and the Morality of Exchange* (pp. 64–93). Cambridge: Cambridge University Press.

Pi-Sunyer, O. (1973). Tourism and its discontents: The impact of a new industry on a Catalan community. *Studies in European Society.* 1, 1–20.

Safi, M. (2017, October 30). Hardline Hindu nationalists campaign against the Taj Mahal. *The Guardian.* Retrieved from https://www.theguardian.com/world/2017/oct/30/hardline-hindu-nationalists-step-up-campaign-against-taj-mahal.

Scheper-Hughes, N. (2003). Keeping an eye on the global traffic in human organs. *Lancet.* 361, 1645–1648.

Seligmann, L.J. (2009). Material politics and religious fervor: Exchanges between an Andean market woman and an ethnographer. *Ethos: Journal of the Society for Psychological Anthropology.* 37(3), 334–361.

Skoczen, K.N. (2008). Almost paradise: The cultural politics of identity and tourism in Samana, Dominican Republic. *Journal of Latin American and Caribbean Anthropology.* 13(1), 141–167.

Smith, V., ed. (1989). *Hosts and Guests: The anthropology of tourism.* Philadelphia: University of Pennsylvania Press.

Stovel, K., & Shaw, L. (2012). Brokerage. *The Annual Review of Sociology.* 38, 130–158.

Strobl, A., & Peters, M. (2013). Entrepreneurial reputation in destination networks. *Annals of Tourism Research.* 40, 59–82.

Stronza, A. (2008). Through a new mirror: Reflections on tourism and identity on the Amazon. *Human Organization.* 67(3), 244–257.

Vidal, D. (2000). Markets and intermediaries: An enquiry about the principles of market economy in the grain market of Delhi.In Dupont, V., Tarlo, E., & Vidal, D. (eds.), *Delhi: Urban space and human destinies* (pp. 125–142). Delhi: Manohar Publishers.

Waters, A.M. (2003). Heritage tourism development and unofficial history in Port Royal, Jamaica. *Social and Economic Studies.* 52(2), 1–27.

Zelizer, V.A. (2011) *Economic Lives: How culture shapes the economy.* Princeton, NJ: Princeton University Press.

Zelizer, V.A. (2012). How I became a relational economic sociologist and what does that mean? *Politics and Society.* 40(2), 145–174.

6   Seeing Fez

Jesse Dizard

I spent approximately 11 months learning the ways of Fez's unofficial tour guides. Theirs is a dangerous job.[1] The guides face jail, extortion, or worse, in addition to the demands of honor and identity that all young Moroccan men and women face. The guides I met survive by forming syndicates, which afford some protection, but also create new demands. The group I came to know is essentially a mutual assistance association drawn from neighborhoods and families in which informal control mechanisms have deteriorated or disappeared altogether.

The guide is adrift in an ocean of relatively wealthy foreigners who are able to sample the planet's cultures as from a box of chocolates. Tourists consume what they take to be the finest the guides' own society affords, paying often exorbitant sums (in relative terms) for so-called peak experiences which none of my informants could ever have afforded, were they not someone's guide.

What is it like to guide, translating bits and pieces of one's own social and material culture to foreigners? How much, and how accurately, does one translate or explain matters of interest or mere curiosity to one's client? I never heard a guide say, "I don't know." In a society of long-standing antipathy toward outsiders, how well or badly do the guides maintain their status as outsider's insiders? Is reality really bargained for? What is hidden from outsiders and why? What risks do guides actually run?

Paul Bowles (1991) has described Fez as a singularly unhealthful place. I would be hard-pressed to disagree. And yet despite the noisome smells, the pallid complexions, the poverty and overcrowding, I found a vigorous and robust quality to the people who guided me through their world. Because of the dislocation their families have experienced, and the often grinding poverty in which they were raised, and in which many continue to live, the guides I knew were sensitive, thoughtful, and tough. Yet they were also fatalistic, mournful, and tragic souls.

Despite my accented Arabic, my status as an outsider, and my ambiguous reasons for being there, a notorious group of guides accepted me as one of their own, showed me their world, introduced me to allies, alerted me to

---

1   This chapter is a revised excerpt from my book *Into Fez* (2008).

enemies, and patiently explained the convoluted network of relationships necessary for survival in Fez's narrow alleys. Ultimately, I "passed": I became a member of their *confrèrie* and spent many hours sharing stories and other pleasures with them. I guided foreign tourists. I "earned" commissions. I was nearly arrested.

Acceptance was perhaps never more than partial, however. I was useful; therefore, I was tolerated and, on occasion, confided in. A quid pro quo was always either explicit or implicit in all our interactions.

To guide successfully is—among many things—a matter of controlling one's clients' means of maintaining an adequate definition of reality. According to the *Oxford English Dictionary*, one of the earliest contextual definitions (ca. 1585) of the English verb "to guide" suggests origins in the Arabic *qada'u*: "He which is the guide goeth before mounted on a camel." Hans Wehr (1980) offers the following translation of the Arabic: "To lead, lead by a halter; conduct, engineer, steer; to drive (a car), pilot (an airplane); to pander, pimp; to be led, to follow, obey, yield, submit, retaliate." Explicit in the Arabic are the binary oppositions of control and submission, delinquency and conformity, resistance and placidity. "I know," one guide told me. "We kill ourselves with our own hands."

As a tale within a tale, my story is framed by what other people thought I was doing. Consequently misunderstanding was a routine feature of my research experiences. I was forced to explain repeatedly that I was not a spy for any organization (although over time I came to have second thoughts about this); that I was working independently; and that I was interested in the guides and industrial tourism in Fez because I wanted to tell the story of tourist consumption of Moroccan culture and how it feeds the local economy. Tourists experience a version of Morocco that Moroccans create for outsiders. Guides contribute by orienting outsiders to culture for sale, which in turn is shaped by Moroccan perceptions of tourists' expectations.

It is a complex story, and it is in every respect cultural in Geertz's sense of comprising webs of significance spun by the players themselves (Geertz 1973). It has aspects of skullduggery: one of my informants murdered his father during the course of my stay in Fez. It has anomalous components: one of the most successful unofficial guides I met is a young woman. It has intrigue: elderly women would often warn the guides of police operations in an effort to help the guides avoid arrest. It has terror: almost all of my informants could count on at least two months in jail each year. It has pathos: informants frequently asked me to write *al haqq* (the truth) so that they could survive the police repression of what they considered to be legitimate entrepreneurship. It has all the passion and joy of satisfaction with a job well done: after a big sale the guides and salespeople involved would relax and spend some of their profits on beer, red wine, whiskey, and hashish, the better to entertain each other with tall tales of the ruses used, the near misses, and the sheer delight of making money by virtue of their wits. My tale of their tales is thus only my version of the experiential raw materials they use to construct and animate the dull interstices of their lives that are, after all, based largely on the whims of tourists' fantasies.

Figure 6.1 Medersa Bou Inania. By Annie Spratt, Unsplash.com

It is difficult to ignore the fact that these words I have fashioned into the stories this account comprises are merely the empty husks of what was once a vibrant tale, animated by the experience of living people, as well as by alcohol and strong hashish. My pallid recreation of their spontaneous outbursts and calculated silences cannot adequately reproduce the power of the words spoken among my primary informant, Al Malik, and his associates, the *geeyad* (guides).

In Fez, behavior resisted neat categorization as "modern" or "traditional" or "postmodern." There[,] tradition and modernity interpenetrated, and postmodernity seemed to be a tangible, palpable reality. The stark juxtaposition of the walled city, Fès al-bali, with the Ville Nouvelle, made the distinction between modern and traditional seem obvious.[2] The Ville Nouvelle boasts billboards, broad boulevards, boutiques, apartment buildings, and wide sidewalks. Fès al-bali within its crenellated walls feels medieval—there are no roads, only narrow alleyways; donkeys carry all goods and supplies in and out of the old city; and one must watch one's step to avoid the slippery evidence of a mule-train's passage. To see a man dressed in a suit and tie was quite normal in the Ville Nouvelle, but the same man dressed that way in Fès al-bali seemed out of place, even alien, given his surroundings. Veiled women looked equally odd in the Ville Nouvelle, whereas in Fès al-bali, they seemed more appropriate to the context: a traditional costume in its traditional milieu.

My confusion about what was modern, and what was traditional, grew greater the longer I lingered in Fez. The view from a rooftop in Fès al-bali proved disorienting, further upsetting the apple cart of categories: I saw many satellite dishes, electrical wires strung from odd angles, as well as the occasional ram hobbled on a roof, being fattened for the eid al-kebir celebrating the end of Ramadan. The coexistence of satellite television and veiled women seemed as profoundly contradictory as Palestinian teens hurling paving stones at the Israeli Defense Forces soldiers during the first Intifada.

One day while wandering through Fès al-bali I watched a wedding procession pass. The bride was borne upon a beautiful palanquin, dressed in rich brocades, her hands stained with a filigree pattern of henna. She was surrounded by crowds of ululating women, each of whom had henna-stained hands as well—though none as elaborately done as those of the bride. "How authentic, how very traditional," I thought to myself as the procession approached. But as the crowd drew near I noticed that the bride was not Moroccan. She was Japanese, and so was her groom. The musicians and well-wishers had been hired by the couple to provide them with a real Moroccan

2   The conurbation that is modern Fez (or *Fès* in French orthography) can be divided into five sections: *Fès al-bali*, the old city—also known colloquially as *al medina; Fès J'did*, the new city—dating from the 13th century Merinide Dynasty; the Jewish quarter, *al mellah*; the French colonial *Ville Nouvelle*, built outside the ancient walls; and the recently erected *bidonvilles* and temporary shelters of the poor.

wedding experience! Clearly, under specific circumstances and within particular contexts ceremony, clothing, and comestibles are only superficial indicators of cultural complexity.

To further complicate matters, a small army of young men besieged the Euro-American visitor offering their services as guides to Fès al-bali and its sights, hidden within the labyrinthine network of alleyways. Inevitably, after a short tour of the most famous and picturesque aspects of Fès al-bali, the visitor is led to a carpet shop and offered the opportunity to purchase an authentic, handmade rug or Berber blanket. The modern guides sell tradition to postmodern tourists. Is this behavior modern? Postmodern? Or is it traditional? I went to Fez in an effort to find out more about the interpenetration of tradition, modernity, and postmodernity.

Authenticity and Tradition

Morocco in general and Fez in particular seemed an excellent place to explore the relationship between religiosity and unemployment/underemployment and the durability of tradition because it is the religious capital of Islam's westward expansion in the seventh century CE (Common Era). Fez is also a complex city fraught with the tensions of other quickly expanding metropolises without particularly robust economies. Of special relevance to my research, Fez happens to boast a relatively unchanged (by colonialism) architectural infrastructure, parts of which date from the city's founding in the eighth century. Fez's old city, the medina, is a massive tourist attraction, and deemed so important that it was recently granted the status of World Heritage City by UNESCO. A fund has been established by that body to "save" the old city from the depredations of overpopulation and poverty. This fund is strictly dedicated to restoring architectural features, however, especially those that might attract tourism. The people who live in Fez's ancient city are apparently less interesting to the likes of UNESCO.[3]

I chose to examine these ideas concerning modernity, tradition, faith, agency, and belonging in a specific urban context—a small neighborhood (*huma*) in Fez, Morocco's imperial and spiritual crown jewel. In doing so, I have been forced to confront an interpretation of agency, faith, and modernity as they were presented to me by my friends and informants, an interpretation based not on the divine, but on the profane, the vulgar, and the material. I am speaking of that emergent subject who results from repeated encounters between "ex-primitives" and "postmoderns," the tour guide.

Now, after September 11th and the wars in Afghanistan, Iraq, Libya, and Syria have firmly established fundamentalist Islam as a replacement for

---

3   In 1994, 40 percent of the households in the *Quarawiyyine* quarter of Fez averaged four to ten people each, and lived in a single room. Nationwide, fully 35 percent of the urban population lived under "precarious" and "illegal" conditions (Ksikes 1994).

Figure 6.2 Fez Market Street, by Vince Gx, Unsplash.com

communism as America's preeminent public enemy,[4] Morocco is ardently trying to position itself as a moderate, modern Muslim state. It is banking on its geographically strategic importance to European and American interests because it occupies the Atlantic and Mediterranean littoral of Northwest Africa. It is also counting on its appeal to tourists seeking the pleasures of sun and sand, both of which Morocco has in abundance. Increasingly, tourism has come to be understood as a means to augment national coffers and

4   The construction of Islam as America's enemy has been building since at least 1979 when Iran's Shah Reza Pahlevi was overthrown by supporters of Ayatollah Khomeini.

help repay a crushing debt to the International Monetary Fund and the World Bank.[5] Morocco's annual budget is $19.3 billion (CIA 2003). Currently tourism in Morocco contributes three billion dollars annually to the national economy (Moroccan American Trade and Investment Council 2008; now subsumed under the Moroccan American Center for Policy, see: moroccoonthemove.com). Approximately 47 percent of Morocco's labor force is employed by the service sector (CIA 2003). The employment figures for Morocco's tourism industry are exceedingly incomplete, however. Many who earn their living from tourism are not considered "employed" for they have no officially recognized capacity as tourism industry employees. Nevertheless, these figures are useful for illustrating just how important tourism actually is to the officially measured Moroccan economy.

Tourism, quite simply, is the largest industry in the world. It has overtaken petroleum and motor vehicles as the leading export earner in the world (Youell 1998). Taken as an ensemble—passenger transportation, hotels, restaurants, and leisure activities (including those advertised as "cultural")— tourism is expected to account for roughly eight trillion dollars globally in 2008 and rising to roughly $15 trillion over the next ten years according to the World Travel and Tourism Council (wttc.org). This growth in numbers will also reflect changes in the kinds of people who travel and the kinds of experiences they will purchase. One can expect generally older tourists who are likely to spend more money per visit.

According to my observations as well as those of *The Economist* (1991, 38), most tourists visiting Morocco come from five countries: the United States, Germany, the United Kingdom, Japan, and France. Due in part to American deregulation of its airlines, travel over great distances has become less expensive and far more common, thereby facilitating tourism and travel in general. And despite 9/11, its aftermath, a weakening US dollar, and rising fuel costs, the World Travel and Tourism Council notes that regional emerging markets in Africa, Asia Pacific, and the Middle East are experiencing higher growth rates than the world average, at 5.9 percent, 5.7 percent, and 5.2 percent respectively (wttc.org).

Tourists are valuable commodities to the vacation-brokers and tourism industrialists, and this is not lost on the Moroccans of humble origins who find themselves unable to realize the economic aspirations that the movies, television advertisements, and situation comedies imported from the West ceaselessly encourage. Because of structural changes in Moroccan society, steady population growth, unemployment, and in particular the growth of industrial tourism, those young Moroccan men lucky enough to live in one of the imperial capitol cities famed for their ancient medinas (Fez, Marrakesh, or Meknès) have been, since the late 1970s, increasingly drawn to work for what is perceived to be easy money earned by guiding tourists.

5   Total external debt as of 2007 is $16.86 billion (CIA 2003).

It is important to note that Morocco has been a destination of distinction for European and American elites ever since France gained political control there in 1912. Winston Churchill spoke of the Mamounia hotel in Marrakesh as "the most lovely spot in the whole world" (Humphreys 2003). More recently, often younger American, German, and Japanese travelers eager for an inexpensive good time, risky sex, and easy access to illegal drugs have arrived buoyed by songs like "Marrakesh Express" by Crosby, Stills, Nash, and Young, the legends of Jimi Hendrix relaxing on the beaches south of Essaouira, or the glamorous parade of celebrities who still go to Morocco.[6] They were, for Moroccans, an easy source of fun, money, and an opportunity to escape the rigid confines of class and status, which relegated them to low-paying menial jobs or worse still, chronic unemployment.

Today, in the face of shrinking legitimate opportunities, guiding is understood to provide a measure of autonomy unavailable to any but the upper classes, hence it is attractive to young, ambitious Moroccans, both male and female. Unofficial guides are considered unsavory characters, harassing outsiders and giving Morocco a bad reputation among tourists internationally, thereby being very bad for business. Indeed, this is not unique to Morocco. As Pruitt (1993) has shown, similar attitudes prevail in Jamaica. Indeed, one would expect this to be the case anywhere those who have been disenfranchised from institutionalized tourism seek direct access to the largesse associated with tourist dollars; they are maligned and persecuted as detriments to the national interest. While governments fail to provide for the interests of the majority of the society, national leaders continue to admonish citizens to cooperate with the establishment's tourism program for satisfying tourists' desires for a carefree, fun-filled holiday (162).

The Guiding Way

My informants were the ones who approached obvious outsiders, tourists, and travelers offering their services as self-styled impresarios of their city's finest cultural artifacts and experiences. Eagerly catering to the Western traveler's desire for illicit pleasure, such as hashish, sex, or alcohol in an "exotic" setting, they were like knights in tailored suits or *jellabas* (traditional hooded woolen gowns). They sought to earn the confidence of tourists in exchange for whatever they could get. They are commonly

---

6 "Now the drugs and sex are (mostly) gone, film keeps southern Morocco's celeb quotient high. The Atlas Studios, in the tiny one-camel town of Ouarzazate, offers cheap film-making facilities to Hollywood. Costs are a fraction of those in America, and there are 300 clear sunny days a year. So Morocco has in recent years become the exotic backdrop of choice for foreign producers, standing in for Tibet in Martin Scorsese's *Kundun*, Somalia in Ridley Scott's *Black Hawk Down*, and Egypt in the French hit *Astérix and Obelix: Mission Cléopatra*. *Hideous Kinky* with Kate Winslet was also filmed there" (Humphreys 2003).

known as illegal or unofficial guides. They called themselves *geeyad* (guides). I called them the Sharks.[7]

I am convinced that where objects of tourists' desire are to be found, tourism itself is having a powerful effect upon the way people, especially the young, conceive of themselves as members of local culture, and upon the long-term nature of local and national economies as these young people come of age in an era of belt-tightening and world economic turbulence. According to MacCannell, the "commercialization of ethnological performance and display co-developed by formerly primitive peoples and the international tourism and entertainment industries is potentially a long-term economic adaptation" (1992, 18). This certainly seems to be the case in Fez, Morocco.

"As people thread their ways through the intricate networks of urban social structure, they choose or forge paths which accommodate their needs, reward their aspirations, and justify their humanity" (Berreman 1972, 584). Though this remark was penned in reference to urban India, this too certainly seems to be true in Fez. In light of this, I think that "the guiding way," as one of my informants put it, ought to be understood as a response to the shrinking opportunity structure of contemporary Morocco. Selling experiences to tourists is a form of deviance that is also modifying traditional attitudes and occupations.

The oldest Muslim kingdom, Morocco has long been a classic site for anthropological fieldwork. Yet few anthropologists have explicitly concerned themselves with the Moroccans many visitors to Morocco would be most likely to meet. Tourists arrive primed by the lustrous enticements of travel magazines touting Morocco as a "world class destination," a "land of forbidden pleasure," and a sensuous escape.[8]

The bulk of my time while in Morocco came to be spent among a group of young men, all of whom had worked or were working as unlicensed tour guides in the city of Fez.[9] Most were still guiding in 1993, six years after I first met them. A few had saved enough money, or had accrued enough support from patrons, to open shops of their own, catering exclusively to tourists. Only two had official licenses to work as guides, and these they had acquired through bribery.

By exploring the guides' fragmented sense of their own power and powerlessness within a context of social and economic change, their search for justice and agency in an unjust world can be understood as a modernizing force

---

7   When I asked one of my informants what he thought of my term, "the Sharks," he made a face and said that he did not like it at all. "Sharks are stupid animals," he told me, "*geeyad* are neither beasts nor fools." While I agree with this opinion, I still like my term because of the association with ruthlessness and voracious appetites. It also reflects the fear that tourists have of the *geeyad*.

8   None other than the romance novelist Danielle Hayes wrote about Morocco (1994), "To be in Morocco is to enter the realm of the senses."

9   I met and interviewed one young woman (19 years of age in 1994) who worked as an unlicensed guide in Fez. Her street name, ironically, was "*al wild*" which means "the boy."

dependent upon an illusion of pre-modern authenticity, and as an effort to resist a repressive authoritarian state. In doing so, they cling to Islam as a core feature of their identity. Despite their sybaritic orientation and fast living, they unambiguously identify themselves as Muslim, even as they contradict every normative orientation to Islam.

I had come to Fez with a preconceived agenda, largely derived from research reports that seemed above reproach. I expected to find that people whose economic aspirations were blocked would be drawn to a harsh evangelical "retrograde" version of Islam. Though I could not manage to penetrate the oppositional mosques' *umma* (community of the faithful), I was able to gain access to a scene in which the people who might have been drawn to the mosque were, instead, drawn to very nearly the opposite. The monarchy is hostile to anti-modern Islamist social movements, so those who were trying to organize and radicalize their *umma* had to be very wary of spies.[10] In a curious way, they were as vulnerable as the Sharks. But the Sharks had to be more open and less risk-averse. Hence, I could gain access to their world, the guiding way.

To put it another way, I went to Fez a structuralist and came out a symbolic interactionist. I began with the expectation that the most disadvantaged members of society would be the most adamantly hostile to the monarchy and the king's version of modernity. Instead, I had to come to terms with resignation, fatalism, and complacency. The structural features of Moroccan society that made my research possible also forced me to consider the ways Structuralism and Symbolic Interactionism require each other. Each, taken alone, distorts and makes it impossible to understand what is going on.

As I waited for my flight from New York's JFK airport to Casablanca on Royal Air Maroc, I found myself sitting with fellow travelers in a sterile, windowless lounge, under the drab glow of full fluorescent lighting, and listened as they swapped stories of vacations in the most far-flung corners of the map: Alaska, China, "Rhodesia." They were elderly white men and women each trying to outdo the other couple's tales of sumptuous lodgings, gourmet meals, or spectacular views. After a while I asked if any of them had been to Morocco. "Yes," said several couples, "but we'll not go back." I heard this sentiment expressed repeatedly in Morocco as well as elsewhere, and it was corroborated by friends who travel a great deal more than I do. When I asked why this might be so, I found a non-specific dissatisfaction to be rather common among tourists returning from Morocco. This was often attributable to what tourists and others describe as personality conflicts with specific Moroccans, and/or the perception of a general expression of resentment on the part of Moroccans toward the outsider.

In an effort to explain this common impression of veiled malevolence, I wish to avoid the abstractions that are alluded to by Entelis (1989), who

10 One informant, not a guide, insisted in very hushed tones that "one in 20 Moroccans is a paid spy for the king."

attributes a certain truculence to "the Moroccan personality." Others are more precise, but the focus is on European representations of Moroccans in Europe (Alloula 1988; Mansouri 1988). Visitors to Morocco may arrive with all sorts of preconceptions, the expectations hyped by romanticized tourist brochures, et cetera, as well as the accreted layers of Orientalist residue.[11] Yet this alone is rarely sufficient to account for such widespread reports of unpleasant results from intercourse (sexual or not) with real Moroccans. I prefer a more materialist explanation, one which may be applicable to a wide variety of situations in which bargaining occurs. Specifically, the economist Ellingson suggests that

> When the pie's size is certain, evolution favors the *fair* strategy; accept any share greater than or equal to one half, reject any smaller share. The unique outcome is hence an equal split. In noisy environments, more flexible behavior tends to appear in equilibrium. Since flexibility attracts greediness, there is then a positive probability of conflict.
>
> (1997, 581, emphasis added)

Conflict in this case arises because the tourist and the Moroccan/guide are frequently each trying to extract maximum advantage in the context of bargaining for services and/or souvenirs.

The Sharks are strategically situated at the intersection of modern and "traditional" conventions. They are quintessential marginal men: they are "in" but not "of" both city and village. They know the limits, as well as the virtues, of both. Occupying a liminal position, they have to know enough of the traditional culture to be able to effectively market that tradition to affluent Westerners; and they have to know enough about the affluent West to be good at appealing to tastes honed by the desire for adventure and the desire to bring back souvenirs of their exotic interlude "outside the passage of time."

The distinction between *geeyad* and official guides bears some scrutiny. The Office Nationale Marocaine du Tourisme licenses the latter. They are essentially the embodiment of Morocco's efforts to distance itself from its bad reputation as a dangerous land of unscrupulous barbarians.[12] Licensed guides represent an effort to make Morocco "safe" and welcoming to timid tourists, but there are those young affluent tourists from Europe, Japan, and the United States who want something more raw, adventurous, and "authentic" than anything the packaged tours and official guides can offer. Hence the market niche for the unlicensed unofficial guides.

11 Following Said (1978), I understand "orientalism" to mean an essentialized realm originally separate from and unsullied by the West, one that has no Cartesian order to it, except that which is imposed by colonialism.

12 According to *The New Shorter Oxford English Dictionary*, the term "barbarian" has its origins in Arabic: "Arab *barbar* (berber); barbaria, land of barbarians (an old name for the western part of North Africa)."

As features of the tourist's imagined landscape, like Scylla and Charybdis, Morocco's unofficial guides' reputations precede them worldwide. Guide books to Morocco are replete with warnings about the touts and guides of Fez, Marrakech, and Tangiers. The popular guidebook *Let's Go! Spain, Portugal and Morocco* (1991) goes so far as to urge visitors to Fez to hire an official guide to avoid the generalized hassles posed by unofficial guides, and also to bring water and other supplies in case one gets lost in Fès al-bali, home to over 200,000 souls. The implication is that unofficial guides are not to be trusted, that they are even dangerous men; that amidst the exotica of a magical medieval (yet modern) Muslim city one is a form of prey.[13] The fact is that the unofficial guides themselves are prey of the Moroccan state: unofficial guides are subject to harassment from corrupt police who extract "protection" money, or even impose arrest for the seemingly trivial offense of guiding without a license. Every unofficial guide I came to know in Fez had either already been through the municipal jail, or had been shaken down by the police's Brigade Touristique.

At the signing of the General Agreement on Tariffs and Trade (GATT) in Marrakesh in 1994, the unofficial guides of that city were rounded up, loaded onto trucks and busses, and driven 50 miles out of town as part of a clean-up campaign. There they were left to make it back to Marrakesh on their own, so the story went among the unofficial guides of Fez. Currently, the unofficial guides are the objects of police repression, subject to arrest if seen with tourists. If caught and unable to provide evidence of a powerful patron's protection (*rkeeza*), the minimum sentence is generally two months in jail, with longer sentences imposed for recidivism.

Jail is a place all the unofficial guides know or at least know of. An unofficial guide who finds himself behind bars has few options: if he has money or goods other inmates value, such as Nike shoes, he must sell or trade them for protection and for a place to sleep. If he has no money or goods of value to trade he is likely to become a "girlfriend" to a powerful inmate. Trading sex for protection is common in Morocco's jails, according to my informants.

The guides feared jail. *Al habs* (the jail) is invoked to frighten and chastise obstreperous or contentious members of the crew I spent time with and learned from. There is a distinct age-grade hierarchy determining who can threaten whom. Younger members of the crew deferred to older, "wiser" members in all matters, and listened with rapt attention to tales of the jail. The normal rowdiness fades when incarceration and police repression are the topics of discussion. No one makes casual jokes about being "queen bottom" (*hissess*) or the "top man" (*zammel*) in the verbal jousts over sexual ability and submission when suffering in jail is mentioned.

---

13 Paul Bowles' "A Distant Episode" (1989), though not set in Fez, exploits this fear as fully as possible.

Unofficial guides are blamed for all sorts of social ills, from petty thievery to prostitution and gambling. I know of no unofficial guide who has committed outright theft—especially from a tourist—nor did I ever find evidence of the guides I knew being involved with gambling operations or prostitution (Rabinow 1977, 68–69), though I suspect such activities do occur. A system of informal codes loosely defines the limits within which the *geeyad* operate.

There is honor among guides. One guide will not muscle in on another's "mark" or client, although they may change horses in midstream if one has a better relationship with a vendor of products the mark seems interested in—or, for that matter, to maximize any number of advantages one guide might have over another. But this is a negotiation: there is always a bottom line in terms of the percentage of profit made from sales to the mark, and how that money is divided among all who aided in the sales effort. There is also a hierarchy of marks. But "counting coup" as it were on other guides is irrelevant except in terms of bragging rights over how much a foolish tourist paid for this or that, or over how subtle (and not so subtle) insults were delivered to the tourist. In general, the guides I met preferred clients in their mid-twenties to mid-thirties. Such marks tend to have more money, and more expensive tastes.

According to the guides themselves, they must maintain scrupulous integrity toward their clients because otherwise they would lose their business. Moreover, since they are not officially employed by a legitimate tourist agency, they are vulnerable in ways that official guides are not. As such, the guides I knew must always protect themselves by being as honest as possible in order to succeed in the dishonest business of selling to tourists.

The guides I met were generally nattily attired young men who had been doing this kind of work since they were school children. They usually begin this work when young because it takes time to acquire and retain the often quite sophisticated expressions and vocabularies of various languages. They must be acutely aware of individual psychology in order to quickly size up marks to determine weaknesses and preferences, the better to present the mark with things they will like and feel good about buying. My primary informant, whom I will call Al Malik ("the King"), understands this all too well when he asserts that above all, he "sells words." Precisely how he does this is a matter of some subtlety.

The guides size up the mark by virtue of their outgoing gregariousness (an essential personality characteristic of any aspiring guide) and try to inspire enough confidence in them that the mark is willing to be led into the labyrinth of Fès al-bali. This is difficult to do, given the reputation of Fez's guides and the hyper-exoticism employed to attract tourists to Fez. Even the best of guides will hedge when asked direct questions about how they go about this crucial phase of what I call "the snag." Once successful, the guide will learn the mark's tastes through conversation and acute observation during the course of a whirlwind tour through the medina. They often concentrate on only a few of the most famous sites followed by picturesque or titillating orientalist set-pieces, such as a narrow alley, or a crowded *souk* (market). From these brief situational tests the guide is often able to quite accurately judge the mark's desires, expressed and unexpressed. One guide went so far as to tell me the colors preferred by various tourist nationalities: Americans, for example, are said to like stripes.

A tourist, or group of tourists, is unlikely to venture very far into the medina without a guide. Those who do happen to wander in will soon find themselves attached to a guide. Even when no such service is requested, and even if nothing is purchased, the guide will tag along doing his best to disorient and confuse the tourist (all under the guise of being helpful), ultimately demanding some money. The game often gets very tense for the tourist who is unused to such in-your-face petty harassment, especially since this is their "holiday." When, on occasion, the tourist becomes exasperated, guides have been known to begin leveling accusations of racism ("You won't hire me because you don't like Arabs!"). This tactic is sometimes effective, resulting in "the snag," or even a handful of change hastily given, just to be rid of the irritating guide and escape the uncomfortable situation.

It is important to distinguish between guides and merchants. The latter are the avowed masters of the deal, the former are like their lieutenants—but with plenty of autonomy to arrange deals of their own for services rendered. Merchants and guides rely upon each other. The merchant greets the mark, makes the mark relax and feel "the genuine warmth of Moroccan hospitality," usually in whatever language the mark is most comfortable with. The successful merchants are the ones who feign disinterest in sales. They repeat to each mark, "It costs nothing to look..." and proceed to show products they suspect the mark will want, usually based upon the guide's insight, gleaned over the course of the tour. They are very good at creating the necessary atmosphere of trust required for the best of cons. For, when the mark feels comfortable, whatever price they pay will seem like a bargain to them: they are indeed buying words.

Tourists are not alone in feeling betrayed. The guides too are accustomed to the petty betrayals that are inflicted by tourists. In the real world, if a relationship is established there is usually a reciprocal obligation involved, if only implicitly. But in the ersatz Morocco, one pays and then leaves. No relationship exists beyond the transaction. In the real Morocco, one leaves and then pays. In other words, a connection has been established and honor requires that one maintain it. Tourists rarely grasp this feature of social life in Morocco, regardless of how much they may profess to be intoxicated by Moroccan hospitality, generosity, and warmth. Rarer still are those who keep their end of the bargain. For example the guides have heard countless promises to send them copies of photographs, or cassettes, or compact discs, or any number of items that might establish genuine sociability. So few such promises are kept that it is not surprising that the guides are fatalistic and cynical not just about tourists, but about most everything. Several examples from my journal illustrate this.

Morocco's soccer team made the World Cup playoffs hosted by the United States in 1993. The city was abuzz with excitement, men and boys played soccer with more than the usual intensity. Morocco was scheduled to play Saudi Arabia for a chance to enter the semi-finals and face Germany. There was a raucous party in anticipation that evening at Al Malik's shop. As the kickoff approached, we moved the party down the alley to another much more sumptuous carpet bazaar where there was a television. We rolled out beautiful *kilims* and stretched out to enjoy the American coverage of the game in luxury. The American network aired short tourist-oriented "background" introductions to each team's country. The introduction to Morocco caused howls of pleasure from those assembled. It relied primarily on abstractions such as sun, sand, mysterious and sensuous veiled women, dark handsome men. There was some discussion among the group about the superficiality of the portrayal. When I asked Al Malik how he felt about Morocco's team playing in the World Cup hosted by the United States, he simply shrugged and said, "Even if Morocco could win, it would not be allowed to happen." Morocco lost to Saudi Arabia.

Also from my journal: After a long December evening of conversation and camaraderie, I decide not to remain in the old city to sleep; I walk instead back to my bed in the apartment I have rented in the Ville Nouvelle about three miles away. The gates of each *huma* used to close at nine or ten in the evening (no one seems quite sure), and the main gates of the medina used to close as well. Some parts of the city still do close. For example, the streets leading to the densest part of the old city, the *souks* of the *kissaria*, are blocked every night except during the first nights of Ramadan, when hordes of young men and boys light firecrackers and small explosives in celebration. But as one friend told me, the primary motive is to frighten their sisters and mothers, and to annoy their uncles and fathers. Such mayhem is still several months away, and the neighborhood's gates remain open.

Chill winds whip through the medina's narrow cobblestone streets at this hour, some time between midnight and four in the morning. I don't know the exact time, having loaned my wristwatch to one of the guides. He asked to borrow it because material goods from beyond Morocco, especially *stazen* (the contracted form of the French noun *les États-Unis*), lend the possessor great status—no matter that my watch has a Japanese-made movement and a dial made in Taiwan. No one but drunkards, "bad men with knives" (so my friends warn me), and I are out so late at night and in this cold. The drunks, *meskine* (a catchall term for unfortunates), are huddled in doorways, bundled in rags, gibbering. The so-called knife fighters lean on corners here and there, staring from beneath their knit caps at everything that moves. I walk steadily, meeting any gaze defiantly from beneath my own knit cap, the sound of my steps echoing like small-caliber pistol shots on the cobblestones. "Get me out of here," I think to myself. But at the same time, I want to be here; for it is at such an unlikely hour that the city streets are most easily navigated and, contrary to popular opinion, quite safe.

One can best appreciate the funnel-like spider web that is Fez at night, orange light from sodium-arc street lamps playing crazily across the slanting stone walls, reflecting off of tile rooftops, and casting shadows that shroud the way in uncertainty. Smells guide me: the bitter acrid scent of strong chemicals used to mask fouler, septic system odors suggests an older, poorer family's home; rotting vegetation means the markets of *Funduk Yehudi*; while the fishmonger's familiar rankness means I've come nearer the *mellah*, and thus will soon break through the walls into the open of the Boulevard Moulay Youssef leading to the Ville Nouvelle. From there it is a straight shot along the wide, well-lit sidewalks of the Ville Nouvelle to the Avenue des Sports, and then across to the train station, and finally up to my street.

Once beyond the medina's walls and past the broad empty expanse of the plaza in front of Fez's royal palace (one of many throughout the country), I nod to the men who nominally guard the apartment buildings' main entrances. These men are potentially my allies and informants, or could cause me unwanted difficulties, for they make it their business to observe all that transpires in their field of view. I made it a point to acknowledge them, hoping that by doing so they would be more inclined toward helping me, should the need arise.

The apartment I have rented is in a building in a newer section of the Ville Nouvelle. Like other modern buildings owned and inhabited by wealthier Moroccans, mine has a night watchman. His name is Ahmed. He has a curious "command post" from which he surveys the ebb and flow of traffic on the street throughout the night. It is a large cardboard box, out of which he has fashioned an all-purpose foxhole. He has a small shelf in front with a hole cut out to hold his glass of very sweet and viscous coffee-flavored milk. He keeps a small transistor radio down below the shelf. His seat is a purloined school chair that he covers with a worn sheepskin. The lines on his face are deep. He smokes strong cigarettes of Moroccan manufacture, "Casa Sports." One night I asked to try one. He refused to let me, and in response to my repeated entreaties said only, "Kmi Casa Sports—li 'l kaboor" (Smoke Casa Sports—go to the cemetery). He leaves around sunrise each morning. Ahmed the night watchman and I exchange a few words about the frigid night. Each time I come home late at night Ahmed teaches me a new phrase and quizzes me about the last one. This time it's "Allah y saub" (Allah makes it so), referring to the fatalistic attitude toward physical deformity: they are that way because Allah willed it to be thus. Period. A comforting way of dealing with adversity, for it attributes specialness by the grace of Allah to what others might be tempted to see as misfortune.

All of my informants entertained fantasies of escaping from Fez. They envisioned themselves eventually finding and marrying a European. Although the full implications of this are rarely confronted, it remains a powerful fantasy. They did not see guiding as a way of life, rather it is a way of postponing the responsibility of adulthood while living well, and being able thereby to enjoy—at least partially—the leisure they see tourists as having. Consumption is therefore a basic component of their worldview. Leisure is to be consumed, replenished by some kind of minimal "work," and then consumed again. The cycle repeats itself ad infinitum. In short, leisure is earned and then used as a marker of success. Unfortunately, durable success is not the common condition. Hence the value of Ahmed's expression, "Allah y saub." "Making it" ultimately means being able to have other people work for you.

In this sense, my primary informant, Al Malik, has made it. He owns a modest carpet shop and controls the labor of a pair of blanket weavers. He also has three young men working for him: Sidi Zitoun, age 31, is a gifted salesman, fluent in French and confident in English, Spanish, and German; Tattoo, age 20, is his apprentice; and Muscles, age 18, is the gopher and general assistant. They sell blankets woven on the premises, and several kinds of carpets (*hanbel, kilim,* and *zarbia*[14]). But, primarily, regardless of the object or experience on offer, words are ultimately the merchandise. Of the approximately 1000 unofficial guides in Fez, a loosely knit group of 20 regularly brings customers to Al Malik's shop where, it is hoped, the words will entice the tourists to buy. The "selling words" have their desired effect often not only because they are indeed mellifluous, but also because of the context in which they are uttered.

Fez itself is seemingly chaotic to an outsider. There is no Cartesian order to the old city (Fès al-bali or simply the *medina*), in marked contrast to the new city (Fès Ville Nouvelle) built roughly one mile from the medina's walls by the French in the early decades of the twentieth century. Fès al-bali is downright bizarre: a walled city of roughly 200,000 souls wherein no cars can pass, for the widest cobblestone "streets" are perhaps 12–15 feet across at their least constricted points. Most alleys are no broader than one's shoulders and two passersby must turn sideways in order to slip past each other. The medina is a canyon land of perpetual shadows, the narrow, twisting passages between structures always cool, except for the quarter hour at high noon when the Sun's light shines directly overhead.

It is among these *ruelles* that the guides ply their trade, for "hidden" from outsiders are the "secret charms" of this marvelous jewel of a city, to borrow the vocabulary of exoticism. Even armed with the best of the guide books available, however, Fez's old city is so strange to an outsider that a guide can be most welcome, doubly so if he or she can be of use in repelling what tourists and other outsiders perceive to be the ceaseless harassment by zealous

---

14 *Kilim* is a word of Turkish origin that refers to a pileless textile for a variety of uses. They are produced by one of several flatweaving techniques that have a common or closely related heritage and are practiced in the geographical area that includes parts of Turkey (Anatolia and Thrace), North Africa, the Balkans, the Caucasus, Iran, Afghanistan, Pakistan, Central Asia, and China (Hull, Luczyc-Wyhowska, and Barnard 2000). *Zarbia* literally means "carpet"; the guides used it to refer to any carpet that is not a *kilim. Hanbel* is the term the guides use to refer to blankets.

Figure 6.3 Fez Alley by Moroccan Zest, Unsplash.com

hustlers hawking goods and services.[15] In fact, one of the guides' primary functions is to protect their clients while reaping profit for themselves in the demimonde of rapacious merchants and hustlers that inhabit this fascinating metropolis.

Daily life in Fez shows how individuals affect what Pierre Bourdieu describes as "structuring structures." According to Bourdieu, the common-sense world of daily life can be described in the abstract in terms of

---

15 The Office Nationale Marocaine du Tourisme's colorful-yet-vague impressionistic maps marked with the main points of interest cartooned onto the tracery of city streets are useful only to mark one as an outsider and, as such, fair game for the hustlers. There is not an accurate map of Fez available to the public. Even the best maps ignore the smaller capillary alleyways; they are simply too small. In a very real sense then, there is no map, only cognitive maps, the fruit of experience.

> systems of durable, transposable dispositions, structured structures pre-
> disposed to function as structuring structures, that is, as *principles of the*
> *generation and structuring of practices and representations which can be*
> *objectively "regulated" and "regular" without in any way being the product*
> *of obedience to rules.*
>
> (1972, 72, emphasis added)

"Structure" for Bourdieu functions here as a verb rather than a noun. The
Sharks obey a code of conduct they themselves might not recognize as such.
By so doing they contribute to the production and maintenance of social
order, even as they act in ways outwardly understood to be disorderly.

Fez's guides are fascinating for their own brand of social banditry, and for
the coarse, transgressive lifestyle associated with their mercantile duplicity.
Their stock-in-trade is both acceptable and offensive, a form of necessary
evil. Someone has to buy the products made by Fez's *artisinat*—the copper
artisans, potters, embroiderers, weavers, tailors, tanners, calligraphers, etc.
Local producers are beholden to guides for help marketing their wares. But
the guides get drunk. They get stoned on hashish before their time,[16] they
seek and enjoy illicit sex with clients, they fail to pray throughout the day,
and they generally do not attend the mosque on Fridays. One may be for-
given for wondering just what specifically links them to Islam, since this
obvious contradiction may seem in need of explanation. The guides I knew
unanimously affirmed their identity as Muslims based on their claim that
they fast (*sawm*) during Ramadan, the holy month. The sacrifices necessary
to keep the fast—especially when it falls during the long, hot days of
summer—are not only an outward reflection of devotion to the abstractions
of religion, but also of the structuring practices contributing to belonging
among the *geeyad* I came to know.

While they use sufficient discretion to be able to claim a minimum of dig-
nity before their parents and relevant elders, in the quasi-separate world of
guiding tourists and selling souvenirs a more louche persona emerges. A particularly well-executed scam affords an opportunity for a great deal of gloat-
ing and derisive pleasure. Guides love to brag and joke among themselves
about the exorbitant prices they have succeeded in persuading tourists to pay.
I have watched guides laugh in front of clients, boasting in Dérija (Moroccan
dialect) of their own prowess and the tourist's stupidity. Often they will crow,
"I really screwed this or that tourist!" But what to them amounts to a great
profit is really only a matter of 10 or 20 US dollars, a negligible sum for all
but the most hard-bitten budget travelers. However, there are naturally
exceptions.

---

16 There are certain cafés where men publicly smoke hashish or leaf marijuana, *kif*,
and there is no particular opprobrium associated with this activity. This is an
activity reserved for those too old to work, a pleasure of *la retraite*.

I watched one day as Sidi Zitoun and another of the geeyad, nicknamed Soap thanks to his inattention to personal hygiene, sold their least valuable pieces—machine-made nylon rugs 3 feet by 6 feet—to tourists for U$55 apiece. Later, when I expressed astonishment at the exorbitant price, the pair laughed saying, "we sell the same crap to Japanese tourists for 300 US dollars!"

On another occasion, two young Canadian women were spotted, wandering around in the medina. One of the guides made a successful snag and gained their confidence; he eventually brought them to Al Malik's shop. They looked over the *kilim* and *zarbia* on display, and Sidi Zitoun could tell that one of the women really liked one of his least valuable pieces. Setting the table, as it were, he proceeded to extol the virtues of a more expensive one instead. The Canadian eventually bought it at a price that was, unbeknownst to her, scandalously low, affording very little profit for all concerned. Their guide was upset, but Sidi Zitoun told him to relax. Later that afternoon, Sidi Zitoun dispatched one of the younger assistants to find the Canadian women and their guide, and bring them back once more to the killing floor. Amazingly (to me), this was easily accomplished and when they arrived Sidi Zitoun greeted them with contrition, saying that he had given them a bad deal on the carpet they had bought from him. In an effort to correct this error, he would now offer them a better price for the one they had really preferred all along. The women agreed, and exchanged the more valuable carpet they had bought cheaply for the cheaper less valuable one, having paid Sidi Zitoun four times its value, thereby increasing everyone's *jabba* ("cut" or "take" from a transaction).

While such impressive profits are not as common as more modest takes, one wonders why people pay so much. I suspect it is partly because they are lied to: "these carpets are made of pure silk." But, more importantly, it is because they like what they see in the context of the bazaar. The same rug elsewhere would surely be much less attractive without the medina's exoticism and the thrill of interacting with swarthy vendors speaking a "guttural" tongue. The transaction would simply lack the seductive "magic" the tourist seeks.

Moroccans I met live in what has often been called a "shame culture" (Misheva 2000). Public humiliation is to be avoided if at all possible. One's reputation is all one can really claim. Exploitation like that practiced by the guides produces real shame. The guides I know were generally seen as "bad elements" by the upstanding solid citizens and pious proletariat alike. The guides know they are bad. Many revel in their badness. Some, like my friend Sidi Zitoun, walk a tightrope between outward conformity and semi-private debauchery. He takes his meals with his parents when it is convenient for him to do so while hiding his penchant for smoking hashish, drinking alcohol, dating Euro-American women, and indulging in pre-marital heterosexual sex—all of which are frowned upon more or less severely by Fez's faithful. Most guides and merchants catering to the tourist trade try carefully to maintain similar distinctions with more or less success. Publicly they conform to cultural expectations just enough so that they cannot be criticized, yet they indulge themselves when out of the culture's "public eye." It is, however, functionally impossible to be invisible. Herein lies a contradiction, a conflict between conformity and desire.

One whom I will call Mustapha was among those most pleased by teaching me obscene words. He is an outwardly conformist Muslim. He indulges in all the illicit pleasures the tourists come to Morocco to enjoy; he smokes hashish, cigarettes, and *kif* (a mixture of hashish and tobacco), gets drunk, and lusts after carefree romance. For him as well as others, the border separating acceptable and unacceptable "lifestyle choices"—or even indulging in the concept of a "lifestyle choice"—is the degree to which one feels compelled to maintain a façade of piety. Though here too there are exceptions.

One afternoon I was on the rooftop of Al Malik's shop in the company of a certain merchant engaged in the tourist trade. The call to prayer was reverberating throughout the city's tracery of corridors and plazas but this man ignored it and his bellowing to friends below on the street actually drowned out the local mosque's *muezzin*. He was shouting for someone to bring him more hashish, of all things!

So on one level these are delinquents who have grown up and now occupy a tolerated place in the community mainly because they commit "victimless" petty fraud and earn a reasonable income by doing so—money that they freely spend throughout the community. At the same time, they are stigmatized and regarded with suspicion by tourist and Moroccan alike.

Agents of Change

Ironically, for the guides of Fez as well as for their analogs in any of the myriad places that have become tourist destinations, in the name of independence and freedom from the restrictive norms of local culture they have become dependent upon outsiders: tourists. In the process of this transformation of dependency from local to global economies, the guides are also exploited. They are vulnerable to the depredations of corrupt police. They work at the whim of fickle tourists. Their freedom is constrained by the psychology of individual tourists as well as the vicissitudes of the global tourism industry.

While leisure has long been a commodity, the industry associated with selling leisure services is fast becoming one of the most powerful economic players in both local and international political struggles. The effects of the leisure industry are a "people spill" not unlike an oil spill. As a consumable "service good" leisure is contingent upon the violence that results from economic and political competition spreading from the site—or sites—of the tour itself, like concentric circles. The guides I knew are but one of these rings.

The deviant behavior the guides display is contributing to an ongoing struggle over the definition of contemporary Islam in Morocco. There is great anxiety and controversy over which direction Moroccan society will go. One option is that it will accommodate modernity, in spite of its *jahilyya* (chaos) and what Ritzer (2000) has called the McDonaldization of society. Or, the fear is that Morocco will fall prey to what Kepel (1994) has called an evangelical form of Islam. By dubious virtue of their liminal position within the demimonde of Fez, the guides are at the sharp end of a wedge driving into the heart of Moroccan society.

Poverty is not necessarily fanatic fundamentalism's incubator. If Fez becomes primarily a temple of consumption, the people who live there and earn their livelihoods by selling their culture may well not care very much, if at all, about the tourists' religion. Theirs is a domestic and secular crusade. Money too works in mysterious ways.

References

Alloula, M. (1988). *The Colonial Harem*. Translated by Wlad Godzich. Minneapolis: University of Minnesota Press.

Berreman, G. (1972). Social categories and social interaction in urban India. *American Anthropologist*. 74(3), 567–586.

Bourdieu, P. (1972). *Outline of a Theory of Practice*. New York: Cambridge University Press.

Bowles, P. (1991). Preface. In Betsch, W., *The Hakima: A tragedy in Fez*. New York: Aperture Press.

Bowles, P. (1992). *A Distant Episode: The selected stories*. New York: Ecco Press.

Central Intelligence Agency (CIA) (2003). *The World Factbook: Morocco*. Washington, DC: United States Government Printing Office.

Economist, The (1991, March 23). Tourism in Morocco, p. 38.

Ellingson, T. (1997). The evolution of bargaining behavior. *Quarterly Journal of Economics*. Cambridge, MA: Harvard University Press. 112(2), 581–602.

Entelis, J. P. (1989). *Culture and Counterculture in Moroccan Politics*. Boulder, CO: Westview Press.

Geertz, C. (1973). *The Interpretation of Cultures: Selected essays*. New York: Basic Books.

Hayes, D. (1994, October). To be in Morocco is to enter the realm of the senses. *Jax Fax Travel Marketing Magazine*.

Hull, A., Luczyc-Wyhowska, J., & Barnard, N. (2000). *Kilim, The Complete Guide: History, pattern, technique, identification*. San Francisco: Chronicle Books.

Humphreys, A. (2003). Stars flock to the land of forbidden pleasure. *The Observer*, June 22.

Kepel, G. (1994). *The Revenge of God: The resurgence of Islam, Christianity, and Judaism in the modern world*. University Park, PA: Penn State University Press.

Ksikes, D. (1994). 35% des logements en ville, précaires et illégaux. *La Libération*. 997, 1. Casablanca.

Let's Go: Spain, Portugal and Morocco (1991). Cambridge: Harvard Student Agencies.

MacCannell, D. (1992). *Empty Meeting Grounds: The tourist papers*. New York: Routledge.

Mansouri, M. (1988). Moroccan tourism image in France. *Annals of Tourism Research*. 15(4).

Misheva, V. (2000). *Shame and Guilt: Sociology as a poietic system*. Uppsala: Uppsala University Sweden.

Morocco on the Move. Moroccoonthemove.com

Pruitt, D. (1993). Foreign Mind: Tourism, identity and development in Jamaica. Doctoral dissertation, University of California, Berkeley.

Rabinow, P. (1977). *Reflections on Fieldwork in Morocco*. Chicago: University of Chicago Press.

Ritzer, G. (2000). *The McDonaldization of Society*. Thousand Oaks, CA: Pine Forge Press.

Said, E. (1978). *Orientalism*. Westport, CT: Praeger.

Wehr, H. (1980). *A Dictionary of Modern Written Arabic*. Edited by J.M. Cowan. Beirut: Librarie du Liban.

World Travel and Tourism Council. Wttc.org

Youell, R. (1998). *Tourism: An introduction*. Boston: Pearson Higher Education.

Part 4

Imagining Tourism and the Production of Place

7 The Tulum Mayan ruins

A place for foreigners

Maria Lauridsen Jensen

On the Caribbean coast of Mexico, nestled in between palm trees, the archeological site of Tulum rises over the magnificent azure sea. The Tulum ruins attract visitors from all over the world, inviting them to a time when Tulum was home to one of the most developed civilizations of the world—the Mayas. The ruins are one among several symbols of the Mayan past, and as a symbol, the site facilitates many interpretations. As anthropologist Anthony Cohen (1985, 15) pointed out, "Symbols do not so much express meaning as give us the capacity to make meaning." A symbol articulates limitless stories. This chapter deals with how the Tulum ruins, as a symbol of Mayas, are expressed in tourism discourses on site, locally, and globally.

Through tourism discourses, ideas about the Tulum ruins and Mayas flow across the globe and influence imaginaries about the place and ethnic group. This chapter is an analysis of tourist discourses on the Tulum ruins and Mayas and of Mayan ethnicity among contemporary Mayas in Tulum. I analyze tourism discourses through a textual analysis of websites,

Figure 7.1 God of Winds Temple, Tulum

information signs at the site, and a guide book for tourists, and I examine social practices connected to the discourse on the Tulum ruins based on observations at the site and interviews with Mayas from the town center of Tulum, "El Pueblo." I gathered the fieldnotes through ethnographic fieldwork in Tulum from August to November 2015. Although I was very open about my role as a researcher, and have consent to use the ethnographic data, I changed the names of my informants to protect them, as well as myself, from potential complications.

The Tulum ruins, which are often identified as "Mayan ruins" in tourism discourse, has become an iconic site of the Caribbean Coast of Mexico. In 2017, the Archeological Zone of Tulum was visited by 2,207,446 people, which makes it the most visited archeological site in the Mexican state of Quintana Roo and the third most visited archeological zone on the Yucatán Peninsula after Chichén Itzá and Uxmal (Instituto Nacional de Antropología e Historia 2018). "Maya" is a term for an ethnic group, and covers several ethnic subgroups in Mexico, Belize, Guatemala, El Salvador and Honduras. In this chapter, my approach to ethnicity is inspired by anthropologists Fredrik Barth (1998 [1969]), Arjun Appadurai (2010 [1996]), and Richard Jenkins (2008). I perceive ethnicity as a social construction and as a dynamic process. On the one hand, ethnicity is determined by what social group we ourselves identify with, while on the other hand, external powers, for example other people, categorize us in social groups. Ethnic groups are social constructs, and group boundaries are negotiable.

Theoretical frame—global flows

In this chapter, tourism is approached as an example of global flows. Anthropologist Arjun Appadurai (2010) argues that our time is characterized by fast-moving mass-mediated images that circulate globally and provide individuals with resources for creating scripts about themselves and others. Appadurai (5) suggests that imagination plays a newly significant role. While images used to be projected as visions by powerful individuals, now, ordinary people pick up elements of globally flowing images and construct their own visions and narratives. Appadurai (33) works with five theoretical dimensions of global cultural flows: *ethnoscapes, mediascapes, technoscapes, financescapes*, and *ideoscapes*. From these five theoretical dimensions, people form images and narratives about the world. Appadurai (44, 53) underlines that people choose from a wider set of possible lives than in the past, and that culture is more an arena of conscious choice and representation than ever before. Following Appadurai, I investigate tourism as an example of global flows, and I study the effects of images of the local as articulated through tourism.

According to sociologist Roland Robertson (1995), the increase of rapid global flows does not necessarily mean that the world has lost a sense of the local. Robertson argued that the global and the local affect each other. Case studies by anthropologists Edward Bruner (2005) and Noel Salazar (2005,

2010, & 2015) confirmed Robertson's point. Using tourist guides in Indonesia as his ethnographic case, Salazar (2005, 637–638) pointed out that locals actively use global images of their area to sell tours. Salazar's tourist guides were very much aware of global ideas about themselves; they used cell phones, they were aware of international sport events, they followed international TV shows, and they are up-to-date on global fashion trends. The guides performed global ideas of the local for the tourists and hid their global identity from the tourists. Salazar (2015, 56) explained,

> To avoid too much friction, guides position themselves in a transitional or liminal space that facilitates shifting between frames. One moment they are playing the native (forced to be looking culturally inwards), and other moments they are distancing themselves from the locals (dreaming of the wide world out there).

Bruner's (2001, 895) findings from Kenya are similar. He asserted that the Maasai were aware of the discrepancy between their lives and the tourist image but, nevertheless, chose to perform. Tourists are often aware that locals perform. But that awareness is somewhat expected, since they perform the role of tourists in the play where the local is exaggerated (Bruner 2001, 899; Cohen 1988, 383; Rojek & Urry 2004, 52–74, Zarkia 1996, 161).

Who are the Mayas?

Throughout this chapter, I illustrate that the word "Maya" has many meanings and usages. In this section, I define the term "Maya" as ethnic identity.

The pre-conquest Mayan Empire flourished between 1500 BCE and 900 CE in what is now Honduras, El Salvador, Guatemala, Belize, and the Yucatán Peninsula in Mexico. The empire was organized as independent city states. Pre-conquest Mayan civilization is known for having been highly developed, and it is famous for its engineers, astrologers, and mathematicians (Bull 2010, 26–27). As a result, the term "Maya" refers to an ancient ethnic group, which has left impressive marks in the American landscape. The Tulum ruins are an example of such a mark.

Here, I focus on the use of the ethnic label "Maya" in Tulum on the Yucatán Peninsula in Mexico. I discuss how the term is used in tourist discourses and how it is used regarding ethnic identification. As the chapter progresses, it will become more and more visible how the term is used to define two different groups of people, which may or may not share blood— Mayas from the past and Mayas of today.

Since the 1960s, anthropologists (Barth 1998; Jenkins 2008) have seen ethnicity as a social construction. Ethnicity is how people identify as a group and distinguish themselves from other groups, and ethnicity is how people categorize each other into certain groups. Before the year 2000, the Mexican government defined "Mayas" as those who speak a Mayan language, but, thereafter, self-identification as Maya is the officially recognized determinant. However, Mayan ethnicity is not completely fluid. As Jenkins (2008) points out, how a person defines themself is one thing, while how they are defined by others is another. When I was looking for informants, I was told on several occasions that "he is not Maya," although the person looked Mayan to me and spoke a Mayan language. Mayas from Tulum differentiated themselves from Mayas from neighboring towns and Mayas from Yucatán state. Mayas from Yucatán state had come to Tulum to work in tourism because of poor job opportunities at home, and Mayas from Tulum categorized them as unreliable, violent, and as thieves. Though Mayas in Tulum divide each other into subgroups, I regard them all as Maya. For clarity, I define "Mayas of Tulum" as the descendants of the followers of the Santa Cruces who settled in Tulum during the Caste War.

Today, descendants of the followers of the Santa Cruces described in the previous section identify themselves with la Iglesia Maya (the Mayan church) (Juárez 2002). Some Mayas from Yucatán state also attend la Iglesia Maya. The Mayan church is an example of syncretism, where Catholicism is mixed with Mayan traditions and beliefs. In contemporary Tulum, Mayan ethnicity, in its organized form, is centered on la Iglesia Maya, and the families who have lived in Tulum the longest live around la Iglesia Maya. All informants I present in this chapter attend la Iglesia Maya and are members of one of the five "founding families" of Tulum (see Everton 2012, 221).

An historical overview of Tulum

The oldest archeological evidence found in the Tulum ruins is estimated to be from 564 CE (INAH 2018). Originally, the ruin site was called "Zama," which means "dawn" in the Mayan language. When the site was explored in the early 1800s, it was renamed "Tulum." Tulum means "walls," and the name refers to the place's significance as a walled city.

During the Caste War of Yucatán (1847–1901), when Mayas struggled for independence from the Yucatán and Mexican government, a miraculous cross appeared in Tulum to guide the Mayan rebels, and, afterwards, Tulum became a power center for them. The cross is known as "la Cruz Parlante" (the talking cross). The Mayas who followed the cross as their guide and protector are referred to as Santa Cruces *or* Cruzoob in regional historical accounts. The Santa Cruces settled down in Tulum and initiated its development from jungle to farming area and town (Consejo Municipal de Tulum 2009; Juárez 2002, 114). From 1902 to 1974, Quintana Roo was Mexican territory. Before 1902, the area was independent. Before statehood in 1974, Quintana Roo was a wild jungle with few inhabitants. In the 1930s, the Mexican government sent teachers to the Yucatán Peninsula to teach Mayas the Spanish language, force all children to attend school, and spread nationalistic feelings through narratives in which the Mexican nation state was portrayed as the savior of the people. The teachers formed schools that functioned as civic churches where the religion was nationalism. Teachers, for example, had girls bob their hair and change their *huipiles* (traditional Mayan dresses) for dresses, and they dismissed Mayan religion as superstition. All of this was part of the government's Mexicanization plan—the construction of one nation where many cultures were united under one grand narrative (see Eiss 2004; Fallaw 2004). According to Michael Billig (1995, 27), "The achievement of national hegemony is well illustrated by the triumph of the official languages and the suppression of rivals." Many of my older informants spoke Maya as their first language and Spanish as their second. But children and young adults were Spanish-language speakers, and only knew a few sentences in Maya.

In 1937, the Tulum ruins came under the control of the National Anthropological and Historic Institute, a government agency. The same year, a landing strip and a hotel were constructed to make it possible for tourists on excursions from the island Cozumel to see the Tulum ruins, and by 1971 there were daily trips from Akumal, 30 km north, to the Tulum ruins (Ramos 2009, 30). Much has changed since then. Tulum was awarded the title of "Mexico's Leading Beach Destination 2017" by the World Travel Awards, and from January to October 2018 the Tulum ruins were visited by 1,819,669 people, which is an average of 181,967 people per month (Instituto Nacional de Antropología e Historia 2018). Tulum is no longer a small settlement in the jungle, but rather a town buzzing with tourism.

As an externally oriented Mexican national economic development strategy, the construction of the resort town of Cancún, 130 km north, began in 1970 (Torres and Momsen 2005b). Since the 1970s, the Mexican government has branded the coastline between Tulum and Cancún as "Riviera Maya." According to Papanicolaou (2012, 42), and Torres and Momsen (2005b), local Mayas were excluded from this process of developing Quintana Roo into a tourist space because of their poverty and their marginalized status. Similarly, Castañeda (2005) points out, in his study of the ruin site Chichén Itzá in the neighboring state of Yucatán, that Mayan vendors who lived close by the ruins were in "wars" in 1983–1987 and 1993–1996 with the Barbachano family, who owned the land. When local vendors entered the site in an attempt to sell their products to tourists, the Barbachano family resisted, insisting that the vendors gave tourists a bad impression. For decades, a discrepancy has existed between Maya as a symbol in tourist discourse and Maya as an ethnicity.

Today, Tulum is mostly inhabited by Mayas from Yucatán who come to try their luck in the tourist business, Mexicans from the capital city, and people from foreign countries who come to swap their ordinary lives with work in the tourist business while they enjoy the weather, nature, and recreational activities in the area.

The Tulum ruins as an image of the past—textual and discursive practices

In material targeting tourists, "Maya" is often used as a sales strategy to evoke potential tourists' excitement for Tulum. Several anthropologists have pointed out how ethnicities, cultures, and landscapes are often described and performed as exotic when the aim is to sell a destination in tourism discourses (see, e.g., Lindholm 2008; MacCannell 1976; Papanicolaou 2012; Salazar 2015; van den Berghe 1994). When something is "exotic," it is different from what we know in our ordinary lives. Indeed, Valene Smith (1989, 1) defines a tourist as "a temporary leisured person who voluntarily visits a place away from home for the purpose of experiencing a change," and Chris Rojek defines a tourist sight as "a spatial location which is distinguished from everyday life by virtue of its natural, historical or cultural extraordinariness" (Rojek & Urry 2004, 52). When an ethnic group is described as exotic, the emphasis is on how that social group is different, and an ethnic boundary is constructed or maintained imaginarily.

In this section, I analyze text on websites, in a guide book, and on informative signs at the Tulum ruins. I draw on the theory and methods of Critical Discourse Analysis as presented by Norman Fairclough (2008). According to Fairclough, language and social practice co-produce each other, and he calls the co-production "discourse" (17). Fairclough (29) argued that discourse can be analyzed on the levels of *text, discursive practices, and social practice*, and he pointed out that the three levels overlap. Following Fairclough's terminology, "discursive practices" are ways discourses are produced, distributed, and consumed (29). When I analyze on the level of text, I touch upon discursive practices as well. The number of texts about the Tulum ruins is vast. I have chosen different authors and text formats for a more representative analysis.

Figure 7.2 An official sign at the Tulum Ruins defining the site as "Cultural Patrimony of the Nation"

When Googling "Tulum ruins" some of the first websites that appear are: tulumruins.net (2018), "Tulum" on Wikitravel (2018), Lonely Planet's (2018) "Tulum ruins—archaeological site in Tulum," "Zona Arqueológica de Tulum" by the National Institute of Archeology and History of Mexico (INAH 2018), and "Tulum ruins" by LocoGringo (2018). The webpages constitute examples of what Appadurai (2010, 35) termed "mediascapes," which are image-centered and narrative-based elements of reality that flow globally. In the following, I examine the webpages on the level of text, employing Fairclough's Critical Discourse Analysis.

On all websites mentioned above, except for LocoGringo (2018), photos next to the text show one person or no people at all by the ruins. The ruins are photographed from a worm's eye view, which makes them appear bigger than they are, and more like important monuments. Focus is on the buildings and the azure-colored sea, a deserted place in paradise. The viewer may get the impression that they can have the place to themself. On all websites, the Tulum ruins are described in the past tense, and, according to the texts, the Mayas abandoned the site completely by the end of the 16th century. The *word choice* and *grammar* (Fairclough 2008, 32–34) that characterize the texts are centered on the word "Maya" (e.g. "Mayan site," "Mayan ruin," "Mayan city," "Mayan settlement," "Mayan port," and "Mayan culture"), and past tense. The use of past tense in the texts leaves the reader with the impression that Mayas no longer exist. The description by INAH (2018) focuses on the architecture, access, cost, and service facilities of the site. On INAH's webpage, Mayas are only mentioned in relation to the architecture and the suggestion that Mayas worshipped water and wind as gods. The only website that gives the reader the impression that Mayas have not completely died out is LocoGringo (2018): "Local Maya continued to visit the temples to burn incense and pray until the late 20th century." According to the articles by Wikitravel (2018) and tulumruins.net (2018), the Tulum ruins are "one of the best-preserved coastal Mayan sites" and "a popular Mayan tourist site." Analytically speaking, if a site is "preserved," it implies that somewhere along the way time stopped. The word "preserved" is contrary to the dynamic processes of lived life. As a result, the reader gets the impression that living Mayan culture does not exist at the site. Ironically, the site is also a "tourist site." Realistically, if the site was a Mayan site and now is a tourist site, the site has developed and therefore it cannot be a completely preserved site. The photos, word choice, and grammar on the webpages are elements of *semiosis*, ways of creating meaning (Fairclough 2008, 93–94). Photos as well as texts produce images of the Tulum ruins as a place of the past, where monuments rather than living culture remain. Both textual and photographic elements produce images of the Tulum ruins as a place for tourists, rather than as a place used by contemporary Mayas. Later, I draw more attention to the dynamics between past and present Mayan identity at the site, as I outline how the site is socially constructed through acts or performance at the site.

The book *Lonely Planet—Cancún, Cozumel & the Yucatán* (Hecht and Bao 2013), a world-renowned travel guide book series for low-budget travelers, provides a similar image of place. First, I must bring attention to the fact that the book cover has a photo of the Temple of the God of Wind at the Tulum ruins as its background. The fact that the Tulum ruins are cover material indicates that the place appeals to tourists. In the photo, five people paddle in clear water near a white beach, with the Temple of the God of Wind in the background. As in the pictures on the webpages, living Mayan culture is out of the frame, and a building photographed from a worm's eye view and the Caribbean Sea are in focus. Inside the book, the authors have created the list "Cancún, Cozumel & the Yucatán's Top 17," in which "Tulum, scenic ruins" are number 17. The text, which accompanies the rating, highlights the beach location of the "Maya ruins" (Hecht and Bao 2013, 15). Another section of the book "Sights & activities— Tulum ruins" likewise emphasizes the "brilliant beach" and "green-and-turquoise waters that will leave you floored." According to the history section of the guide book, the Tulum ruins were abandoned about 75 years after Spanish conquest, but Mayan pilgrims continued to visit the place and indigenous refugees hid in the ruins during the Caste War (Hecht and Bao 2013, 113).

The Lonely Planet book follows the discourse of the analyzed webpages. In photos and text, the Tulum ruins are portrayed as an archeological site next to an amazing beach—a place separated from real, quotidian life. Or rather, in the texts, the site is constructed as a place where all lived life is tourism. Though it is not their main focus, the Lonely Planet book and the LocoGringo website give hints of Mayan lived life on the ruin site in recent times, but make no connections between contemporary Mayan life and the site. Travel guides are written as if the readers know nothing about the place. The writer gives advice and hopes to inspire the reader. That makes up the *force* of the text (Fairclough 2008, 32, 39–42). The purpose of writing a travel guide book is to sell the book, to inform readers, and to inspire people to travel to the described places. The purpose of the websites is to inform readers and to inspire them to visit the described places. Overall, the aim of written travel guides is to sell place. Appadurai (2010, 8) termed a group of people who imagine and feel things together a "community of sentiment." When people across the globe feel excited about visiting the Tulum ruins, nestled between palm trees and azure water, they form a community of sentiment. Their decision to visit the ruins is based on images of and text on the place and is an example of the effect of images in tourism discourses. As Appadurai (2010, 7) argued, images have power to create social change and to move people. Tourism provides great examples of the power of images. It is no wonder then that governments have secretaries devoted to tourism.

This brings me to another type of textual production about the Tulum ruins worth mentioning: informational signs located on the site. The authors of the text on the signs at the ruin site are representatives of the governmental agencies INAH (National Institute of Anthropology and History), SEP

(Secretariat of Public Education), and Conaculta (the National Council for Culture and Arts), and so these texts appear as officially recognized truth. The signs are elements of the social construction of the Tulum ruins as a museum of national cultural heritage and an "archeological zone," and part of the production of a discourse in which the Tulum ruins are an educational and historical space. With the 1992 constitution, Mexico became a multicultural nation, and that is reflected in the signs at the ruin site. One sign, for example, carries following text, "TULUM ZONA DE MONUMENTOS ARQUEOLÓGICOS—PATRIMONIO CULTURAL DE LA NACION" (Tulum Zone of Archeological Monuments—Cultural Patrimony of the Nation). Another signs states, "HELP US TO PROTECT OUR CULTURAL HERITAGE. THIS IS A NATURAL AND HISTORICAL AREA," "HELP US TO PROTECT YOU AND OTHER VISITORS AT THE SAME TIME AS YOU PROTECT THE CULTURAL HERITAGE OF MÉXICO," and "THE CONSERVATION OF MEXICAN NATIONAL AND CULTURAL HERITAGE IS A RESPONSIBILITY THAT INVOLVES EVERYONE." According to the signs, the Tulum ruins are part of the common cultural heritage of all Mexicans.

Appadurai (2010) argued that, today, representations of culture are more deliberate than before. The informative signs are examples of how Mexican culture is presented to the world. One sign, titled "Historical viewpoint," describes a Mayan armed uprising against the exploitation of indigenous people, and that the ruin site was an important place for the Cult of the Talking Cross (the Santa Cruces), where rituals were carried out in the beginning of the 20th century. The brief mention of the connection between the ruin site and lived Mayan life ends with the statement that the Mexican government took over the site in the mid 1930s. There is no explanation of what happened to the Mayan rebels or to those who used the place for their rituals before the takeover. The signs describe the Mexican government as "investigators" and "protectors" of the Tulum ruins. That word choice, similar to the use of "preserved" on the websites, gives the impression that lived life is separate from the site. Quintana Roo has only been a Mexican state since 1974; Mayas of the Yucatán Peninsula revolted against the federal government in the mid 19th century. Thereby, the Mexican government's interest in associating with Mayas and Mayan culture has shifted throughout the last century, and so has Mayas' interest in collaborating with the government. The function of the Tulum ruins has changed. Moreover, the historical insight hints that it is important to consider the information on the signs from a critical perspective and remember that it is part of a social construction of Mexican heritage. On all the informative signs at the archeological zone of Tulum, Mayan culture is described in the past tense, and there is no information about what happened to the Mayas. The visitors are left with the impression that Mayan culture has died out. Yet, is the government "protecting" Mayan cultures by taking charge of the site? Who profits from Mayan history, ethnicity, and heritage? Who is in control of the production of Mayan-culture-for-others? To answer these questions, I will draw on voices of Mayan informants. However, first, I will describe social practices at the site.

The ruin site—social and discursive practices

In this section, I analyze on the levels of social and discursive practices based on my observations at the archeological zone of Tulum. I look at how the place is constructed spatially, and I give insight into how place is performed by people at the site.

The Tulum ruins are located 4 km from El Pueblo, the city center of Tulum. Locals refer to the parking lot area for the ruins as *centro comercial* (commercial center). Centro comercial is composed of a mix of international restaurant and café chains including Starbucks, Subway, and Häagen-Dazs, and Mexican artisanry, taco restaurants, and small roadside stalls selling fresh coconuts and pineapple juice. Handicrafts, tacos, and coconuts are sold from simple stalls or *palapas* (palm shelters). Subway and Starbucks are concrete houses with air-conditioning; when entering, one might as well be in the United States as in Mexico. Centro comercial is located strategically; visitors cannot avoid passing through the area if they arrive from the highway.

Centro comercial is a good example of *glocalized* space (Robertson 1995), and is characterized by *global flows* (Appadurai 2010, but with reminders— the taco stands, the Mexican artisanry, and text and talk about Mayas—that the visitor is in Mexico. As I mentioned, I use Appadurai's framework (2010], 33) of five dimensions of global flows to demonstrate how the space is touched by globalization. The five dimensions are: ethnoscapes, mediascapes, technoscapes, financescapes, and ideoscapes. Appadurai uses the suffix -scape to underline that these theoretical terms are perspectival constructs or "building blocks of imagined worlds." In other words, every person who visits the Tulum ruins creates his or her own narrative from the elements at and about the site. The site of the Tulum ruins is influenced by global flows of *ethnoscapes* in the form of tourists; *technoscapes* of ATMs, computers, and cappuccino makers; *financescapes* of earning money from tourists from Mexico as well as from other countries; *mediascapes* such as the texts analyzed in the previous section; and *ideoscapes* of nationalism and environmentalism. As outlined in the previous section, the ruin site is administered by the Mexican nation, and the government has put up many signs about the history of the Mayas, narrated as the history of the Mexican nation. Tulum is also constructed as a place that promotes environmentalism. By the ticket booth there are several bicycle stands; the site has many trash cans labeled *inorgánica* and *orgánica,* and information signs encourage visitors to help "preserve nature and the archeological heritage of this place." The ruin site is separated from centro comercial by a fence, and you pass through the ticket office to enter. The fence creates a boundary between museum space and the real world. On the museum side of the fence, pathways guide visitors' movements in space. The path is made of gravel and bordered by a rope that separates the pathway from grass or archeological buildings. The ropes signal that a visitor can see but cannot touch. In some places, the symbolic message of the rope is emphasized by "No Entry" signs. Thus, the movement of the visitors is controlled. If someone dares to step off the pathway to enter the monuments, a guard or a guide quickly makes sure they step back on the path. Yet many visitors step off the path to walk on the grass instead. The pathway and the ropes are elements in the social construction of the Tulum ruins as a museum like the signs analyzed in the previous section. Moreover, the pathway is a component in constructing the discourse on the Tulum ruins, separating buildings from present life. The spatial organization of the archeological zone and the texts analyzed in the previous section feed into each other. If we draw attention to how place is performed, the performance likewise feeds into the already mentioned themes of the discourse on the Tulum ruins. Tour guides lead groups of visitors on the paths while they inform them about the Mayas of the glorious past, and many visitors without guides stop to read the information signs. Most visitors take photos with their cameras or smart phones and many use selfie sticks. They see Tulum as worth remembering, and their photos as proof of their visit. The many iguanas in the archeological zone catch the tourists' attention and are often surrounded by people who take photos of them; interest in the iguanas feeds into the discourse that the ruin site has nature worth protecting because it is unique to the area. Many visitors combine their historical sightseeing with a swim in the Caribbean— another element of the area's unique nature emphasized in the analyzed text. The spatial arrangement of the site encourages visitors to go swimming; one of the pathways leads from the temples to the beach.

Figure 7.3 Pathway from the ruins to the beach

Continuing the analysis of how space is performed, we move back to centro comercial. There, local vendors are active and direct in their selling strategies. Through their language and actions, they co-construct the Tulum ruins as a space. The vendors use the terms "Mayan calendar," "Mayan art," and "souvenir" to sell their goods, and though vendors often claim that their goods are handmade, there is a remarkable similarity between the different vendor's products. The vendors co-construct a global mediascape about Mayas through the stories they tell and the objects they sell, whereby the objects become symbols of Mayan ethnicity. As a result, the vendors take part in ethnic image production, yet another example of discursive practices. When vendors mention the Mayan calendar or claim to be Maya themselves, they keep imaginaries alive, and they might even add to the tourists' narratives about Mayas. Tourists bring the stories and the objects home where they relate their travel stories of Mayas and the ruins, and introduce images about Mayas and the ruins to imaginations of people who have never visited Tulum. The vendors are reminiscent of Salazar's (2010) tour guides, who strategically use their knowledge about tourists and the world to create an "authentic local" atmosphere for the tourists, and Bruner's (2001, 895) Maasai in east Africa, who are aware of the discrepancy between their lives and tourists' image and choose to perform the image. According to MacCannell (1976), Lindholm (2008), and Salazar (2011), it is the idea of authenticity that draws tourists.

Street performers at Tulum dress up as caricatured indigenous people, and dance and pose with their snakes and iguanas for tourists' photos. Covered by body paint and feathers, they perform as Mayan warriors. However, in this case, there is no doubt that "the Mayas" are performers. Yet, the performances which emphasize the exotic feed discourse on the Tulum ruins as a historical Mayan place. Pi-Sunyer and Thomas (2015, 98–99), who have also conducted field work in Tulum, argued that Mayas' role in tourism is to give the popular imagination a touch of authenticity. My findings support that argument.

In his studies of the social construction of Chichén Itzá, the biggest ruin site on the Yucatan Peninsula, Quetzil Castañeda argued:

> The ruins are clearly an artifact of (primarily) Western science. They are a representation of the ancient city, constructed through the techniques of early twentieth-century archeological science. Chichén Itzá is a life-size scale-model replica of "itself": It is *hyperreal*. The traces of the constructed authenticity of Chichén are scandalously and continuously concealed and effaced in memory even as they are brought to consciousness.
> (Castañeda 1996, 104, emphasis in original)

The Tulum ruins are discursively constructed as a physical manifestation of Mayan culture now presented to tourists in museum-like style. Yet as Castañeda argued in the case of Chichén Itzá, the Tulum ruins can be considered a life-size scale-model replica of itself. What appears as "untouched" remains of Mayan civilization have been excavated from the jungle that once hid them, rearranged, and reconstructed (see Peissel 1963 for an ethnography on Tulum before the tourist boom). The Tulum ruins are likewise constructed through archeological science and presented to tourists like every other archeological site in the world. Narratives about the ruins, told on information signs, online, and in guide books, the spatial organization of the zone, and the performances at the place produce and reproduce discourse on the Tulum ruins.

Pi-Sunyer and Thomas (2015, 98–99) and Castañeda (1996, 98) argued that in the discursive practices in which Maya as symbol is constantly rewritten, Maya has more to do with the present than the past. I agree: ethnic image production of Mayas in the archeological zone of the Tulum is constructed in present time. "Maya" is partly constructed by the Mexican government, which has multicultural nationalism and money-making as its agenda, and by people in the tourist business, who have an eye for what tourists like and dislike. In the archeological zone, "Maya" is a commodity. Visitors are given the role as consumers and locals take on roles as servants or sellers.

Mayan voices on the "Mayan ruins"—social and discursive practices

Torres and Momsen (2005a, 314) pointed out that locals of Cancún called their city "Gringolandia," arguing that the term reflects the Disneyesque quality of the hybrid space where elements of Mexican, Mayan, and American culture combine in new ways when presented for tourist consumption. Torres and Momsen compared the Americanization of Cancún to an invasion, leaving readers with the impression that Mexican Mayas and Mayan culture are under threat. Friedman (1990) and Kirtsoglou and Theodossopoulos (2004) argued that tourism can strengthen ethnic identity construction. But Kirtsglou and Theodossopoulos (2004, 146) underlined that if the production of ethnic images is controlled by external forces, tourism can be experienced as causing loss of identity. The Mexican nation state is the author of the information signs at the Tulum ruin site and is responsible for oversight, archeological investigations, conservation, and tourist visits to the archeological zone. So, what are contemporary Mayas' perceptions of the ruin site?

Contemporary Mayas of Tulum distance themselves from the so-called "Mayan ruins" of the town. While the Tulum ruins are constructed discursively through text, performances, and souvenirs as a physical manifestation of Mayan culture, my informants describe the site of the Tulum ruins as a place for foreigners, tourists, and business. When I asked questions about the Tulum ruins, I was often told, "Puro negocio" (pure business).

Several informants told me that the Mayas who built the ruins are another kind of Mayas than themselves. Carlos, one of the most prominent men of the Mayan community told me:

Los de las ruinas de Tulum es aparte por el proceso. Bueno, fue de los mayas también, pero mayas que termino ser, acabo de la rasa. Porque los que están hicieron de las pirámides, dónde agradaron cemento? Dónde agregaron material hasta la fecha? No, no es el mismo.

(Those of [the Mayas who built] the Tulum ruins are apart from the process. Well, they were also Mayas, but Mayas that no longer exist—their race ended. Those who made the pyramids; where did they find cement? Where did they collect material at that time? No, they are not the same.)

"Mamá Maya," who called me "hija adoptiva" (adopted daughter) during my daily fieldwork visits, likewise classified those who built the ruins as a different type of Mayas. She described them as "otro generación. Hombres chiquitos. Puro trabajo de mano" (another family. Short people. Only manual work). For Carlos and Mamá Maya, the Mayas of the ruins have died out, and there is no connection to Mayas of today.

Figure 7.4 The figures in the myth are over the windows

Power is woven into discourses; particular narratives spread and influence people's perceptions, often without the awareness of their narrators (see Appadurai 2010; Fairclough 2008; Foucault 1991; Jenkins 2008). The Mexican government's nationalization agenda potentially has shaped my informants' perceptions. Anthropologists likewise influence those they write about. I present two concrete examples of the effect of ethnographic texts and discourse on the level of social and discursive practices.

The first deals with Antonio, a man in his thirties who married into one the founding families of Tulum and who self-identified as Maya. When I interviewed Antonio about the Tulum ruins, he quoted a passage from a book about the meaning of carvings on one of the temples. He first retold the story from memory, then brought the book to read a passage to me. Antonio later lent me his book, which I discovered was written by anthropologist Guillermo Goñi (1999). Antonio retold the story from a first-person point of view; he used it as an element of his *internal definition of identity* (Jenkins 2008, 55). As he retold it, he added his own interpretation. I present the case as an excerpt of an interview I conducted in September 2015:

INFORMANT: "¡Oh, sí, sí, sí! Un americano y uno de indio, donde el americano sube arriba de ir a caer, como cae del edificio. El otro sube. Este significa que aquí en Tulum va a ver muchos extranjeros, extranjeros, turistas, y los que están de acá, los mayas van a estar abajo, pero cuando caiga el otro ese sube. Este es el significado." (Oh yes. An American and an Indian, where the American goes up and is about to fall off the building, the other rises. That means that here in Tulum, one will see many foreigners, tourists; and those from here, the Mayas, will be below, but when the other falls, they rise. That is the meaning.)

ME: "¿Quién son los extranjeros? ¿Son de otras partes de México también?" (Who are the foreigners? Is that people from other parts of Mexico too?)

INFORMANT: "Extranjeros pueden ser americanos, europeos, todo así." (Foreigners can be Americans, Europeans, and the like.)

ME: "¿Pero de otra partes de México también"? (But also those from other parts of Mexico?)

INFORMANT: "También de otra parte—como México [DF]. Ellos vienen para poner negocios toda estas cosas." (Also those from other parts—like Mexico City, they come to set up businesses and all that.)

ME: "¿Ellos van a caer también?" (They will fall as well?)

INFORMANT: "Todos." (Everyone.)

ME: "¿Solo los mayas van a subir?" (Only the Mayas will rise?)

INFORMANT: "Sí, porque dicen que están bendecidos. Aquí están los mayas así, y los protegen así." (Yes, because they say they are blessed. The Mayas here are protected like that.)

ME: "¿Cómo bendecidos de Dios?" (Like they are blessed by God?)

INFORMANT: "Aha." (Aha.)

ME: "¿Qué va a pasar después? ¿Qué significa que los mayas suben y los otros caen? ¿Los otros van a morir?" (What will happen afterwards? What does it mean that the Mayas rise and the other descend? Do the others die?)

INFORMANT: "Como una destrucción. Van a sobrevivir nada más los mayas." (A destruction. They, only the Mayas, will survive.)

ME: "¿Ppiensas que es verdad?" (Do you think that is right?)

INFORMANT: "Pienso que sí. Es dicho así." (I think so, yes. That is how it is told.)

Antonio transformed a myth, collected and retold by an anthropologist, into a story about himself and those with whom he ethnically identified. When he used the anthropological text to explain his social reality, the story became discourse on the level of social practices. Antonio suggested Mayas have lost power over the territory to foreigners, but that the power relation will change with time. The story provides elements about the social situation of Mayas, and according to the script Antonio formed, there is no need to act because change will come when the time is right. His attitude toward his social situation and that of other Mayas is passive. Although he drew a parallel between his group identity and the Tulum ruins, for Antonio, social life of contemporary Mayas in Tulum is separated from the Tulum ruins.

My second example involves Canche Jr., whose father Pablo was a main informant of anthropologists Michael Peissel (1963), Richard Luxton (Luxton & Balam 1986 [1981]), and Macduff Everton (2012). Pablo was described as very emotional about "the Mayas' loss" of the Tulum ruins to the Mexican nation; Canche Jr. is quick to distance himself from the site. In *Sueño del camino Maya*, Pablo connected the Tulum ruins with his ethnic identity and loss of place to the government:

> Todos los hijos de los abuelos hicieron fiestas para ellos, allá en las ruinas. Incluso en años que yo recuerdo esto ha sido así. Pero si vinieran ahora a pedir permiso para llegar a las ruinas, Bueno, pues no se concede el permiso. Ahora gobierna alguien distinto. El español ha tomado posesión para explotar las cosas de un modo distinto. Nuestra costumbre, se puede decir, se ha olvidado. El español no quería que existiera.
>
> (Luxton & Balam 1986, 92)

> (All the children of the grandparents held parties for them, there in the ruins. Inclusively, in years I remember they did it like that. But if you go there now, to ask for permission to enter the ruins, well, one is not allowed. Now, another one governs. The Spanish have taken possession to exploit things in a new way. Our custom, one can say, is forgotten. The Spanish did not want it to exist.)

Pablo defined the place as a symbol of Mayan ethnicity. But when I asked Pablo's son about the quote, he told me that the ruin site is "puro negocio" (pure business) and that he did not like to go there. He told me that the site is for artists and tourists, and complained that he cannot use the beach or go fishing there as he used to. His wife added, "Ahora cobran todo. Solo turistas van. Tú tienes que pagar" (Now everybody must pay. Only tourists go. You must pay). As Basso (2001) and Ingold (1993) argued, landscape is a symbolic ordering of space, socially constructed and dynamic. For Mayas living in Tulum, the ruin site is no longer related to Mayan ethnicity, but, instead, primarily linked to tourism.

But the Tulum ruins also evoked local pride. Carlos told me that entry fees to the ruins go straight to the Mexican government "to make everything better for everyone." In his opinion, the money should be used locally to make Tulum more presentable to tourists. He told me, "El turismo ve muy mal porque puro baches" (All the potholes are very bad for tourism). A quote from Rosa, a Mayan woman in her twenties, is an example of how tourism facilitates local pride in Tulum:

Es como ellos nunca han conocido estas partes. Ellos vienen y les gusta tan el lugar. Y ellos cuando regresen otra vez lo recomiendan, recomiendan a la gente, a los demás: "Yo fui a esta cenote y me gusto, te lo recomiendo y llevo a tu familia. Está bien bonito." Es lo que dicen la gente mayormente. ... Cuando vienen lo que buscan es cenotes, agua fresca o las ruinas.

(It is because they [tourists] have never seen these parts. They come here and they very much like the place, and when they go back home, they recommend the place to other people: "I went to this *cenote* [sinkhole] and I liked it, I recommend it to you and your family. It is very beautiful." That is what people mostly say. ... When they come, they look for *cenotes*, fresh water, or the ruins.)

Mayas study tourists at least as much as tourists study them; they are aware of the preferences of tourists, and they want to spread a positive image about their place to the world. Rosa's quote is one of many examples of Mayas expressing the importance of tourists' impressions of Tulum and the unique sites the place offers.

Conclusion

Tulum evokes opposing narratives, and Maya is a symbol with many interpretations. People who are involved in the tourist business in Tulum have a financial investment in the production of a particular discourse about Tulum; the Mexican government has interests in the ruins in relation to national economy and the construction of Mexican nationality. While the Archeological Zone of Tulum is officially described as a physical manifestation of Mayan culture, my Mayan informants identify the Tulum ruins as "a place for foreigners" and as "pure business." Barth (1998) argued that the boundary between ethnic groups is constantly renegotiated. As my research shows, "Maya" contains distinct, and at times overlapping, meanings that facilitate tourism, nationalism, and academic and ethnic imaginaries.

References

Anderson, B. (1991). *Imagined Communities: Reflections on the origin and spread of nationalism*. Revised and extended edition. London: Verso.

Appadurai, A. (2010 [1996]). *Modernity at Large*. Public Worlds Series, no. 1—Cultural Dimensions in Globalization. Minneapolis & London: University of Minnesota Press.

Barth, F., ed. (1998 [1969]). *Ethnic Groups and Boundaries: The social organization of culture difference*. Illinois: Waveland Press.

Basso, K. (1996). *Wisdom Sits in Places: Landscape and language among the Western Apache*. Albuquerque: University of New Mexico Press.

Billig, M. (1995). *Banal Nationalism*. London: SAGE.

Boissevain, J., ed. (1996). *Coping with Tourists: European reactions to mass tourism*. Providence: Berghahn.

Bruner, E.M. (2005). *Culture on Tour: Ethnographies of travel*. Chicago: University of Chicago Press.

Bull, B. (2010). *Latinamerikanske utfordringer*. 1st edition. Kristiansand, Norway: Høyskoleforlaget AS.

Castañeda, Q.E. (1996). *In the Museum of Maya Culture: Touring Chichén Itzá*. Minneapolis: University of Minnesota Press.

Castañeda, Q.E. (2004). "We Are Not Indigenous!": An introduction to the Maya identity of Yucatan. *Journal of Latin American Anthropology*. 9(1), 36–63. doi:10.1525/jlca.2004.9.1.36.

Castañeda, Q.E. (2005). Tourism "wars" in the Yucatan. *Anthropology News*. 46(5), 8–9. doi:10.1525/an.2005.46.5.8.2.

Cohen, A.P. (1985). In Hamilton, P. (ed.), *The Symbolic Construction of Community*. London: Routledge.

Cohen, E. (1988). Authenticity and commoditization. *Annals of Tourism Research*. 15, 371–386.

Consejo Municipal de Tulum, ed. (2009). *Génesis, realidad y visión de futuro*. Tulum.

Edensor, T. (1998). *Tourists at the Taj: Performance and meaning at a symbolic site*. London: Routledge.

Eiss, P.K. (2004). Deconstructing Indians, reconstructing Patria: Indigenous education in Yucatan from the Porfiriato to the Mexican Revolution. *Journal of Latin American Anthropology*. 9(1), 119–150.

Everton, M. (2012). *The Modern Maya: Incidents of travel and friendship in Yucatán*. Austin: University of Texas Press.

Fairclough, N. (2008). *Kritisk diskursanalyse: en tekstsamling* (A social theory of discourse). 1st edition. Copenhagen: Hans Reitzel.

Fallaw, B. (2004). Rethinking Mayan resistance: Changing relations between federal teachers and Mayan communities in Eastern Yucatan, 1929–1935. *Journal of Latin American Anthropology*. 9(1), 151–178. doi:10.1525/jlca.2004.9.1.151.

Foucault, M. (1991). Governmentality. In Foucault, M., Burchell, G., Miller, P., & Gordon, C. (eds.), *The Foucault Effect: Studies in governmentality: with two lectures by and an interview with Michel Foucault* (pp. 87–104). London: Harvester Wheatsheaf.

Friedman, J. (1990). Being in the world: Globalization and localization. *Theory, Culture & Society*. 7(2): 311–328.

Goñi, G. (1999). *De Cómo Los Mayas Perdieron Tulum*. 1st edition. Córdoba, Mexico: D.R. Instituto Nacional de Antropología e Historia.

Hecht, J., & Bao, S., eds. (2013). *Cancún, Cozumel & the Yucatán*. 6th edition. Footscray, Victoria: Lonely Planet.

Ingold, T. (1993). The temporality of the landscape. *World Archaeology*. 25(2), 152. doi:10.1080/00438243.1993.9980235.

Institute of Archeology and History of Mexico (INAH) (2018). Zona Arqueológica de Tulum. Retrieved from http://inah.gob.mx/es/zonas/99-zona-arqueologica-de-tulum.

Instituto Nacional de Antropología e Historia (2018). Estadística de visitantes. Retrieved from http://www.estadisticas.inah.gob.mx/.

Jenkins, R. (2008). *Rethinking Ethnicity.* 2nd edition. London: SAGE.

Juárez, A.M. (2002). Ecological degradation, global tourism, and inequality: Maya interpretations of the changing environment in Quintana Roo, Mexico. *Human Organization.* 61(2), 113–124.

Kirtsoglou, E., & Theodossopoulos, D. (2004). "They are taking our culture away": Tourism and culture commodification in the Garifuna community of Roatan. *Critique of Anthropology*, 24(2), 135–157.

Lindholm, C. (2008). *Culture and Authenticity.* Malden, MA: Blackwell.

LocoGringo (2018). Tulum Ruins—Tulum. Retrieved from https://www.locogringo. com/mexico/ways-to-play/mayan-ruins-archaeological-sites/tulum-ruins/.

Lonely Planet (2018). Tulum ruins—archaeological site in Tulum. Retrieved from https:// www.lonelyplanet.com/mexico/tulum/attractions/tulum-ruins/a/poi-sig/1159761/361702.

Luxton, R., & Balam, P. (1986 [1981]). *Sueño del camino Maya.* Mexico: Fundo de cultura económica.

MacCannell, D. (1976). *The Tourist: A new theory of the leisure class.* London: The MacMillan Press.

Papanicolaou, A. (2012). Authenticity and commodification: The selling of Maya culture in Mexico's Mayan Riviera. In Moufakkir, O., & Burns, P.M. (eds.), *Controversies in Tourism* (pp. 41–52). Wallingford, UK: CABI Publishing.

Peissel, M. (1963). *The Lost World of Quintana Roo.* 1st edition. New York: E.P. Dutton & Co.

Pi-Sunyer, O., & Thomas, R.B. (2015). Tourism and the transformation of daily life along the Riviera Maya of Quintana Roo, Mexico. *Journal of Latin American and Caribbean Anthropology.* 20(1), 87–109. doi:10.1111/jlca.12110.

Ramos, Y. (2009). Quintana Roo: Turismo y cambios en su mapa político. *Ketzalcalli.* 2, 29–37.

Robertson, R. (1995). Glocalization: Time-space and homogeneity-heterogeneity. In Featherstone, M., Lash, S., & Robertson, R. (eds.), *Global Modernities* (pp. 24–44). London: SAGE.

Rojek, C. & Urry, J (2004 [1997]) *Touring Cultures: Transformations of Travel and Theory.* London: Routledge.

Salazar, N.B. (2005). Tourism and glocalization—"Local" tour guiding. *Annals of Tourism Research.* 32(3), 628–646.

Salazar, N.B. (2010). *Envisioning Eden: Mobilizing imaginaries in tourism and beyond.* New York: Berghahn.

Salazar, N.B. (2011). Tourism imaginaries: A conceptual approach. *Annals of Tourism Research.* 39(2), 863–882.

Salazar, N.B. (2015). Becoming cosmopolitan through traveling? *English Language and Literature.* 61(1), 51–67. Smith, V.L. (1989). *Hosts and Guests: The anthropology of tourism.* 2nd edition. Philadelphia: University of Pennsylvania Press.

Torres, R.M., & Momsen, J.D. (2005a). Gringolandia: The construction of a new tourist space in Mexico. *Annals of the Association of American Geographers.* 95(2), 314–335. doi:10.1111/j.1467-8306.2005.00462.x.

Torres, R.M., & Momsen, J.D. (2005b). Planned tourism development in Quintana Roo, Mexico: Engine for regional development or prescription for inequitable growth? *Current Issues in Tourism.* 8(4), 259–285.

Tulumruins.net (2018). Retrieved from http://www.tulumruins.net/.

van den Berghe, P.L. (1994). *The Quest for the Other: Ethnic tourism in San Christobal, Mexico.* Seattle: University of Washington Press.

Wikitravel (2018). Tulum. Retrieved from https://wikitravel.org/en/Tulum.

Zarkia, C. (1996). Philoxenia receiving tourists but not guests. In Boissevain, J. (ed.), *Coping with Tourists: European reactions to mass tourism* (pp. 143–173). Providence: Berghahn.

8 Tropicality, purified spaces, and the colonial gaze

Exclusionary policies in cruise tourism and its impact on the Caribbean

Matthew Nelson

Anthropologist George Foster (1986) saw opportunity in cruise tourism research. It was a new field, and could elucidate tourism and its role in greater global processes. He held that the cruise industry represents "a major frontier for tourism research." Interestingly, the complex relationships that the cruise industry maintains with its patrons are particularly helpful in determining what tourists want, how they get what they want, and how they change and leave impressions on the commodities they consume. While cruise tourism in the Caribbean is exceptionally rich in potential research on globalization, society, colonization, and other fields, this chapter examines the dynamic relationships between the Caribbean cruise tourism industry and the product and/or people they commodify for the consumption of their customers. The first section will review the exclusionary practices that are at work in cruise tourism, specifically in the Caribbean where package deals and enclave resorts yield "lost" individuals who are left on the periphery of their own homes. Further, the colonial nature of the Western tourist space, which is created through the gentrification processes that so widely characterize cruise tourism to the Global South, will be described.

The second section incorporates tourist narratives into the discussion of colonial fantasyscapes. These stories all revolve around a single port of interest, specifically Labadee, Haiti, where Royal Caribbean International (RCI) leases a small peninsula for a nominal fee. In examining this port-of-call, the discussion of colonial impact via enclave tourism is further clarified from the tourist perspective. The narratives were solicited both in person and electronically from publicly available sources. Most are from Western tourists, who illustrate their desire for liminality and fantasy—precisely what cruise tours propose to offer. In probing these narratives, a tropical ideal can be imagined as constructed in the minds of tropical cruise tourists. This very image is captured and reconstructed in Labadee for the fantastic *excursions* (RCI 2008a) of elite tourists that walk its beaches.

Finally, the third section attempts to link colonial themes, Western tourist narratives, and the national identity of Haitians. As local inhabitants grapple with their acceptance of RCI and in turn shape their identity around it, government officials strive to give Haiti's image a face-lift, elevating it from a portrait of violence, poverty, disease, and political unrest to a potential para-dise for travelers. In this light, RCI takes on new meaning when locals sup-port its colonizing themes in an attempt to reconcile with a national tourism agenda. As Haiti strives to reconfigure its image, the enclave system may turn out to be of greatest benefit to a democracy in its infancy. Like the bubbles and physical containers that partition potentially harmful forces into man-ageable units, Haiti's all-inclusive resorts may potentially keep the damaging and degrading forces of tourism at bay.

Colonial exclusionism in the Tropics

As in any consumer-based industry, a product must be marketed and con-structed in a way that appeals to your target customer base. Cruise lines like Royal Caribbean International employ experiential marketing in a way that produces themed fantasy at a latitudinal level, where any desire can be pur-portedly fulfilled. These staged and performed tourist sites/sights characterize the liminal space that is constructed both onboard the ship and in various ports or enclaves.

Urry (2002) suggested that experts manipulate place and space to cultivate a collective and individual tourist gaze. They remove

> modern-day litter and quotidian/practical items from their resort beach fronts, jungle trails or ethnic tourist sites, and add "primitive" or "nat-ural" features such as palm trees, sand and "ancient" wood or stone carvings to (re)create a picturesque landscape suitable for the tourist gaze.
> (Law, Bunnell, & Ong 2007, 144)

It is the commodification of sites/sights via the tourist gaze that has people in communities like Labadee packaging and performing particular kinds of authenticity for tourist consumption (MacCannell 1973, 1999).

Producing fantasy

Royal Caribbean International (RCI) offers a vast collection of consumable experiences to its potential tourists. This collection of highly produced and constructed products of *fantasy* is at the continual disposal of the ship's pas-sengers both in and out of port. As *fantasy* is a wide and vague concept, tourist industries provide this through experiential marketing, which leverages tourist encounters into a "holistic Gestalt" (Schmitt 1999, 53). In a letter from RCI to a potential repeat cruiser, the company furthered their claim as a gatekeeper to *experience* by stating, "On a Royal Caribbean cruise vacation, you don't just see places like Alaska, Europe, Mexico and the Caribbean, you feel like you're a part of them" (RCI 2008b). In the cruise industry, experi-ential marketing tactics are commonly used; a delicate balance must be maintained between immersion and absorption on one plane, and passive and active participation on another. These bisecting planes of activity create what some scholars suggest are four *realms* of tourism experience, namely: education, entertainment, escapist, and aesthetic (see Pine & Gilmore 1998). According to Alistair Williams (2006), a tourist's richest encounter encompasses all of these *realms* while accounting for the five senses. In this light, sites such as Walt Disney World are assumed to offer one of the richest tourist experiences available. Similarly, the McDisneyfication (Ritzer & Liska 1997) of the cruise industry, which incidentally includes Disney Cruise Line, strives for this balanced approach when marketing its services to potential cruisers. Royal Caribbean International (RCI) markets itself as completely comprehensive, insomuch that on the second page of their Caribbean Cruise Vacation Planner guide, they imply that all senses, moods, and ideas of a vacation are met aboard their amenity-clad ships:

> It really all comes down to this one question: What does adventure mean to you? And the best part is there are no wrong answers. Because whatever your concept of adventure, you're pretty much guaranteed to find it when you cruise with Royal Caribbean International .... And don't worry—there's something for every energy level, whether you're in the mood for power snorkeling or power shopping. (RCI 2008a)

Themes are important in the construction of fantasy for Williams (2006, 489), who further explains that inadequate themes "give consumers nothing to focus on," which may limit the success of the experience. Subtle cues hint toward themes that not only evoke a heightened coherence of the vacation as a whole, but also produce a lasting memory of the experience—important for cruise tourism indeed. RCI likewise attempts to produce a theme through clever cues and marketing. *Adventure* and *relaxation* are two of the key themes with which consumers identify in their narratives. The author's own experience as a tourist aboard a Royal Caribbean cruise yielded a simulacrum of the *adventure* theme, specifically *colonialism*.

Caribbean cruise tourism

Cruise tourism is one of the fastest-growing tourist enterprises in the world. As industry giants have shifted their target from upper and upper-middle classes to a wider market, cruise tourism has soared in popularity (Wood 2000). Massive growth in the amount of cruise ships and berth capacity has marked the last 20 years, with the number of cruise ships growing by 25 percent over the period 1988 to 2002 and the number of berths by 50 percent during that same period (Mintel 2003). As cruising became more accessible over the last two decades, islands in the Caribbean are seeing a considerable increase in cruise-based tourists relative to stopover tourists (Holder 1993), minimizing economic benefit for the host destination. In light of the

heightened popularity, competition between cruise lines escalated and continues today, as the pressure to add exotic ports-of-call is intense.

Mark Gottdiener's (1997) "themed spaces" are the primary vectors that
RCI uses to introduce ideas of *exploration* and *adventure* to its passengers.
This is done on cruise ships and their ports through "highly encoded shopping malls, festival marketplaces, heritage sites, cultural quarters and water-
front attractions," which "comprise an expanding sector of tourist space"
(Edensor 2001, 66). Robert Wood (2000) calls these themed spaces *fantasyscapes*, where inspiration is drawn from all over the globe. Likewise, cruise
ships are more equipped with ludic toys that are "linked thematically and
spatially," presenting "glamour, fame and beauty, projecting fantasies of
power and desire" (Edensor 2001, 67).

As the themed spaces on cruise ships become more elaborate and comprehensive, they begin to resemble floating theme parks (Showker & Sehlinger
1998) that you may encounter in Las Vegas—complete with multiple casinos,
golf courses, ice-skating rinks, and theaters onboard. The ships themselves
become the destination, while the ports-of-call are secondary. Further, archi-
tect Vittorio Garroni Carbonara (1997) foresaw these artificial islands replacing real-life destinations. Tourist narratives such as Clark's (2008) confirmed
the importance placed on the boat during cruise tours, and how many of the
"ports begin to blend in to each other," while "the ship never disappoints."
According to Reiner Jaakson (2004, 46, my emphasis), "a cruise ship is a
place designed exclusively for tourists and those who serve them."

Schmitt (1999) envisioned the future of tourism in companies like RCI,
agreeing with Pine and Gilmore's (1998, 98) assertion that the "next competitive battlefield lies in staging experiences." As illustrated earlier, experiential
marketing and fantasy production have taken firm hold in the cruise industry,
insomuch that the cruise itself has become its own "secure, comfortable, and
tightly controlled" tourist bubble (Jaakson 2004, 57).

Figure 8.1 Partitioned space for selected local vendors in the marketplace

Fantasy islands: Bubbles, enclaves, and staging tourism

Staging fantastic experience is at the core of Royal Caribbean's mission. The 2008–2009 Caribbean Cruise Vacation Planner guide addresses its potential passengers regarding what it offers those who book a cruise with them. "Truth is, we show you around these warm-weather playgrounds like no one else can .... We'll even let you in on some secret pink-sand beaches" (RCI 2008a). RCI is not marketing Haiti, Jamaica, Mexico, or other places, but is clearly marketing the liminal environment that is found aboard the ship itself (McElroy & de Albuquerque 1998). Playgrounds and secret beaches are offered. In clarifying this marketing maneuver, Jaakson's (2004, 47) study of tourist bubbles indicates:

> The controlled and safe cruise ship environment has been replicated on shore by companies that have purchased a private island or a fenced-off costal enclave made available for shore visits to what is presented as a secure haven isolated from the local population.

In his illustration of the closed tourist bubble that exists onboard the ship, an extension can easily be made to include tourist ports that replicate the ship's environment. Perhaps this explains why many passengers elect to stay onboard while docked at their respective destinations (Dahl 1995). They simply do not see the need to experience the ship's environment transposed to land. Indeed this was mentioned in tourist narratives (TripAdvisor 2008), as many repeat cruisers skipped a visit to the shores of Labadee.

Wood suggested that the

> ultimate in fantasyscapes on Caribbean cruises is not on the ship ... it is to be found on *fantasy islands*, privately owned by the cruise companies, off-limits to all but their passengers and employees, and marketed as the true Caribbean experience—only better.
>
> ((2000, 361, my emphasis; see also: Sorkin 1992)

Fantasy islands act as all-inclusive tourist preserves, where everything is constructed and staged, and cruises can operate as the "ultimate product-placement scheme" (Cabezas 2008, 26). Many tourists who visited Labadee did not feel that this was unreal, but a representation of hyper-reality that was framed perfectly around previous constructs of what a tropical paradise should look like (Cohen 1995; Law et al. 2007; Williams 2006). Umberto Eco (2000, 4) called this idealization a "real copy of the reality being presented," yet it "must be absolutely iconic" for tourists. Similar to how Disney World encapsulated a richly sensory tourist event in the discussion above, Disney also epitomizes "the symbolic American utopia" through simulation of various aspects of American reality (Venturi 1995, 67).

The fantastic staging of tourist ventures occurs in a variety of places:

On beaches and mountains, in cities, heritage sites, museums and theme parks. These settings are distinguished by boundedness, whether physical or symbolic, and are often organized—or stage-managed—to provide and sustain common-sense understandings about what activities should take place. (Edensor 2001, 63)

Edensor (2000) described how physically demarcated areas, known as *enclavic* regions, like Labadee, clearly provide an influence for acceptable and encouraged behavior. Tourists felt free to engage in ludic behavior as they abandoned previous roles for novel actions that the staged event prompted. Further, Sibley (1988) commented on how these *purified spaces* are superstructured and regulated, requiring continual upkeep to minimize underlying ambiguity and contradiction. Continuity in these highly produced sites is of great importance to the cruise companies that are "shielding potentially offensive sights, sounds, and smells" (Edensor 2001, 64) through *soft control* techniques that Ritzer and Liska (1997) elaborate. The intent is to keep their guests in a manipulative state of being, where inner conflict and agency are minimized.

The tourist gaze is occupied by key visual cues and codes (Freitag 1994). As these visual cues and codes are cycled through the tourist body, a shared understanding of what is worthy of the romantic gaze (Urry 1992, 2002) circulates and further produces the tourist site/sight that can be found on Labadee among other Caribbean island destinations. Through these producing mechanisms, Mark Neumann (1988, 24) suggests,

Tourists are rarely left to draw their own conclusions about objects or places before them. Instead, they more often confront a body of public discourse—signs, maps, guides and guide books—that repeatedly mark the boundaries of the significance and value at tourist sites.

Since Labadee is only marketed by Royal Caribbean, or third-party companies that book RCI tours, the body of public discourse is consistent. The message from several tourists is that Haiti is dangerous, Haitians are poor, and Labadee is safe at the core of the bubble.

Labadee exemplifies the elements that go into any theme park. As Sorkin (1992, xv) explains, "The theme park presents a happy regulated vision of pleasure ... and it does so appealingly by stripping troubled urbanity of its sting, of the presence of the poor, of crime, of dirt, of work." Labadee has been gentrified insomuch that locals who represent the poor and the dirty sting of urbanity are kept out by fences, walls, and, at times, armed guards (Orenstein 1997). This island fantasy that RCI promotes as an exclusive destination is not marketed as Haiti at all, but as an imaginary paradise that carries a bastardized name, which many locals will correct as actually being Labadee—the name of the nearest town. Marketed as Hispaniola, RCI is promoting a timeless and etic imaginary paradise—one with colonial roots

Figure 8.2 Wall extending from perimeter to the beach, hiding local activity from tourists

that are evocative of the ultimate colonizer, Christopher Columbus. Lefebvre (1991, 353) termed these purified places as "the space of the dream," where the mundane is suspended and the extraordinary is assumed. It is the charge of the experiential cruise industry to maintain this construct of dream space for its fantasy-seeking tourists (Carter 2001). As Orenstein (1997, 29) further clarifies, Labadee is the "best of the Caribbean" because no Caribbean people are living there. In mentioning why Labadee is so great, an RCI instructor commented that, "it's super-cheap, it's pretty, and there's minimal contact. Contact is disturbing to the passengers." As illustrated in the tourist narratives and discussed later, contact at the peripheries of the tourist bubbles was disturbing to many.

The colonizing fantasy

Amalia Cabezas (2008, 25) describes how modern cruise tourism favors the all-inclusive deal:

> A comprehensively controlled tourist experience in which the familiarity of the brand and the security of the travel experience are more important than local differentiation. The all-inclusive tourist package allows tour operators and travel agencies to combine all the components of a destination's attractions—recreation, meals, food, lodging, and transportation—into a single product paid for at the point of origin [thus confining] the profits to the global North.

Cabezas (2008, 29) further describes the enclave tourism she sees in the Dominican Republic, which shares the island of Hispanola with Haiti, characterizing them as compounds that "provide electricity, sewerage, paved roads, and running water for their pleasure—and leisure-oriented guests" while leaving neighboring shantytowns without such greatly needed amenities.

"This neglect," she claims, "represents a hidden cost to the host society and a further appropriation of social and environmental resources by foreign capital."

In an increasingly globally connected world, cruise companies frequently take advantage of the mobility inherent in cruising. Companies headquarter themselves in countries like Norway that do not have strict employment standards in order to garner the greatest amount of work per dollar. Standards like *mandatory time off* or *minimum wages* are not enforced as the employees are subject to the labor laws that pertain only to the country in which the ship is flagged, allowing Caribbean cruise companies to pay wages as low as US$1.55 per hour (Wood 2000). By strategically flagging ships, the cruise industry can successfully exploit their labor, save US$30 million a year in US taxes (Frantz 1999), and dump waste in water proximal to the Caribbean nations it visits (Wood 2000). Further, Caribbean nationals represent just a minority of onboard staff, in spite of the rampant unemployment that exist, particularly in Haiti. Wise (1999) estimated that no more than 7 percent of the Caribbean cruise onboard workforce represent people from the area. In 2008, tourist employment in Haiti represented only 5.8 percent of the total workforce (WTTC 2008). RCI provides only 60 coveted jobs to locals, who claim that only those with ties to power are granted access to these positions (Orenstein 1997).

In Jamaica Kincaid's (1998, 18) poetic book *A Small Place*, she illuminates some of the inequalities that she notices in tourist development in the Caribbean:

> Every native of every place is a potential tourist, and every tourist is a native of somewhere. But some natives—most natives in the world—cannot go anywhere. They are too poor. They are too poor to go anywhere.

"Poverty in the region averages roughly 38 per cent of the total population, ranging from a high of 65 per cent in Haiti to a low of 5 per cent in the Bahamas" (Wood 2000, 363). In Jamaica's excerpt, it appears economic constraints on the Global South, particularly in one of the most popular tourist destinations in the world—the Caribbean—the poor are responsible for servicing the desires of the elite, while these elites desire no reciprocal notion of responsibility, especially while on vacation. Tourism is viewed by scholars such as Britton (1996, 155) as something that "perpetuates existing disparities, fiscal problems, and social tensions" (see also Greenwood 1989). Further, it marginalizes Caribbean locals who face the US and Western Europe in their dominance over the global travel infrastructure. Lanfant, Allcock, and Bruner (1995) suggest that this dominance is manifested seemingly peacefully via political jockeying and financial control in the markets of the South. As Urry (1996, 215) explains regarding the economics behind the power gradient, "only 22–25 per cent of the retail price remains in the host country."

As the seminal figure of colonization in the New World, Christopher Columbus is celebrated throughout tourist sites in the Caribbean. Haiti, like other Caribbean nations, claims a piece of this history to aid in their appeal as a tourist destination. According to third-party travel agencies that market for Labadee, "Christopher Columbus named Labadee when he chose this secluded spot to take a break from his voyages to the New World" (iCruise 2008). Although themes of colonialism are relatively easy to see in the exploitative practices of the tour companies, the inherent structural violence that accompanies such colonization is reshaped by tourist-driven entities into something more acceptable to the tourist. It is changed into *adventure* and *exploration* to be digested more easily by the tourist. What could be more iconic than relaxing in the enclavic space of Labadee, with subjected locals partitioned to their respective bubbles, basking in the shadow of your superiority, which is symbolically portrayed by your luxury ship?

Tourist perspectives of Labadee

Similar to Jaakson's (2004) discussion of Zihuatanejo, Mexico's port acting as a "tourist façade," Labadee likewise is a veneer that hides the poverty and social ills that the name *Haiti* connotatively totes as it travels through tourist discourse. Labadee is situated on a small peninsula off the northern coast of Haiti, nearest to the village of Labadie. High mountains and dense jungle seem to insulate this place naturally, as many tourists did not remember noticing the 10-foot fence that moves intricately with the terrain in such a way that it stages the natural in methods commonly used by zoos and aquariums. Jane Desmond (1999, 242) points out that "notions of freedom and wildness must be retained, while the fact of the imprisonment ... must be papered over."

Quest for liminality

"I didn't spend all that money to feel bad" (Clark 2008), remarks a passenger regarding the feelings he had while visiting some of the Global South destinations that Royal Caribbean calls home. In elaborating, the passenger recalled an uncomfortable feeling that may have been the result of the clear class contrast that RCI, among other cruise companies in the Caribbean, perpetuate through private beaches, islands, and enclaves. This is a common feeling among passengers who notice the disparity that exists between the opulence of the cruise ship and the ports-of-call they visit. Inherent in the existence of tourist bubbles of affluence and their interactions with local environmental bubbles, peripheral views of what is *outside* begin to illustrate just how stark the disparity in the Caribbean can be (Judd 1999). As touched on earlier, Edward Bruner (1995, 238) identifies colonial themes in that many tourists "accept no moral or political responsibility for the people they visit." However, as illustrated by the passenger above, some cruise tourists appreciate an inner struggle that is symbolized by the dichotomous images that grace their vacation scrapbooks and computer desktops at home, a symbol of the affluent West—the cruise ship, docked in the untouched, purified spaces of the primitive other.

This image, which is clearly marketed by RCI through a variety of methods, is evocative of many Western themes of colonialism. As was brought up in tourist narratives regarding Labadee, many visitors recognized this sight to "look like the old King Kong movies," or how it was like "being on a movie set" (TripAdvisor 2008). Interestingly, the romantic gaze that is common at Labadee features three levels of meaning that are displayed in many pictures brought home from the site. These three levels produce a colonizing gaze that displays an empty paradise, which an explorer/colonizer/tourist has *discovered* and *conquered*. The base or background layer captures a small portion of the wild jungle and untamed mountain terrain; the second or middle layer illustrates the cruise ship, a symbol of Western dominance; the third or top layer contains the colonizers/tourists themselves, standing on the beach, illustrating the familiar scene of the conquistador coming ashore, or maybe even Christopher Columbus, whose very name graces a beach on this fantasy peninsula. This three-layer image of framed colonialism is overwhelmingly the most common photographic representation of Labadee among tourists.

Visitors to the shores of Labadee were often struck by the iconic beauty it seemed to naturally present. However, this was disrupted by perforations in the RCI Western tourist bubble, which were extant on the guarded peninsula. These perforations occurred in places near the periphery of the various bubbles that interact, namely the tourist bubble, and the "local" or "native" bubble. In the craft market, where Haitian vendors are strictly contained in small booths, tourists were granted access to a calculated sample of the Haitian bubble. Many reacted negatively toward this, as it was inconsistent with the cruise's overall theme, although some felt that it meshed quite well. "If you could somehow block out the locals" was a reaction that had numerous simulacra throughout tourist narratives. "They would hound you like starving animals" (TripAdvisor 2008).

Figure 8.3 Opulent cruise ship in local Haitian harbor

Figure 8.4 Example of frequently taken photo at "Columbus Cove"

Figure 8.5 Periphery of the bubble, showing fencing in the background near pro-
hibited-use road, and wild dog with military guard personnel sitting
against building

Supporting the production

Those few tourists who felt that the perforations between the Western and Haitian bubbles were congruent with the theme of the ship, acted in like manner, illustrating how even this different view yields a colonial feel. In expressing his distaste with the craft market and the desperation exhibited in the vendors' selling tactics, one tourist mentions that these Haitians "were no match for my wife." Chuckling, he quotes the vendor after his wife had been bargaining with him for a while, "Madam, you're killing me!" She responded that she did not want to kill him, but was only trying to get a *fair* price for the wares (TripAdvisor 2008). In colonial fashion, the woman represented in this travel narrative wants to preserve the native inhabitant, while extracting what he produces for little or no cost to her, given her station as the colonizer.

Many tourists in Labadee commented on the "amusing locals/natives" who were humorous in their selling approach at the peripheries of the bubble—in vendor tents and on the water. Some found it very pleasurable to be "greeted by native people," which crystallized the image of Columbus coming ashore to be greeted by the amusing natives, offering drinks, beach chairs, massages, and more.

Implications for Haiti

As these dynamic relationships between *tourist* and *place* only increase in number and complexity through time, the various hosts of these exclusionary and enclavic sites take on a variety of roles. More research is needed on how these sites are received by the local population. In this section, I outline the position that Haitian government officials are taking through an analysis on the few but poignant responses of the local people. Finally, I address how Haiti's desire for a new image may potentially be best served through these colonial enclaves during a time of adjustment and change.

Government agendas

Government and other tourist officials in the island nation of Haiti are conflicted about the tourist activity that occurs therein. As political unrest and military coups have characterized the region since its celebrated independence from France at the turn of the 19th century, tourists are difficult to attract. Officials claim that although the enclavic practices reinforce a colonial gradient between themselves and the Global North, tourism industry and revenue is "better than nothing" (Harman 2006, 1). Local Jean Cyril Pressoir expressed that although she was angered in the past about the way RCI excludes locals in their own land, she says today that, "We have an image problem and this is the way to get people to give the country a chance ... We really need tourists" (1). Further, support for these enterprises exists in Haiti as some tourism officials recognize that "we should have ten more Labadees" (1). Perhaps this national push toward creating a tourism industry in the newly democratized nation of Haiti is also leading locals to grapple with their place in new enterprises, just as locals on the peripheries of enclaves grapple with their positions.

Local support

Of the more than 100 tourist narratives collected, only a few were from Haitian national tourists or locals. One of the Haitian tourist narratives necessarily complicates the relationship that enclavic paradises have with the local populations. Isaiah is primarily positive throughout his description of Labadee, as he is preoccupied with ensuring that in light of the highly publicized poverty, Labadee truly represents his country, specifically saying, "This is Haiti" (TripAdvisor 2008). To Isaiah, the highly produced and staged authenticity that resembles no "real" place in time or space is his nation's identity. Similar to how national parks propagate an iconic image of their respective nations, Labadee, although unofficial, represents hope to many Haitian locals. Orenstein (1997, 29) reported that although local men seem to incriminate the ship—"it took their beach, they say; it only hires the local boss's friends; the fish are all gone"—they concede that they would like to see "more ships to Labadee." Interestingly, as locals are torn by their responses to the Global North's encroachment, many tourists are also torn by the mere presence of locals in their respective space or bubble.

Bubbles and containers revisited

As the Haitian reaction to the colonial exclusionary practices of RCI is complicated, Labadee and other enclavic destinations in the Global South begin to take on new meanings. In light of the local acceptance and pride in some of these destinations, the Haitian government is considering an embracement of such tourism. Like national parks in the United States and elsewhere, Labadee may offer greater support in an unstable political environment. Perhaps Haiti recognizes the degrading and destructive aftermath of open tourism and has decided to contain the dangers of Western tourist exploitation, like the roads that permit cars to explore national parks, to safe zones or bubbles where they are easily managed (Louter 2001). Interestingly, this thought is reciprocal as tourists are also under the impression that the fences and gates exist to keep danger out. However, perhaps they are the danger that the "real" Haiti is trying to keep in check.

Conclusion

As Caribbean cruising is soaring in popularity, the population of the Global North increases its interaction with the Global South. Labadee's "private paradise" was set in the colonial Caribbean, in a timeless and static state, catering to a collective *old* Caribbean gaze. Although this environment was clearly not the Haiti you read of in Paul Farmer's (2005) writings of poverty and disease, passengers accepted this as staged authenticity or hyper-reality. The port at Labadee represents a closed, extremely secure system of produced fantasy, which occasionally allowed for the transcendence of borders through the merchant tent and other peripheries of the bubble. Both the tourist and local appreciated these interactions reciprocally. However, arguably only the tourist can reconcile the inner conflict that is motivated by such encounters, as he/she can return to the Global North, rich with exploited experience, souvenirs, and pictures that were largely appropriated from the impoverished; while the local remains in the destructive gaze of the colonial tourist that arrives each week on floating magnificence. Although Cabezas (2008, 33) calls on the tourist industry to ensure "reciprocal leisure travel," this would require significantly more effort to divert the global North-to-South tide that drives such exploitation in this industry.

References

Britton, S. (1996). Tourism, dependency, and development: A mode of analysis. In Apostolopoulos, Y., Leivadi, S., & Yiannakis, A. (eds.), *The Sociology of Tourism: Theoretical and empirical investigations* (pp.155–172). New York: Routledge.

Bruner, E. (1995). The ethnographer/tourist in Indonesia. In Lanfant, M.-F., Allcock, J., & Bruner, E. (eds.), *International Tourism: Identity and change*. Thousand Oaks, CA: SAGE.

Cabezas, A. (2008). Tropical blues: Tourism and social exclusion in the Dominican Republic. *Latin American Perspectives*. 35, 21–36.

Carter, E. (2001). The space of the dream: A case of mis-taken identity? *Area*. 33(1), 47–54.

Clark. (2008). Personal interview—recorded tourist narrative. M. Nelson (ed.).

Cohen, E. (1995). Marketing paradise, marketing nation. *Annals of Tourism Research*. 22, 404–421.

Dahl, J. (1995). Why go ashore when the ship's so nice? *The Wall Street Journal*, B1 and B9.

Desmond, J. (1999). *Staging Tourism: Bodies on display from Waikiki to Sea World*. Chicago: University of Chicago Press.

Eco, U. (2000). Travels in hyperreality. In Hartley, J., & Pearson, R. (eds.), *American Cultural Studies: A reader*. Oxford: Oxford University Press.

Edensor, T. (2000). Staging tourism: Tourists as performers. *Annals of Tourism Research*. 27, 322–344.

Edensor, T. (2001). Performing tourism, staging tourism: (Re)producing tourist space and practice. *Tourist Studies*. 1, 59–81.

Farmer, P. (2005). *Pathologies of Power: health, human rights, and the new war on the poor*. Berkeley: University of California Press.

Foster, G. (1986). South Seas cruise: A case study of a short-lived society. *Annals of Tourism Research*. 13, 215–238.

Frantz, D. (1999). Sovereign Islands (a special report): Gaps in sea laws shield pollution by cruise lines. *The New York Times.*

Freitag, T. (1994). Enclave tourist development: For whom the benefits roll? *Annals of Tourism Research.* 21, 538–554.

Garroni Carbonara, V. (1997). Futuristic cruise liners. Conference speech presented at Seatrade Asia Pacific Cruise Convention. Singapore, December 4–7, 1996. Retrieved from http://www.cybercruises.com/garronispeech.htm.

Gottdiener, M. (1997). *The Theming of America.* Oxford: Westview Press.

Greenwood, D. (1989). Culture by the pound: An anthropological perspective on tourism as cultural commodification. In Smith, V. (ed.), *Host and Guests: The anthropology of tourism* (pp. 171–186). Philadelphia: University of Pennsylvania Press.

Harman, D. (2006). Could this paradise really be poor, desperate Haiti? *The Christian Science Monitor.* Jan 25.

Holder, J.S. (1993). The Caribbean Tourism Organization in historical perspective. In Gayle, D., & Goodrich, J. (eds.), *Tourism Marketing and Management in the Caribbean* (pp. 205–219). New York: Routledge.

iCruise (2008). https://www.icruise.com/cruise-lines/royal-caribbean-labadee.html.

Jaakson, R. (2004). Beyond the tourist bubble? Cruiseship passengers in port. *Annals of Tourism Research.* 31, 44–60.

Judd, D. (1999). Constructing the tourist bubble. In Judd, D., & Fainstein, S. (eds.), *The Tourist City* (pp. 35–53). New Haven, CT: Yale University Press.

Kincaid, J. (1988). *A Small Place.* New York: Farrar, Straus Giroux.

Lanfant, M. -F., Allcock, J., & Bruner, E., eds. (1995). *International Tourism: Identity and change.* Thousand Oaks, CA: SAGE.

Law, L., Bunnell, T., & Ong, C. -E. (2007). *The Beach,* the gaze and film tourism. *Tourist Studies.* 7, 141–164.

Lefebvre, H. (1991). *The Production of Space.* London: Basil Blackwell.

Louter, D. (2001). Glaciers and Gasoline: The making of a windshield wilderness, 1900–1915. In Wrobel, D., & Long, P. (eds.), *Seeing and Being Seen: Tourism in the American West* (pp. 248–270). Lawrence: University Press of Kansas.

MacCannell, D. (1973). Stages Authenticity: Arrangements of social space in tourist settings. *American Sociological Review.* 17, 589–603.

MacCannell, D. (1999). *The Tourist: A new theory of the leisure class.* Berkeley: University of California Press.

McElroy, J.L., & K. de Albuquerque. (1998). Tourism Penetration Index in small Caribbean islands. *Annals of Tourism Research.* 25, 145–168.

Mintel (2003). Cruises, Leisure Intelligence.

Neumann, M. (1988). Wandering through the museum: Experience and identity in a spectator culture. *Border Lines.* Summer, 19–27.

Orenstein, C. (1997). Fantasy island. *The Progressive.* August, 28–31.

Pine, B.J., & Gilmore, J.H. (1998). Welcome to the experience economy. *Harvard Business Review.* July/August, 97–105.

Royal Caribbean International (RCI) (2008a). 2008–2009 Cruise Vacation Planner.

Royal Caribbean International (RCI) (2008b). 2008–2009 Vacation Planner Cover Letter, M. Nelson (ed.): Personal Communication.

Ritzer, G., & Liska, A. (1997). McDisneyization and post-tourism: Complementary perspectives on contemporary tourism. In Rojek, C., & Urry, J. (eds.), *Touring Cultures: Transformations of travel and theory* (pp. 96–112). New York: Routledge.

Schmitt, B.H. (1999). Experiential marketing. *Journal of Marketing Management*. 15, 53–67.

Showker, K., & Sehlinger, B., eds. (1998). *The Unofficial Guide to Cruises*. New York: Macmillan.

Sibley, D. (1988). Survey 13: Purification of space. *Environment and Planning D: Society and Space*. 6, 409–421.

Sorkin, M. (1992). *Variations on a Theme Park: The New American City and the end of public space*. New York: Hill and Wang.

TripAdvisor (2008). www.tripadvisor.com/Attraction_Review-g147306-d150230-Revi ews-Labadee-Haiti.html.

Urry, J. (1992). The Tourist Gaze revisited. *American Behavioural Scientist*. 36, 172–186.

Urry, J. (1996). The changing economics of the tourist industry. In Apostolopoulos, Y., Leivadi, S., & Yiannakis, A. (eds.), *The Sociology of Tourism: Theoretical and empirical investigations* (pp. 193–218). New York: Routledge.

Urry, J. (2002). *The Tourist Gaze*. Thousand Oaks: SAGE.

Venturi, R. (1995). Distorted imagination. In Appignanesi, R., & Garrett, C. (eds.), *Postmodernism for Beginners*. Cambridge: Icon Books.

Williams, A. (2006). Tourism and hospitality marketing: Fantasy, feeling and fun. *International Journal of Contemporary Hospitality Management*. 18(6), 482–495.

Wise, J. (1999). How cruise ships shortchange the Caribbean. *Fortune*. 139, 44–45.

Wood, R. (2000). Caribbean cruise tourism: Globalization at sea. *Annals of Tourism Research*. 27, 345–370.

World Tourism Travel Council (WTTC) (2008). *Haiti: 2008 travel and tourism economic research*.

Part 5

Hosting Sustainable Tourism and Global Geopolitics

9 Setting the tourism landscape

Ethnic tensions and economic development on a small island in Mexico

Brandon Melecio Fischer and Todd Pierce

Global economic tensions affect localized sustainable tourist-based living wages, often lead to community disputes, and can raise issues of worth, racism, and conflicting community goals. This chapter discusses these issues on the island of Isla Mujeres, Mexico. Though small, Isla Mujeres is among the top tourist destinations on the planet and regarded as the antithesis of Cancun for the traveler looking for a more authentic Mexican beach vacation. In March of 2014, after Isla Mujeres was voted among the top ten best beaches on the planet via TripAdvisor member rankings, the local government of Isla Mujeres passed a town ordinance banning beach vendors and many street vendors. The government decision caused much debate and heated emotional discussions within the foreign immigrant, tourist, and local isleño community. The discourses that followed the government decision reflected community ownership, efficacy, local versus non-local, and ethnic ideologies. The TripAdvisor ranking, as fleeting as it may be, stirred tensions between the government, local isleños, and expat/tourist groups, with many individuals left feeling their economic security has been sacrificed for the sake of possible future investment.

Across the globe, transnational economic influences significantly affect the working conditions of those living in tourism-based settings, no matter how sustainable the economic design. Economic tensions can quickly lead to disputes within communities living and working in tourism sites that are rooted in conflicting visions for the future. These conflicting visions generate concerns around aesthetic representations of the local that can give way to racist differentiations of who is able to participate and belong within tourism economies. This chapter discusses how these tensions and their effects were made manifest on the small island of Isla Mujeres in southern Mexico in early 2014, spurred by a performative move on the part of local officials that had repercussions both in the front and back stage of the island's landscape. During this time, the municipal government and police force removed an entire segment of the workforce during an opportune moment to purportedly improve the island's brand as a premier tourism destination. By tracing the events that unfolded during this active and controversial moment in time, it becomes clear how performative acts serve to call certain modes of power into being at the expense of already vulnerable communities.

To begin speaking about tourism in Mexico, it is important to first consider the role that tourism plays in the country's agenda for economic growth. Mexico is among the most visited countries in the world and has a tourism industry that is a driving force in its economy, accounting for an estimated 12.6 percent of the country's GDP,[1] and placing it in the ranks of the most lucrative and sought after tourist destinations in the world alongside Spain, France, and the United States. In effect, tourism is an industry of national interest, one that the country is committed to strengthening through a robust administrative framework for infrastructural development.

For decades, Isla Mujeres has been a permanent fixture in the booming Mexican tourism economy. Situated eight miles off the coast of Cancun, Isla Mujeres is a sleepy island roughly five miles long and a half-mile wide at its widest point. Although small in size, Isla Mujeres is among the top tourist destinations in the world, designed to provide an experience distinct from its shoreside neighbor, Cancun, by offering a less manicured though no less idyllic alternative to the Mexican beach vacation. In March 2014, Playa Norte, a more popular beach on the northern shore of Isla Mujeres, was listed as one of the top ten beaches on the planet by TripAdvisor. The designation not only drew the attention of international tourists, but also set into motion a series of initiatives by the municipal government.

That same month, the local government of Isla Mujeres began to advance a series of policies that included a local ordinance that, when implemented, effectively banned mobile beach and street vendors, or *vendedores ambulantes*, from engaging in commerce. The ordinance was expected to produce a safer beach environment during a time in which the local government sought two internationally recognized eco-tourism accreditations, Blue Flag and White Flag, that would catapult Playa Norte and, consequently, the island into the ranks of Cancun and various other premier tourist destinations along the southern Mexican coast, further imprinting Isla Mujeres as a permanent fixture on the global eco-tourism map. Over the course of the implementation of the ordinance, an estimated 150 migrant vendors were forced to close shop, many of whom identified as or were considered local *isleños*, residents of the island, and had worked as vendors for over 20 years along Isla's beaches.

Shortly after its implementation, the decision by the local government caused heated and emotional discussions within the non-Mexican immigrant population, tourist, Mexican national, and local *isleño* communities. Tourists who regularly visited the island felt that local officials went too far in their decision to clear the beaches of *vendedores ambulantes* and in the forceful implementation of the ordinance. The debate that followed the government decision across

---

1   According to the World Travel and Tourism Council, travel and tourism generated 12.6 percent of Mexico's GDP in 2013 as a total of direct, indirect, and induced GDP impact. Benchmarking Travel & Tourism in Mexico: Summary of Findings, November 2013. http://www.wttc.org/-/media/files/reports/benchmark%20reports/country%20results/mexico%20benchmarking%202013.pdf.

these four groups came to a boiling point, centering around topics of community ownership, local versus non-local identity formation, and highly charged racial discourse that was rooted in already existent ethnic divisions. This singular event, the forceful and at times aggressive removal of vendors from the beaches of Isla Mujeres, demonstrates how performance in tourism can serve as public pedagogy in which the aesthetic foregrounds the intersection of politics, tourist sites, and embodied experience (Alexander 2005).

This chapter examines discourse across five groups: non-Mexican immigrants, tourists, local isleños, Mexican nationals, and local government and police officials who either were present during or engaged with these activities. We deploy a multimethods approach, including participant observation, informal interviews, and virtual exchanges as well as surveys of local online and print media. Across these various platforms and mediums, ideas of a more sustainable tourism industry are negotiated, as are the consequences of striving for a particular economic model that thrives at the expense of peripheral economies and the ethnic minorities they employ. Through an analysis of the events that unfolded on Isla Mujeres in 2014, this chapter will demonstrate the intersection of performance and performativity in the deployment and marking of the racialized *chiapaneco* subject on the island, the worker from Chiapas who is employed in the informal economy, during a moment of performative intervention by the local administration on the island that, in Langellier's words, "situates performance narrative within the forces of discourse" (1999, 129). By approaching the forces of discourse through performativity in this way, we trace how the dramaturgical staging of identity, race, community, belonging, and aesthetics stoked the refusal of particular communities already marginalized throughout Mexico who did not quite accommodate the cosmopolitan aesthetic and ideal.

In focusing on performance in tourism space and practice, this chapter draws upon various scholars who have analyzed the ways that tourism is staged. Following Kirshenblatt-Gimblett, we hold that tourism is made up of encapsulated contingent events that are quotidian in nature (Kirshenblatt-Gimblett 2008). Though, as this chapter shows, the events that produce tourist stages can also be directed and performative, at times conflicting with other stagings. As Edensor reveals, tourism is a constant practice of (re)production, a process that "involves the ongoing (re)construction of praxis and space in shared contexts" (Edensor 2001). This very (re)construction may well be interrupted by other staged events, ideologies, and spaces.

Setting the stage

Isla Mujeres (the island of women) is a small Caribbean island located off the coast of Cancun in the southern Mexican state of Quintana Roo. Although a small island, it is home to an estimated 13,000 residents, many of whom travel to and from the island on a regular basis given its proximity to other tourist destinations and urban centers in Mexico and states along the border of the

Figure 9.1 Photo of Isla Mujeres by Philip Edge, 2018

United States. Over the past ten years, Isla Mujeres has been called the 17th most colorful city, best island to escape to, 6th best island on the planet, and 10th best beach on the planet by sources such as TripAdvisor and the *Telegraph*, and Playa Norte has been ranked the best beach in all of Mexico. What was once a sleepy, lightly populated fisherman island has become a premier tourist destination. In particular, Isla Mujeres attracts eco-tourists looking to enjoy the clear turquoise waters and the silky beaches, to swim with whale sharks and large manta rays, to dive and snorkel the reefs and underwater museum, and to experience the release of baby sea turtles. It also attracts cultural tourists who enjoy the slow pace of life on the island, the musical and food traditions, and the history and cultural diversity the island offers.

Throughout the course of the past several decades, the island's economy has been supported primarily by the tourism industry. An integral part of the cultural landscape that gives shape to this tourism industry has been mobile vendors, or *vendedores ambulantes*, who sell their artisan crafts, hammocks, clothing, and food items along the beach, many of whom bring their business directly to beach dwellers who rest casually along the island's sandy beaches. For the tourist, these interactions were not a nuisance, rather they allowed them to feel more integrated into the fullness of island life, a participant in local economies. For a few pesos and a moment of their time, they got a souvenir and a conversation, a reciprocal exchange, a seat at the front of stage of tourism activity on the island. In this staging, the tourist was both audience and participant in an immersive dramaturgical experience in which the *vendedores ambulantes* are those performing island culture and an integral part of the tourism landscape.

However, in the summer of 2014, the municipal government of Isla Mujeres enacted a range of measures to comply with standards set by two eco-tourism accreditations, White Flag and Blue Flag, the former, an accreditation that paved the way for the second, a global accreditation. The effort to become accredited in both certifications immediately followed the listing of Isla Mujeres' Playa Norte as one of the top ten beaches in the world by TripAdvisor user polls, and was to further galvanize and expose the image of the island. Of the image of the island, the mayor at the time stated,

> Isla Mujeres is a world class destination. One of the compromises of this administration is that visitors leave with a positive vision of the island. As a society and government, we should work together so that tourists leave with an image of a municipality that is safe and secure.[2]

In principle, Blue Flag would contribute to the preservation of Isla's prized marine wildlife and ecology, the safety and cleanliness of its beaches, and the established eco-tourism economy. As an international mark of distinction in the eco-tourism industry, Blue Flag would further impress Isla's beaches and marinas upon the map of the world's premier eco-tourism destinations. In their interpretation of standards set by Blue Flag and White Flag, the municipality took a performative and pedagogical approach, enlisting the Department of Control and Fiscalization to police all beaches for trash and pollution, and to attend to concerns around health and sanitation compliance. According to the local municipality's interpretation of eco-tourism standards vis-à-vis health and sanitation regulation, informal vending and income-related activities fell outside of the scope of legal compliance. By expanding the interpretation of health and sanitation concerns to all informal commerce, the beach "clean up" ordered by municipal government and implemented by the local police extended to all informal economies including those employing *vendedores ambulantes* regardless of whether such a risk was present.

On March 23, 2014, this regimen went into effect. Municipal police of Isla Mujeres took to the island's tourist-laden port entry, beaches, and other public throughways demanding that vendors evacuate the premises. Wielding arms and a mandate from the local government to effectively "clean the beaches" (*limpiar las playas*), police forcefully removed and confiscated vendors' products and carts throughout the months that followed. One by one, local authorities escorted vendors to the Palacio Municipal, the island's center of municipal offices, where they were later charged fines of $900 to $1500 pesos and ordered not to return to their vending sites again. Local officials urged that the island's high-trafficked areas were to remain clear of all informal commerce, trash, and other "nuisances" in order to uphold standards of cleanliness and safety that fell in line with the administration's tourism development agenda.

2 Translated from the original Spanish: "Isla Mujeres es un destino de clase mundial y uno de los compromisos de esta administración es que los visitantes se lleven una buena imagen. Como sociedad y gobierno debemos trabajar unidos para que los turistas se lleven la imagen de un municipio limpio y seguro." http://islamujeres.gob.mx/2017/09/02/mantiene-gobierno-municipal-y-zofemat-playas-limpias-y-seguras/.

Figure 9.2 Women vendors from Chiapas on Playa Norte, Isla Mujeres, just before sunset. Photo by Jennifer Miner Pierce, 2013

This government intervention set the tone for the strategic removal of the island's beach and street vendors from main throughways for months to come. From March 23 onward, police and sanitation officials conducted routine inspections in targeted locales around the island. During and prior to these interventions, representatives from various departments within the municipal government were in conversation around strategy and response. Likewise, the local population erupted into conversation. The effects variably impacted multiple constituencies, both the "true residents" of the island, or isleños, and migrant labor communities.

This chapter contextualizes the complex terms of belonging and citizenship being negotiated during these interventions by the municipality of Isla Mujeres with an emphasis on the role of performance. By performance, we draw upon Burke, focusing on the actors, purposes, scripts, stories, stages, and interactions present during this time (Burke 1969). The argument is elaborated in three parts. First, we situate practices of "beach cleaning" within the material realities in which they are embedded, illustrating the informal conditions at the back stage of the tourism landscape. Second, we will focus on aspects of labor and identity vis-à-vis administrative discourse at the front of stage of Isla Mujeres' tourism economy. This discourse actively produces standards for Mexican citizenship that include expectations for how the citizen is to contribute to the economy and the labor force that supports tourism industry. Here, ethnographic material shows just how this discourse travelled through the regulatory force of municipal practice governing labor in performative events as well as the tourists' reactions to these events. This ethnographic material will be placed in conversation with existing scholarship on tourism in Isla Mujeres and the state of Quintana Roo more broadly, which describes how the terms of citizenship in the region are being marked ethnically through administrative discourse and practice. The chapter will conclude by contextualizing both the back and front stage of Isla's tourism economy with a reflection on how performative interventions by the local administration produced certain modes of belonging and citizenship that drew upon existing stratifications rooted in economic and ethnic differences.

As the chief administrative body overseeing tourism in Mexico, the Ministry of Tourism, or SECTUR, is responsible for strengthening the country's tourism industry by setting into motion strategic policy directives that produce priorities in the services that are offered through tourism. SECTUR communicates their vision for tourism culture as follows:

> When we speak of the touristic culture we are making a reference to the participation of people looking for possible ways to generate more tourist activity; this implies the commitment to learn about tourism in order to contribute to its growth and in order to benefit from its amenities, dedicating the necessary attention to develop tourism into the sustainable activity that it should become.[3]

This quote articulates specific expectations for those who participate in Mexico's tourism industry, expectations expressly rooted in terms of economic profit and growth. As part of a broader framework of economic citizenship in Mexico, this discourse puts in place standards for economic activity that are designed to support the tourism development agenda set forth by the municipal government.

In conversations with representatives from the office of the president, the Federal Maritime Land Zone (ZOFEMAT), and the Departments of Control of Sanitation, Economic Development, and Social Development on Isla Mujeres, these standards for economic activity grounded each of their expressed concerns and priorities around internal migrants who come to the island for work in informal markets. In particular, their concerns were directed toward those beach and street vendors who come from Quintana Roo and the Yucatán, especially migrants from the state of Chiapas (the "*chiapanecos*") who have been working off the grid from formal tourism economy and thus, in their view, do not contribute to the formal development economy. Although this group of internal migrants is employed in irregular labor markets, they do indeed contribute to the tourism economy and landscape.

Based on interviews with local officials, Isla's vendors did not adequately contribute to the tourism economy that they aspire to develop. For these officials, vendors reportedly came to the island from Chiapas with a low level

3 SECTUR. http://www.sectur.gob.mx/wb2/sectur/sect_9070_breviario_de_cultura, accessed 17 July 2014. Translation by Ilda Jimenez y West, 2008.

of education, poor English-language ability, and no technical skills, so they did not provide the abilities required for Isla's economic growth. Instead, they reportedly took advantage of government spending and present a host of problems for Isla's society such as substance abuse, domestic abuse, uncleanliness, manipulation, and, as revealed in the events of summer 2014, failure to comply with safety and sanitation regulations. By purportedly demonstrating these and other unfavorable behaviors, the community of migrant vendors and, more specifically, the *chiapanecos* employed in the sector, created obstacles for the municipality's future development agenda. During these exchanges around *vendedores ambulantes* and the characteristics this group purportedly espoused, the use of the *chiapaneco* category often carried a specific connotation with reference to an ethnic minority, namely that of indigenous descent.

A rather different perspective on these events was communicated by beach and street vendors that migrated to Isla Mujeres for work from elsewhere in southern Mexico. From their standpoint, the restrictions of belonging and citizenship imposed upon them during the performative and pedagogical moment in which the police cleared the beaches were marked by ethnic exclusions, which drastically changed their position and experience at the front stage of the tourism landscape. Their living conditions, at the back stage, remained the same, though were still out of view in Isla's tourism landscape.

The back stage: Living conditions

The high degree of mobility that characterizes Isla's resident and tourist population makes it difficult to find clear boundaries of the isleño category. Many *vendedores ambulantes* who sell *paletas*, or popsicles made of fresh fruit, are considered isleños who have been vending on the island for decades. Many other *vendedores ambulantes* came to the island from other parts of the country, primarily from the state of Chiapas. While a portion of these migrant vendors live on the island, a still larger portion live on the mainland, either within the Cancun city limits or the mainland area of the Isla Mujeres municipality, often referred to as the "Continental Zone."

The following ethnographic reflection, recorded during the summer of 2014, describes an afternoon spent exploring the residential sites that are home to many of the migrant vendors. These informal settlements, which are situated on the outskirts of Cancun and along the Continental Zone, provide an important gaze into the back stage of Isla's tourism economy.

After passing the city limits of Cancun, the bus winds up on a single stretch of road extending before me into the horizon. We can see a handful of structures scattered along our route—a labor syndicate, a gas station, a school bus stop. We exit the *taxi colectivo* and step onto the dry and barren earth of Rancho Viejo, an informal settlement just outside of Cancun. Ambling past a Catholic church, my guide, Josue, points us toward the residential area of La

Invasión, a squatter settlement that is nearly entirely off the municipal grid. We approach a neighborhood of encampments—a patchwork of salvaged planks of wood, rusted aluminum sheets, and blue polyethylene tarps. Passing the first row of houses, we notice a makeshift shop with an adjoining residence and enter. The shopkeeper, Rosa, is cautious, but welcomes our questions. She has little to say of her neighbors, despite her holding shop there for some three years. She knows no one, she tells us. For Rosa, all that has been consistent in La Invasión is movement of material and of identity within the community.

Rosa lives beside some 2000 other migrants in an informal settlement bordering Cancun. These are internal migrants who have traveled to the region to work in tourism. They have been deterritorialized, unable to reside within tourism centers due to their extreme poverty and policies that make permanent their irregular labor status, particularly in the case of *vendedores ambulantes*. They are left with no option but to work with an irregular status if they wish to remain in the sector. Day in and day out, Rosa and her neighbors live the permanence of transience.

This experience with Rosa in Rancho Viejo makes clear the physical and economic conditions at the back stage of Isla's tourism economy, and adds context to the events described. The vendor who enters the island as an internal migrant does so with precarious social and economic standing from the onset. Lacking the privileged "true local" or isleño status, the vendor who works as an internal migrant is discouraged, through institutionalized forms of exclusion and discrimination—at times linguistic, ethnic, and socioeconomic—from accessing educational opportunities and entry into the formal economy. Likewise, the *chiapaneco* who works as a migrant vendor, a Mexican citizen, is accused of not paying municipal taxes and of stealing the isleños' job opportunities that are "rightfully theirs," mirroring the discourse around undocumented Mexican immigrants in the United States. The migrant vendor feels like a blemish to Isla's aesthetic of cleanliness and safety, evident in the government-led program to "clean the beaches." When all is said and done, the vendor is still expected to fully contribute to the demands of Isla's eco-tourism economy as well as its aspirational model for development despite all of these obstacles. This view of the *chiapaneco* worker existed well before the events of summer 2014, but was further present and consequential in and around the time of the municipality's performative move to clean the beaches.

Labor and identity: A flash point

One of the most characteristic of vendors on Isla Mujeres are the "*paleta*" or popsicle vendors, which are typically local businesses run by families who have been on the island for several generations. The family produces several flavors of popsicles by hand at night. Each morning, the older men of the families transport their bulky carts of popsicles, mini refrigerators with no electricity, from the middle to the most northern end of the Island. These carts are able to stay cold for many hours, though their cargo must be sold by the end of the day.

Often, the men push their carts over two miles to reach their target customers, the tourists on Playa Norte and other beach areas and sidewalks along the main beach road. Once they arrive at the beach, the vendors push their bulky carts through the soft sand, traveling between beach umbrella and beach blanket, selling their popsicles for 20 pesos each. Although the objective is to sell the entire supply, selling out is difficult given work conditions. Vending is demanding physical labor that is practiced under high heat and humidity. Once the day ends, as cars and golf carts pass them by, the vendors make a 2.5-mile trek back home to the residential neighborhood where they live, located near the center of the island. That same evening, the process to prepare stock for the next day's sale begins.

The popular image of the *paleta* vendors, as conceptualized in the front stage of tourism on the island, is an idyllic "true isleño," a resident and local who is dedicated to their labor and to the well-being of the island. Through the romantic gaze of a participant at the front stage, the *paleta* vendor is an honest, hard worker who takes much pride in his trade, much like fishermen

Figure 9.3 A local isleño popsicle vendor's cart is confiscated for vending on the beach. Photo posted on a popular public Facebook group

or carpenters. *Paleta* vending, like other manual trades, is often passed along generationally; children learn the trade of their parents or relatives very early, master it throughout their lives, and pass the knowledge on to their children. At a particularly critical moment during the clearing of the beaches, a *paleta* cart was confiscated by the city for vending on the beach. Once word spread that the *paleta* vendors were also implicated in the policing of the beaches, the intervention became further politicized. For many living on the island, the right to access employment was based on how long one lived on the island, which, once contradicted, led to public reproach.

The confiscation of the first *paleta* cart catalyzed an especially contentious debate around who has the right to participate in the tourist economy, based in large part on the owner being isleño, or resident of the island. Seizing the cart made the tensions between isleños and their local government more immediate, and added to strains already present with the affected community members from other parts of the country. Many of the local isleños' reactions posted in online public forums expressed outrage at the government for confiscating the popsicle cart. They were upset that the new policy affected vendors who had been selling their wares on the beaches for many years, and, for some, decades. Those vendors have become part of the social landscape of the island, actors that were expected on the front stage. Some reactions were of pure outrage:

> This is justice? These people are the living, working to earn a bite ... not like you, you are just sitting in your chair scratching your ... they walk from sunrise to sunset ... while you're getting fat. God will not forgive you ... but for them, punishment ... What do you say? ... How can you punish men that work from sunrise to sunset and earn very little money?

There were calls for public protests "so that we can protect our physical and moral integrity." Protests occurred. Those who protested were declined official vending licenses. This is not to say that all "locals" (isleño and Mexican nationals) were opposed to the government's actions. One resident expressed, "a congratulations to our president [mayor] for being the first president to clear our city street vendors and informal trade efficiently and effectively by removing the bad image of the streets which are mostly not even islanders." As responses to the events became more heated, many fixated not only on difference in terms of the point of origin in geographic terms, but also on ethnicity, by focusing on certain types of vendors who were not from the island, but from the state of Chiapas. Those vendors look and dress differently, and generally come with a different socioeconomic standing. Now thought of as causing problems with health and sanitation for the island, they are furthermore seen as uneducated and dirty, a blemish to the island.

The local versus migrant worker distinction in discourse is reflected in economies around the world. In the United States of America, we can trace the tensions over time easily, from the Irish immigrants of the early 1900s to the Latin Americans of the 21st century. "Locals" often feel that "outsiders" are taking away from the economy, as opposed to becoming an essential part of it. In the case of Isla Mujeres, we see how these distinctions are reinforced by a directed staging of tourism by the municipal government at a moment when economic incentives were especially present. This directed staging was made possible by the boundedness of tourism spaces.

As Edensor writes, "[tourist] settings are distinguished by boundedness, whether physical or symbolic, and are often organized—or stage-managed—to provide and sustain common-sense understandings about what activities should take place" (2001, 63). However, this directed staging reaches its limit, which was manifest in the form of a backlash from tourist and resident populations, revealing a paradox inherent in tourism design. Edensor explains this paradox: "the production of tourist space concerns the intensification of attempts to design and theme space, and the increasingly promiscuous nature of tourism, whereby tourist stages proliferate" (64). In the case of Isla Mujeres, existing local and resident communities drew upon and produced such boundaries based on who is and who is not able to participate in the tourism economy.

The front of stage: Tourist reactions

Tourist responses came as rapidly as local ones, but for very different reasons. The removal of vendors was quickly noticed by tourists, and was reflected in a flurry of social media exchanges that inquired into why. The tourists that the government was trying to please by attempting to improve the image of the island were unconvinced and, at times, upset with the direction that the local administration and police force had taken. There are many tourists who think of Isla as their own little secret island, or at least one of the best least-known islands. They love its quaintness and non-commercialized aspects (e.g. there are no chain businesses on Isla). There were hundreds of responses on various social media platforms (like TripAdvisor and Facebook) opposing the government decision. One public post by a TripAdvisor user gives the general impression felt by most:

> Please let ISLA be ISLA. We don't care about the top 10 of anything. We love the locals and admire their perseverance and hard work. Let them continue to sell on the beaches. This is their island and home, just leave them alone.[4]

---

4   TripAdvisor, Beach vendors gone???? https://www.tripadvisor.com/ShowTopic-g150810-i360-k7302965-o10-Beach_vendors_gone-Isla_Mujeres_Yucatan_Peninsula.html#57002607, accessed 2014.

Economic security

As the tourism economy grows, so too does the demand for labor. Migrant laborers from many different states in Mexico, like Chiapas, travel to Isla Mujeres, seeking to participate in the booming economy, even though their labor rights and protections do not equal those of the local workforce. As Torres and Momsen (2005, 279) indicate, "in Quintana Roo, rapid growth of the tourism industry has reinforced existing unequal relations of domination and subordination, while also producing new social, political and economic hierarchies manifest in patterns of uneven development." The government creates programs to educate and train the workforce to fill the jobs needed to sustain this economic growth, but has its own economic constraints. Many migrant workers encounter various obstacles to accessing social services currently offered, either from not knowing about them, feeling like they do not qualify, or experiencing linguistic and social barriers. The government is struggling to create a system that can assist isleños, while also facing a "brain drain" of those who are educated, as they leave the island for better economic prospects elsewhere.

Residency and locality have taken on deep political significance as the island's diverse population vies for access to work and a sustainable livelihood for themselves and their families. Unstable claims to true residency cast the isleño, or the "true islander," as a model citizen who carries entitlements to the island's growth through eco-tourism and related opportunities. In this way, the performance of island residency and, ultimately, of belonging, became central themes throughout the course of events that took place during the beach "clean up." Meanwhile, the municipality's migrant labor populations compete for what few minimum wage jobs there are available and are blamed for taking these jobs from their rightful recipients, the isleños who most deserve to have the option should they so choose. This nebulous category of local identity is an important factor in who is allowed at the "front of the stage" in this tourist economy. The issue of who should be assisted most and who should be included in the economic future of Isla Mujeres leans more to those residents who claim true isleño status, leaving those who do not come from families who have been on the island for generations feeling lost.

By reflecting upon the perspectives of the migrant vendor community alongside administrative discourse on tourism, it becomes clear that the politics of locality has a direct impact on how or whether the Ministry of Tourism's standards are attainable. More specifically, where one comes from plays a major role in determining who may take part in economic activities that are perceived to contribute to the growth of tourism. However, there is an important check on the practice of governmentality at play here. The municipality of Isla Mujeres cannot readily deport the internal migrant vendor as they are legal citizens of the country. Instead, Isla's municipal leadership must mobilize other normative parameters to justify revoking vending licenses and access to work for large segments of the migrant community.

Aesthetic preferences for cleanliness have given new meaning to the municipality's efforts to "clean the beaches," reducing the migrant vendor to a blemish that must be rubbed out. In her analysis of tourism on Isla Mujeres, Ilda Jimenez y West describes connections among ethnicity, citizenship, and notions of cleanliness. Through tourism, Jimenez y West argues, specific ideals of cleanliness have been etched into Isla's semiotic landscape. These ideals of cleanliness are shaped by assumptions around what is attractive to the cosmopolitan consumer. These are often values of Western import, and, according to Jimenez y West, of whiteness. In effect, whiteness and cleanliness have become integral to the design process as tourism architects strive to create a more positive image of the island. "Isleños' perceptions of cleanliness in their island is grounded on their conscious ideology of race founded on a historical legacy of colonization."[5] In the process, enduring structures of racism produce economic and social stratification through a specific aesthetic of cleanliness supported by the tourism industry itself.

To put in context the clean-up of beach vending orchestrated by the local government of Isla Mujeres, one only needs to look to Cancun to find an historical connection between social stratification and tourism development in Mexico more broadly. Following the completion of Cancun's hotel zone, Mexico became a global leader in state-directed Planned Tourism Development. From its inception, Cancun was anticipated to serve as an engine for regional development and equitable growth. However, the planned tourism has only increased social stratification. As geographers Rebecca Torres and Janet Momsen argue, "While Planned Tourism Development [in Cancun] has proved to be a highly profitable model of tourism development for transnational corporations, entrepreneurial elites and national governments, it does not necessarily translate into regional development, nor does it guarantee poverty alleviation for marginalised people" (2005, 279). Instead, Torres and Momsen argue that Cancun's tourism industry has only continued to produce uneven development that reinforces existing systems of social stratification while also producing new social, political, and economic hierarchies.

Concluding thoughts

In tracing the activities during and after the "beach clean-up" of *vendedores ambulantes* on Isla Mujeres in the spring and summer of 2014, this chapter illustrates the intersection of performance and performativity in the deployment of the racialized *chiapaneco* subject in discourse across different groups, including local isleños, tourist communities, and the municipal government and police force, each with different conceptions of the island's future. The

---

5   Jimenez y West, Ilda. Good Hosts as Ideal Citizens: Crafting Identity on Isla Mujeres Jimenez y West, 18

discourse was situated within the staging of a premier tourism economy on the island, and framed the local administration's performative and abrupt removal of the vendors from the beaches as a form of public pedagogy. In this chapter, we describe the ways this event brought into question the economic security of a few hundred people who were directly affected during the time of the beach "clean ups." We argue that the "beach clean up" served as a performative move to shift the tourism landscape toward a cosmopolitan ideal at the expense of particular vulnerable communities, and ruptured both the front and back stage of Isla's tourism industry.

References

Alexander, B. (2005). *Performance Theories in Education: Power, pedagogy and the politics of identity*. Mahwah, NJ: Erlbaum.

Burke, K. (1969). *Rhetoric of Motives*. Berkeley: University of California Press.

Edensor, T. (2001). Performing tourism, staging tourism: (Re)producing tourist space and practice. *Tourist Studies. 1(1)*, 59–81.

Jimenez y West, I. (2008). *Good Hosts as Ideal Citizens: Crafting identity on Isla Mujeres*. VDM Verlag Dr. Mueller e.K.

Kirshenblatt-Gimblett, B. (2008). *Destination Culture*. Berkeley: University of California Press.

Langellier, K.M. (1999). Personal narrative, performance, performativity: Two or three things I know for sure. *Text and Performance Quarterly. 19*, 125–144.

Torres, R., & Momsen, J. (2005, July 15). Planned tourism development in Quintana Roo, Mexico: Engine for regional development or prescription for inequitable growth? *Current Issues in Tourism. 8(4)*, 279.

10 Elephants are coming

Safaris, community, and Botswana's hunting ban

Frances Julia Riemer, Kgosietsile Velempini, Tonic Maruatona

> The long drive from Gaborone, Botswana's capital, to Chobe National Park and the Okavango Delta is on two-lane tarred highways, bounded on either side by bush. North from Nata, elephants lounge on the side of the road, cross at will, or more often linger in the middle of the road mornings, afternoons, and evenings. When elephants linger, we wait at a safe distance. Sometimes for ten minutes, sometimes longer, depending on the size of the vehicle and one's comfort with elephants. Giraffes and ostriches loiter on the edges of the road, but it's the elephants that we need to watch. Elephants are big and temperamental.
>
> (fieldnotes, January 2016)

Botswana boasts the largest concentration of wildlife in southern Africa and the largest remaining elephant population in Africa. Tourism and big game animals go hand in hand; elephants have made Botswana a prime destination for both bucket list safaris and high-end sports hunting. Botswana's official tourism website offers photos of zebras entwined at the neck, safaris on the backs of elephants, and a hippo, mouth wide open as it rises up from a river. Ninety percent of all tourists to Botswana come "primarily for a wildlife based vacation" (Ministry of Commerce & Industry 2000). The Botswana government has set aside 17 percent of its land area for national parks and game reserves, and has designated an additional 22 percent as wildlife management areas, in which wildlife is the primary form of land use. Its eight national parks and game reserves[1] encompass a cumulative 18,992 square miles and span from wetlands, fossil lakebeds, savannah, riverine forests, and grasslands, to the Kalahari's largest sand basin in the world. The parks are home to Africa's Big Five: lions, leopards, buffalos, rhinos, and elephants, in addition to giraffes, brown hyenas, warthogs, wild dogs, cheetah, red lechwes, kudu, and springboks.

---

1   Central Kalahari Game Reserve, Chobe National Park, Linyanti Reserve, Makgadikgadi Pans National Park, Mashatu & Tuli Game Reserves, Nxai Pan National Park, Okavango Delta & Moremi Game Reserve, and Savuti Channel.

For many of us in the Global North, the idea of experiencing animals in the African wild is intoxicating. The all too rare connections to wildlife and natural environment are moments to which we return (emotionally and intellectually, if not physically) again and again. These imagined spaces (Anderson 1983) remind us of a pristine Garden of Eden, of what was and soon may be no longer. They have become items on our bucket lists, those powerful accumulations of our dreams, lying somewhere between hope and possibility.

An African safari is often at the top of the bucket list, and Botswana is a prime destination. But the reality is that a safari, hunting or photographic, has long been part of global movement, born of colonial aspirations and assumptions of supremacy, sustained by constructed narratives and media accounts, and shaped by state ideologies and geopolitics. In this chapter, we draw on Arjun Appadurai's (1990) dimensions of global flow, in particular, *ethnoscapes, financescapes, mediascapes,* and *ideoscapes,* to tell the story of safari in Botswana. We are anthropologists, ethnographers, critical theorists, and educators who have followed Botswana's community-hosted safari tourism initiatives over the past 20 years. Based on primary and secondary data sources and employing ethnographic data and media and policy analyses, we trace safari from colonial enterprise and bucket list imaginary to community asset and human–wildlife conflict. We argue that safari rose from colonial images of taming the wild and continues to be shaped by neocolonial models of Western wildlife management (Adams & Mulligan 2002).

First a warning: Hold on to your pith helmets. This is Botswana. Elephants are coming your way.

The bucket list safari

Safari has always been a financescape (Appadurai 1990), a movement of capital across global landscapes. From the 11th century onwards, large caravans of Arab and African traders on camels crisscrossed the African continent carrying ceramics, silk, and beads from Europe and Asia, silk and ceramics from India and China, ivory, gold, and nuts from West Africa, and wood and slaves to Arabia. Safari, from the Arabic *safar* or "to journey," and then *safariya,* the noun for a voyage or expedition, originally connoted travel along trade routes.

Our current image of safari has been traced back to William Cornwallis Harris' two-year expedition and hunting trip from Grahamstown to Kuruman, in what is now South Africa. Harris, an English military engineer, artist, and hunter, wrote of what he described as a hunting safari in his *Narrative of an Expedition into Southern Africa during the Years 1836 and 1837.* Harris (1840) sketched, observed, and killed animals, and along the way "discovered" and introduced the sable antelope to the world.

The British had colonized east and southern Africa, and enthusiasm for European control over and exploitation of the colonies was fostered through these kinds of travelogues. Safari was part of the colonial mediascape, an "image-centered, narrative based account of strips of reality ... a series of elements ... out of which scripts can be formed of imagined lives, their own as well as those of others living in the place" (Appadurai 1990, 299). Coinciding with the popularity of print journalism, exploration narratives allowed the public to accompany explorers and share their adventures in which white subjugated black, and man subdued animal. David Henry Livingston's 1857 *Missionary Travels and Researches in South Africa* was one of the most popular books of the time. The book, based on Livingston's field diaries, was both science and a narrative packaged for public consumption by Livingston's publisher, John Murray (Henderson 2009). *Missionary Travels* made Livingston a national hero in the UK and made the image of the African explorer, clad in pith helmet and safari jacket, iconic. In the US, we had Teddy Roosevelt's (1910) photographs of himself as great white hunter on his 1909 safari, a year-long trek that included 250 porters and guides traveling from Mombasa in East Africa west into the Belgium Congo before heading north to the Nile and ending in Khartoum (see Figure 10.1).

These real-life African adventure narratives were coupled by an emerging literary genre of safari exploits that included Jules Verne's 1863 *Five Weeks in a Balloon* and H. Rider Haggard's 1885 *King Solomon's Mines*. Edgar Rice Burroughs gave us Tarzan in his 1912 *Tarzan of the Apes* and 23 sequels, and the 1930s brought the Johnny Weissmüller version, complete with loin cloth and pith-helmeted colonials to the screen. Inspired by Teddy Roosevelt's exploits, Ernest Hemingway's safaris in Kenya and Tanzania resulted in big game trophies, the novel *Green Hills of Africa* and the short stories "The Snows of Kilimanjaro" and "The Short Happy Life of Francis Macomber." Exploring the great white hunter in popular culture, Hemingway used the image to write at the intersections of colonialism, masculinity, and bravery. For Hemingway, there was always conflict at the intersection, conflicts within oneself, conflict with the wild, conflict with women.

For Isak Denisen, the nom de plume of the Danish author Karen von Blixen-Finecke, there was conflict, but there was also romance, romance that touched women, as much as the lure of big game may appeal to men. The 1985 film version of *Out of Africa*, based on the von Blixen-Finecke's memoir, sealed the deal in terms of images of safari. Clad in what costume designer Deborah Nadoolman Landis described as "romantic linen and khaki costumes" (Junker 2011), Meryl Streep and Robert Redford played Karen von Blixen and Denys Finch Hatton in the film. They fell in love, listened to Mozart on safari, and had high tea on the Serengeti Plains. The colonial safari was reflected in First Lady Melania Trump's first solo trip abroad, when she donned desert tones, a safari jacket, and a pith helmet to conduct her official duties in Kenya (Friedman 2018).

Figure 10.1 Theodore Roosevelt, three-quarter-length portrait, standing next to dead
 elephant, holding gun, probably in Africa. Edward van Altena photo-
 grapher, ca 1909–1919. Library of Congress Prints

The safari has provided an "imaginary" (Strauss 2006) for colonial
engagement with and control over Africa, the land, the animals, and the
peoples. It has been the map for missionary and colonial explorations, mental
and physical control over the wild (animals, land, people), and a gauge of
what a big man is worth. Safari is also part of the ideoscape of North–South
colonial and neocolonial interactions. It is a construction, a simulacrum that
has been created in the press, in fiction, and in film to romanticize the cruelty
of colonial power. According to his press people (Brown 1990), Ralph Lauren
launched his image of the safari woman in 1990 without ever actually visiting
Africa. A designer line complete with furniture, clothes, and signature per-
fume, Lauren argued that the collection was "a fantasy of what colonial life
might have been like, as interpreted by modern times." He added, "I don't
think my designs are idyllic. They are what people want to see." *The New
York Times* film reviewer Vincent Canby (1985), in his review of *Out of
Africa*, captured a not completely dissimilar sentiment. The Africa of Karen
Blixen, Canby wrote, "exists only as she perceives it—an exotic landscape
designed to test her soul." Yet "a fantasy of what colonial life might have
been like" intentionally cloaks the reality of colonial power.

As critics of Ms Trump's fashion choices might agree, romance in khaki
safari-wear obscures the economic effects of colonial domination and dis-
tracts from a history of dramatic income inequities. Colonial exploitation is

washed clean in neatly pressed linen and other safari imaginaries that glorify exploration and domestication.

Managing safaris and other natural resources

African safari tourism continues to produce significant dollars for host countries. Tourism in Botswana accounts for 12 percent of the country's Gross Domestic Product (GDP) and is the country's second largest economic sector. In Kenya, tourism is 11.9 percent of the country's GDP, in Tanzania, 12.4 percent, and Zimbabwe, 10.2 percent, percentages that translate to jobs and incomes. This cross-border movement of tourism dollars catalyzes questions about benefits from that revenue, and has pitted national governments against local communities, the old against the young, dominant against subordinate tribes, and nationals against expatriates.

In contemporary Africa, the wild has been configured back stage by a new ideoscape. Framed as an attempt to address these concerns, safari has become part of a neocolonial conversation around wildlife management and community development. Since the early 1970s, Community-Based Natural Resource Management (CBNRM) has been the buzzword when international funding agencies, and governmental and non-governmental organizations talked about tourism, natural resource management, and economic development. CBNRM has been described as a "paradigm shift in conservation and natural resource management" (Shackleton et al. 2002, 1). Instead of the government as caretaker of and funder for its country's natural resources (i.e. veld products, wildlife), local community members become both the direct stewards and beneficiaries of those resources.

CBNRM is a global proposition, often conceived and generally designed by expatriates, "exogenous to local communities, promoting the agenda of external actors" (Musavengane & Simatele 2016) and funded by external donor agencies. A development mechanism pushed by the Global North, the global players are on board for this devolution of state management policies: WWF (World Wildlife Foundation), UNDESA (United Nations Department of Economic and Social Affairs), IFAD (International Fund for Agricultural Development), UNDP (United Nations Development Program), at times through GEF (Global Environment Facility), the World Bank's IDA (International Development Association), and USAID (United States Agency for International Development). The World Bank offers case studies of CBNRM projects that cross 75 countries around the world. The popularity stems from all that CBNRM promises: poverty reduction, natural resource conservation, and good governance (Blaikie 2006; Breen 2013; Brosius, Tsing, & Zerner 1998, 2005; Child & Wojcik 2014; Western & Wright 1994). Linking social justice, environmental management, and community, CBNRM circulated (Kellert et al. 2000; Twyman 2000) to every country in southern Africa— Mozambique, Malawi, Zambia, Zimbabwe, Botswana, South Africa, Lesotho, Namibia, as well as Kenya, and Tanzania, in east Africa.

The US government embraced community-based natural resource management as part of a regional strategy in southern Africa.[2] Starting in 1989 and for the next ten years, the United States Aid for International Development (USAID) nurtured Botswana's pilot program by funding the National Resource Management Program (NRMP) housed in Botswana's Ministry of Wildlife Environment and Tourism. NRMP hired expatriate Natural Resource Management Advisors, all with degrees in forestry, mostly from the US. Their efforts paid off, in terms of numbers anyway. The advisors worked with international partner organizations and convinced more than 150 communities nested around Botswana's controlled hunting areas, buffer zones outside conservation areas, to register CBNRM projects.

With the backing of American non-profit Conservation International, Ian Khama, the country's former president and an active supporter of these conservation efforts, hosted the first Summit for Sustainability in Africa as a time for "all stakeholders to come together and find a balance between what is economically feasible, socially desirable and environmentally sustainable" (Piet 2012). In his 2012 State of the Nation address, Khama announced "the shooting of wild game purely for sport and trophies is no longer compatible with our commitment to preserve local fauna as a national treasure, which should be treated as such" (Michler 2012). Two years later, then president and a self-proclaimed conservationist, Ian Khama, banned all hunting in Botswana. The only country in the region to then ban hunting, Botswana was described as being on "the cutting edge of conservation in southern Africa" (Barbee 2015).

Widely accepted as a universal goal, environmental conservation is a powerful set of concepts, a related ideoscape that has circulated from north to south for more than a century. Environmental conservation is a meta-narrative about our relationship to the flora and fauna, validated and disseminated by multinational NGOs, including Greenpeace, Conservation International, and the World Wildlife Fund. A mediascape of social media images background Ian Khama's imposition of Botswana's hunting ban: photos of white hunters, the Trump sons included, standing proudly next to their dead prey (Hauser 2018; Lartey 2017), followed by newsfeed of the tracking of Cecil the Lion in Zimbabwe's Hwange Park by American recreational big game hunter, Walter Palmer (Clemons 2017; Loveridge 2018). The killing resulted in international media attention, caused outrage among animal conservationists, criticism by politicians and celebrities, and

---

2   From 1989 to 2005 the US, through USAID (nd), also funded CBNRM programs in Zimbabwe, Namibia, and Zambia. In Zimbabwe the programme was called CAMPFIRE (Communal Areas Management Programme for Indigenous Resources); in Namibia, LIFE (Living in a Finite Environment); in Zambia, a less compelling acronym, ADMADE (Administrative Management for Game Management Area); and in Botswana, NRMP (Natural Resources Management Programme).

a strong negative response against Palmer. Five months after the killing of Cecil, the US Fish and Wildlife Service added lions in India and western and central Africa to the endangered species' list, which includes Cecil's subspecies, making it more difficult for United States citizens to legally kill these lions.

In addition to globally circulated social media images, Khama's decision was catalyzed by dire estimates of wildlife decimation provided by Elephants without Borders' (2010) fixed-wing aerial survey of northern Botswana (Smith 2011). We see again here the global flow of ideas, images, and money around safari tourism policy. The survey was part of the Great Elephant Census, a pan-Africa survey of savannah elephants funded by Microsoft co-founder Paul Allen. With the hunting ban, as a "Distinguished Fellow" of Conservation International (McCloskey 2018), and spurred by Elephants without Borders, Khama, the self-declared founder of Botswana's Anti-Poaching Unit, also situated himself as a leader in international efforts to protect elephants.

Botswana's hunting ban in Controlled Hunting Areas (CHAs) was gradual in coming, one big step after several smaller ones. The hunting of lions was banned in 2002, reopened in 2005, and closed again in 2007, and all trophy hunting in the country's Okavango Delta was seriously curtailed in 2009. According to the country's Minister of Environment, Wildlife, and Tourism, the ban on hunting was "necessitated by available information which indicates that several species in the country are showing declines" (Fitt 2013). As a side note, high-end trophy hunting at registered game ranches, that is, private fenced game ranches, was exempted from the ban.

We share three cases to illustrate the flow of ideas about, funding for, and images of safari tourism, community, and Botswana's back stage wildlife management. The Chobe Enclave Community Trust stretches across multiple villages, Sankuyo Tshwaragano Management Trust is focused in a single village, and the third, Cgaecgae Trust, is hosted by indigenous communities in the northern Kalahari. All three communities were allocated a hunting area and wildlife quotas. It's important to note that while at some point the three communities benefitted financially by the grand idea of community-based natural resource management, all struggled with the challenges of shared governance, stakeholder power, and accountability (Centre for Applied Research 2016; Dikobe 2012; Mbaiwa 2004; Twyman 2000). All three were negatively affected by the 2014 ban on trophy hunting in Controlled Hunting Areas (CHAs). And all three have been enacted in the wave of globally circulating, externally imposed ideoscapes, financescapes, and mediascapes of safari.

Four elephants to one person: Chobe Enclave Community Trust (CECT)

Bounded by Chobe National Park on one side and flood plains that extend out flat to the Chobe River on the other, the area is verdant, and I'm struck again that this is "prime real estate." The Chobe District's five villages—Mabele, Kavimba, Kachikau, Satau and Parakarungu—rise out of bush, and spread out in wards organized around extended families. Not all that long ago, everybody lived in traditional Basubiya[3] huts of reed and thatching. Now the gleam of tin roofs dot the landscape. People raise cattle, grow watermelon, cassava, and corn. Gabo and her friends, sitting just outside the village-run shop in Mabele, tell me people are unhappy. "There are so many elephants. They are destroying our crops." With a population estimated at 10,000 people and 40,000 elephants (Elephants without *Borders 2010*), a four to one ratio has translated to both an economic boom and a real nuisance.

(fieldnotes, January 2016)

When in 1989 the Botswana government decided to try a pilot tourism project, it set its sights on Chobe and this prime real estate. The process was what local expert O.T. Thakadu (2005) called a "planner-centered approach." The government funded a workshop on community management of natural resources, with Kalahari Conservation Society, the big NGO in Botswana, as host. People came; they formed the Chobe Enclave Conservation Trust (CECT), wrote and registered a constitution, and organized themselves into ten-member Village Trust Committees (VTC), with two members of each

Figure 10.2 Elephants on the A3 Nata/Kasane Road, the main route to Chobe National Park

3   The Basubiya are one of the major non-Setswana speaking groups in Botswana.

VTC sitting on CECT's ten-member Executive Board. The initial effort cost the US Government $165,000, which paid for a Community Development Advisor (CDA), who coordinated project activities and trained a CECT-funded local Programme Officer (PO) to take over when he left. It also built offices in Kavimba, bought office furniture, constructed a house, and purchased a vehicle and motorbike for the CDA, offered bookkeeping skills training for youth, and organized and facilitated capacity-building workshops for committee members. After two and a half years of work, CECT received a wildlife quota and a resource use lease for wildlife and tourism.

The next year, the Executive Board decided to tender its wildlife quota to Rann Safaris, which, according to its website, was "the longest operating hunting outfitters in Botswana specializing in dangerous game" (Rann Safaris n.d.). Rann charged its tourists $59,500 for a ten-day elephant safari.[4] According to Rann's website, the fee included daily rates and concession fees, license fees and trophy fees, elephant skin shipping supplement, government surcharges, fees, and taxes. The tendering process was increasingly profitable for CECT. Each of the five villages earned the equivalent of US$23,000 annually, adding up to a total of about US$116,000 a year, or nearly US$1.3 million during the decade after CECT's founding (Bond et al. 2006).

Money was coming to the villages. After paying overhead costs and setting aside funds for administrative use, CECT divided the remaining funds equally across the five villages. Villagers rank ordered village projects in Participatory Rural Appraisal (PRA) workshops. The Village Trust Committee in Mabele opened a shop run by the community, which also offered secretarial services. Satau financed a vending machine for Botswana Power Corporation (BPC) unit cards. Parakarungu constructed a grinding mill. Kavimba built a campsite. The campsite, however, quickly fell into disrepair, and by 2007 had disappeared completely from the tourist radar.

In 2011, the trust partnered with a private company, Ngoma Management Project, to open Ngoma Safari Lodge just outside Chobe National Park. The trust's US$200,000 investment produced employment for 42 of its members at the lodge. According to Africa Albida Tourism (2018),

> This boutique lodge, an oasis in a wildlife wonderland, offers unrivalled panoramic views over the game-rich floodplain and Chobe River. It is on the doorstep of Chobe National Park, also known as the "Land of the Giants," as it is home to the largest population of elephants on Earth.

All this comes at a substantial per person price at High Season (June to October) of $1219 a night for a single, $975 sharing a double (decreasing to $565 in December to March or Green Season) and includes accommodation, full board, all house beverages, up to four activities per day, road transfers

---

4   Prices and other relevant finances are cited in either US dollars or Botswana pula as per the original source.

from the Kasane border or Kasane Airport, park fees, and community fees. This was good news for the trust. In addition to the creation of jobs for community members, CECT received annual net income from lodge operations that increased from US$1641 in year one to US$56,526 in year five.

CECT has been the shining star of Botswana's CBNRM efforts (Arntzen 2006). The most profitable initiative to date, it has had the advantage of its maturity and location. CECT hasn't paid cash dividends; the benefits have been the community projects and around 40 jobs (Johnson 2009). There have been challenges: management of the trust tended to be top heavy and lacked transparency. Only a small percentage of community members were involved, and those that were involved sorely lacked the skills needed to run what is basically a community bank.

But the 2014 hunting ban upended the balance of generating income while protecting wild animals. As Gabo and her friends at the trust's shop complained, "People are unhappy. There are so many elephants. They are destroying our crops." Kamwi Masule, the CECT manager, explained. "There are so many elephants, so many animals." The trust hadn't started photographic tours yet, the proffered alternative to safari hunting. Masule explained:

> Since 2014, we've had trouble with the management plan. It was to be completed by a government contracted consulting company. The funding was dropped, and then the government contracted with another consulting company without telling us. Now we've heard that contract isn't going through. We want to go outside the Department of Wildlife, and find a funder for the management plan ourselves.

Trust members were increasingly frustrated. People were starting to plow their fields, and everyone was afraid. They corralled their animals, Masule added, "because wild animals, elephants, hyena, come and destroy the fields. It's not that people want hunting, but there are too many animals. Hunting is part of management."

The community in the driver's seat: Sankuyo Tshwaragano Management Trust (STMT)

> Sankuyo is on the eastern edge of the Okavango Delta. The land is sandy, dotted with thorny acacia trees, and most houses are constructed of reeds and thatch. Sankuyo's 700 or so residents are riverine people. As long as people remember, they traveled Delta waterways in dug out canoes called mokoros, fishing with nets and traps. They work as tour guides and despite marauding elephants, attempt to dryland farm, planting melons and sorghum. Those who can afford to keep goats. The women weave baskets, men carve, and they sell their crafts in tourist shops in Maun. Several men and women tell us they would be grateful for a few heads of cattle. But the area is just north of the Southern Buffalo fence, on the wildlife side of the cordon where cows are not allowed.
>
> (fieldnotes, January 2016)

Located on the eastern edge of the Okavango Delta, Sankuyo was the second community in Botswana to implement community-based management of the area's wildlife resources. The homesteads that make up the village of Sankuyo are on the southern tip of Botswana's Moremi Game Reserve and just west of Chobe National Park. It's equally prime real estate: Moremi is home to 30 percent of the world's wild dog population, in addition to white and black rhino, elephant, buffalo, leopard, lion, cheetah, giraffe, and hippo.

The backstory of Sankuyo's Tshwaragano Management Trust is not very different from CECT's. Jumpstarted by the USAID's National Resource Management Program (NRMP) and Botswana's Department of Wildlife and National Parks (DWNP) with the same playbook, community members, then a meager 382 residents, wrote a constitution and registered as a trust in 1995. The following year, the trust received a 15-year lease for the Controlled Hunting Area in which Sankuyo is located (Mearns 2004). In 1996, the trust tendered a portion of its wildlife quota to Game Safaris, which paid the community the equivalent of US$600,000 over the following two years. Once money starting coming in, community members engaged in strategic planning, which resulted in vegetable gardens, grass and reed harvesting, and two tourist facilities—a camp ground and cultural village—which brought in additional income.

Figure 10.3 Sankuyo Tshwaragano Management Trust's Maun office

Described as eco-friendly on websites (i.e. Agoda, SafariNow, madbookings), Kaziikini Community campsite offered ten campsites and four twin-bed rondoval huts with beds, along with a central ablution block, complete with solar-powered flush toilets and warm water, a curio shop, the Hippo Hideout Bar, and Mogogelo Restaurant. A grant from the Japanese government funded two tents with en suite bathrooms and viewing decks. The campsite was ranked 15 out of 17 specialty lodgings on TripAdvisor, and described as "rustic camping," "basic but clean," and "reasonably priced" at about US$20 a night per person for camping, $50 for a rondoval. Shandereka Village, just opposite the campground, organized nature walks, traditional dances, and demonstrations about traditional healing, basket weaving, wood carving, and grain storage. The cultural village and campsite together employed over 400 people (Khayae 2012).

In 2001, the trust was awarded the concession for the adjacent Controlled Hunting Area along with a neglected lodge run by a commercial safari company. Banking on its experience running a campsite and cultural village, the trust decided to add a safari lodge to its holdings with a grant from USAID funneled through African Wildlife Foundation, an NGO that, according to its website works with local people to "ensure the wildlife and wildlands of Africa will endure forever" (African Wildlife Foundation 2018). The trust's members renovated Santawani Lodge, restoring six chalets and the reception area. Twenty community members were trained to manage the lodge. It was an even split, with the trust due to receive 50 percent of the operating profits. However, the lodge was difficult to run, and the trust partnered with a seasoned resort owner, Peter Sandenbergh and his Lodges of Botswana, to reopen in 2009 as Sankuyo Plains Camp. Praised as an unusual example of a successful trust-run tourism enterprise (Johnson 2009), Princes William and Harry of the UK stayed there as part of their support for Tusk International.

Despite ongoing challenges posed by running the tented lodge, the trust has been a financial success. It generated two million Botswana pula (BWP), or more than US$300,000 in the decade from 1997 to 2007. Unlike CECT, Sankuyo was always a community-driven model; it's just one relatively small village, and the trust's constitution identifies the community as its decision-making body. The trust was described as "super active" (Johnson 2009) partly because of its very energetic meeting schedule. Trusts averaged about three or four meetings a year. Sankuyo Tshwaragano Management Trust met 60 times, which was more than a meeting a week.

This strong base is reflected in the ways the trust has spent its funds. The village built a school and clinic, bought a maize grinder, and sunk a borehole. Over time the list grew to include household water connections, water system toilets, shelters for the poor, supplementary pension money for villagers over the age of 60, financial support for a football team, training support for young people, grants for funerals, and support for HIV/AIDS orphans. Tourism became the leading employer in the village; that experience was important both financially and psychologically. As a 26-year-old woman in

Sankuyo explained, "I did not work before CBNRM. I did not know what it means to work by then; now I know. I can find a job in other tourism enterprises in the Okavango Delta" (Mbaiwa & Stronza 2010, 645).

But with the hunting ban, the possibility of tendering their animal rights vanished, vital earnings evaporated, community finances once again became precariously low, and the links between villagers and conservation frayed. "That's what made people appreciate conservation," explained Gokgathang Timex Moalosi, Sankuyo's chief. "We told them, that lion or elephant has paid for your toilet or your standpipe" (Onishi 2015, A6). When those financial arrangements were upended by the ban on hunting, Sankuyo Tshwaragano Management Trust's income dropped from 3.5 million to 1.8 million pula, and 35 jobs were lost (Morula 2018).

Suddenly, wild animals were no longer an economic opportunity. Instead, in Sankuyo, lions prowled at night looking for errant goats and donkeys. Elephants invaded livestock's water supply during the dry season. "We are living in fear since lions and leopards now come into our village," the chief complained. "Elephants cross the village to go to the other side of the bush. The dogs bark at them. We just run into our houses and hide" (Onishi 2015, A6).

A story of indigenous peoples: Cgaecgae Tlhabolo Trust, Xai Xai

> The Kalahari Desert is sandy—reddish brown; sand dunes alternate with dry pans. Xai Xai is in far northwest Botswana at the end of a very long 200 km. dirt track after the A3 turn off from the tarred Maun/Ghanzi Road. It is a dry place, a scattering of reed huts just ten km. east of the Namibian border. Any rain quickly soaks through the sand so surface water is nearly non-existent. But there are animals. We see giraffes, zebras, elephants, buffalo, tsessebe, impala, and many ostrich, and men offer us antelope pelts for purchase. At night big cats and other predators—lions, cheetahs, leopards, wild hunting dogs, and foxes—roam at the edge of the settlement.
>
> (fieldnotes, October 2012)

In 1996, Xai Xai was a settlement of 500 residents made up of two ethnic groups. Seventy percent of the people were Ju/'hoansi,[5] one of the indigenous San groups living in remote western Botswana. The other 30 percent are Babandero-Mabandero, an ethnic group closely tied to the Ovaherero, cattle people, whose grandparents came to Botswana in the early 1900s to escape the violence of German colonization in neighboring Namibia. Relations between the two groups had never been easy. Both the Ju/'hoansi and the Ovaherero are minority ethnic groups in Botswana. But in the ranking of minorities, the indigenous people are at the bottom of the list, and the Babandero-Mabandero were

---

5   Ju/'hoansi is a term referring to the San from the area around Xai Xai in Botswana and across the border in Namibia. Ju/'hoansi (singular: Ju/'hoan) is how the people usually refer to themselves, and is most commonly translated as "the real people."

successful in gaining political dominance in the area. The Ju/'hoansi, like other San groups throughout the country, are poor, without cattle of their own.[6]

Xai Xai is famous in anthropologists' circles. In the 1950s, its Ju/'hoansi residents and their daily practices were extensively documented over 12 years in photographs and texts by Laurence, Lorna, and their children Elizabeth and John Marshall. In the 1960s and 1970s, they were the focus of the Harvard Kalahari Research Group's multidisciplinary teams of researchers and their graduate students, who collected data on their hunting and gathering economy and organized the Kalahari Peoples Fund anthropological advocacy group (Biesele 2003; Lee 2012).

The Netherlands Development Programme (SNV) came to Xai Xai in 1994 to pursue its focus on sustainable tourism and natural resource management. With the guidance of an SNV expatriate Natural Resources Management Advisor (NRMA), the community organized !Kokoro Crafts, a cooperative that by the end of 1996 had 80 members (Gujadhur 2000). Cooperative members surveyed the local crafts market and contracted with a shop in Maun, the tourist hub for the Okavango Delta, to sell their ostrich shell jewelry and traditional bows and arrows. Two community members were trained to manage the coop, which soon empowered crafts people and brought income into the community. The craft cooperative financed !Kokoro Semausu, a shop that sold basic food items. The businesses' success also helped convince community members that they could manage their wildlife resources and benefit from the country's new quota system. The shift from the special hunting licenses that were provided to members of Botswana's San communities to communal management of a wildlife quota had initially worried the settlement's Ju/'hoansi, who had the most to lose by giving up their licenses. However, SNV offered a model for its work with remote area dwellers throughout the country that felt fair to everyone. Quota management was organized around the settlement's 11 family groups or wards, with two representatives from each group, preferably one man and one woman, joining a village-wide quota management committee. The arrangement was representative of village demographics, and increased access for both Ju/'hoansi and Babandero-Mabandero. The Ju/'hoansi had some political clout. Their Babandero-Mabandero neighbors were equally pleased with the arrangement. They had been unable to obtain the special hunting licenses that the San received in the past, but quota management gave them access to the area's wildlife.

Individuals talked about coming together as a group across ethnic lines to write a constitution for Cgaecgae Tlhabolo Trust (CTT). "We are working well together," people proclaimed during one of our first visits to the area. In

6 When work is available at all, it involves herding their neighbors' cattle. They augment meager government rations by collecting wild fruits and vegetables and by hunting, either illegally or with a special hunting license issued only to the country's San inhabitants.

Figure 10.4 Ostriches on dirt track to Xai Xai

1997, the community decided to self-manage tourism (Gujadhur & Motshubi 2003; Zeppel 2006) and started offering photographic cultural safaris. Xai Xai Ju/'hoansi residents took small groups of tourists into the bush by vehicle or horses for a two- or three-day trip. The men explained how they tracked and snared animals. The women showed how they identified and gathered veld products. Evenings offered traditional dancing and storytelling. A manager was hired to oversee tourism activities, construction and !Kokoro Crafts. In 1999 CTT decided to sell 30 percent of its hunting quota from its Controlled Hunting Areas (CHAs) 4 and 5 to Safari Hunting Company and retain the remainder of the quota for subsistence hunting. The company also agreed to provide the settlement with meat from its hunts. The following year, the government increased the community's quota to six elephants and two lions plus four leopards (up from two the previous year) and the trust's profit also increased, from BWP 70,000 (US$8645) to BWP 380,000 (US$46,930) a year. The trust was working, and people were happy.

But the expatriate advisor departed in mid 2001, and without his oversight the community did not sustain the work of !Kokoro Crafts and the cooperative closed. Lured by the possibility of an increase in external funding, the board then decided to sell its entire quota of animals to Greg Butler Safaris, which advertised 12-day elephant safaris in Botswana at $60,000 per person, with a trophy fee refund of $10,000 if there was no shoot. Seven-day buffalo safaris were $30,000, with $4000 trophy fee refund if not shot.

This decision was not at all popular with the settlement's residents. Regardless of whether hunting and gathering were age-old activities for the Ju/'hoansi or the result of relatively recent dispossession of cattle (Alverson 1978), they regarded hunting as an integral part of their diet and their culture. The sale of the entire quota deprived the Ju/'hoansi of their hunting rights, weakened their faith in the trust, and dampened any sense of empowerment that had begun to stir. It was a decision made by the Executive Board rather than the community at large. And although the Ju/'hoansi residents had fair representation on the Board, they were not well versed in democratic decision-making, and were unable to advocate for their interests.

Things went downhill quickly (Garner 2012). !Kokoro Crafts closed. Unlike CECT or Sankuyo, Cgaecgae Trust was unable to develop either a tourist camp or lodge. Two visits to the area by Ian Khama, Botswana's then president and environmental advocate, one in 2010 and a second in 2012, give a good idea about the settlement's economics at that time. Botswana Television videotaped the president during a 2010 Christmas gift-giving visit to the settlement. "The resulting clips that showed the abject poverty afflicting people here motivated calls for members of the public to come together to address the basic need for shelter" (Office of the President 2012). As a follow-up gesture, in May 2012, Khama organized the donation of 25 one-roomed houses to residents of Xai Xai, who, according to the *Mmegi* newspaper reporter, "live in abject poverty despite the abundance of potential in community tourism in the area that can be harnessed though their Xaixai Tshwaragano Community Trust" (Keakabetse 2012). The donation was part of the president's Housing Appeal for the Needy, a project initiated after Khama's previous visit to Xai Xai and supported by "concerned entrepreneurs."

Cgaecgae Tlhabolo Trust continued to offer the cultural safaris, including bow-and-arrow hunting, gathering veld foods, traditional dancing, singing and storytelling, exploring nearby Gcwihaba (Drotsky's) Caves, and horseback riding. The caves are on the tentative list for UNESCO World Heritage sites; the area is both "ethnically and ecologically exotic" (Gujadhur & Motshubi 2006). Currently the trust has seven employees. The board has been elected and trained, but the trust is not generating any revenue (CBNRM Report 2017–2018).

Neocolonial models of Western wildlife management

A safari is the stuff of imagination—an imaginary—an item on travel bucket lists and in tourist longings. But safari is also an artifact of an ideoscape constructed of colonial relationships with colonized landscapes, Western-style conservation, pro-hunting camps, and animal rights activism. Safari, the colonial proposition, becomes safari, the community initiative, and then safari, the conservation effort. Safari is maintained by images promoted in media, social media, advertising, and messages disseminated through conferences, cartoons, films and books, and embedded in a financescape of global donors, government credit sheets, tourism operators, non-profit endeavors, and community initiatives.

It is not a stretch to describe safari tourism as a racially defined endeavor, constructed, conceived, organized, reorganized, and packaged both front and back stage by the Global North (Lindsey et al. 2006; Mbaiwa & Ogada 2017), to create dependence on export markets and foster foreign control of the tourist sector. While international agencies promoted participatory discourse around wildlife management to mitigate external influences, across sites local participation posed challenges (Cooke & Kothari 2001). And just when communities coalesced, organized, and received training, the government changed the rules without any warning to the trusts.

Elephant herds have grown in Botswana, but profits have disappeared (Motlhoka 2018). Members of the Chobe Enclave Community Trust (CECT) reported that the annual income of the trust dropped from BWP 6.5 million to BWP 3.5 million in 2014, and 15 jobs including game trekkers, escort guides, and skinners have disappeared (Mbaiwa 2018). The Sankuyo trust had close to BWP 150,000 in 2012, and in 2015 after the hunting ban, the amount accrued was far less than BWP 50,000. Reporting from the field, Onishi (2015, A6) wrote,

> Galeyo Kobamelo, 37, said he had lost all 30 goats in the kraal just outside his family compound to lions and hyenas since the hunting ban. Elephants had destroyed his fields of sorghum and maize. With the hunting ban, his family no longer receives the free meat that hunters left behind. His mother, Gomolemo Semalomba, 58, no longer receives a pension, about $100 twice a year. Now we don't eat meat anymore, she said, pointing to a table with plates of cabbage, beans and maize meal.

The central government and local officials offered photographic safaris as the next big income-generating activity. But even in the best of times, safari hunting by communities generated almost two-thirds of the tourism revenue, with only a third of community revenue coming from photographic tourism (Johnson 2009; Mbaiwa 2018). And according to Joseph Mbaiwa, the Okavango Research Institute's acting director, "Photographic tourism is not that viable in those peripheral areas" (Onishi 2015, A6).

Urged by local community members and their Members of Parliament (MPs) concerned about the increase in danger to humans and property and the decrease in trust income, lawmakers requested a review of the legislation (Cornish 2018; Mguni 2018). Worried about the political fidelity of rural voters, in June 2018, Botswana's parliament decided to review the ban, and Botswana's current president, Mokgweetsi Masisi, scheduled a series of meetings with researchers and village groups. He met privately with Prince William, Duke of Cambridge, to discuss hunting as conservation during an October 2018 conference on illegal trafficking in wildlife (Webster 2018).

Their meeting was held not long after Elephants without Borders reported that an aerial survey found 87 elephant carcasses with tusks removed in northern Botswana. The charity pointed to poaching, although government officials claimed the killings were grossly exaggerated, and that the report was generated to influence the ongoing debate over the hunting ban. Instead of 87, the country's wildlife officials reported 19 dead elephants, six killed by poachers, with the remainder dying "of natural causes or in conflicts with villagers" (de Greef 2018). In response, Global March for Elephants and Rhinos (2019) has collected over 15,000 signatures on a petition that supports Botswana's hunting ban and the rearming of anti-poaching units to Botswana's vice president and the MP from Maun East under the hashtag #SaveOurWildWorld.

A report on the hunting ban, developed by a president-appointed subcommittee and released in February 2019, advocated "regular but limited elephant culling." The response from the international conservation community, who called the lifting of the hunting ban a potential "blood bath," was immediate (Hayes 2019). Nonetheless, in late May 2019, the Government of Botswana announced it was lifting the ban on hunting after the five-year prohibition. Celebrities in the US have already called for a boycott of Botswana until the ban is reissued (de Greef & Specia 2019). Conservation for increased animal population is positioned against hunting as wildlife management, and international animal rights activists and non-profit organizations continue to duke it out with expatriate pro-hunting groups, tourism operators, and local communities for control of Botswana's safari ideoscape, financescape, and mediascape.

References

Adams, W., & Mulligan, M. (2002). *Decolonizing Nature: Strategies for conservation in a post-colonial era.* New York: Routledge.

Africa Albida Tourism (2018). Ngoma Safari Lodge. Retrieved November 21, 2018 from http://www.africaalbidatourism.com/where-to-stay/ngoma-safari-lodges/.

African Wildlife Foundation (2018). Website. Retrieved November 21, 2018 from https://www.awf.org/.

Alverson, H. (1978). *Mind in the Heart of Darkness: Value and self-identity among the Tswana of southern Africa.* New Haven, CT: Yale University Press.

Anderson, B. (1983). *Imagined Communities: Reflections on the origin and spread of nationalism.* London: Verso.

Appadurai, A. (1990). Disjuncture and difference in the global cultural economy. *Theory, Culture & Society.* 7, 295–310.

Arntzen, J. (2006, January). Case study of the CBNRM programme in Botswana. IUCN-South Africa office, USAID Frame project. Gaborone, Botswana: Centre for Applied Research.

Barbee, J. (2015, March 21). Botswana seems to show the way ahead in conservation—but poaching is still on the rise. *The Observer Botswana*. Retrieved September 2017 from https://www.theguardian.com/world/2015/mar/21/botswana-game-hunting-ban.

Biesele, M. (2003). The Kalahari Peoples Fund: Activist legacy of the Harvard Kalahari Research Group. *Anthropologica*. 45(1), 79–88.

Blaikie, P. (2006). Is small really beautiful? Community-based Natural Resource Management in Malawi and Botswana. *World Development*. 34(11), 1942–1957.

Bond, I., Davis, A., Nott, C., Nott, K., & Stuart-Hill, G. (2006). *Community Based Natural Resource Manual*. Wildlife Management Series. Nairobi, Kenya: World Wildlife Federation.

Breen, C. (2013, June 5). *Community-Based Natural Resource Management in Southern Africa: An introduction*. Gainesville, FL: Center for African Studies at the University of Florida.

Brosius, J.P., Tsing, A.L., & Zerner, C. (1998). Representing communities: Histories and politics of community-based natural resource management. *Society & Natural Resources: An International Journal*. 11(2), 157–168.

Brosius, J.P., Tsing, A.L., & Zerner, C. (2005). *Communities and Conservation; Histories and politics of community-based natural resource management*. Lanham, MD: AltaMira Press.

Brown, P.L. (1990, March 25). Way out of Africa when Ralph Lauren envisioned the "safari woman." *The New York Times* News Service. Retrieved April 18, 2013from http://articles.sun-sentinel.com/1990-03-25/features/9001310377_1_ralph-lauren-safari-retail-sales.

Canby, V. (1985, December 18). "Out of Africa," starring Meryl Streep. *The New York Times*. Retrieved April 18, 2013 from http://www.nytimes.com/packages/html/movies/bestpictures/africa-re.html.

CBNRM report (2017–2018). Ngamiland district. Gaborone, Botswana: Government of Botswana.

Centre for Applied Research (2016). 2016 Review of Community-Based Natural Resource Management in Botswana. Report prepared for Southern African Environmental Programme (SAREP).

Child, B., & Wojcik, D. (2014). *Developing Capacity for Community Governance of Natural Resources Theory: Theory & practice*. Bloomington, IN: AuthorHouse.

Clemons, M. S. (2017). Cecil the Lion: The everlasting impact of the conservation and protection of the King of the Jungle. *Villanova Environmental Law Journal*. 28(1), 51–69.

Cooke, B., & Kothari, U. (2001). *Participation: The new tyranny?*London: Zed Books.

Cornish, J. -J. (2018). Botswana reconsidering ban on elephant hunting. WN Eyewitness. Retrieved November 15, 2018 from https://ewn.co.za/2018/09/13/botswana-reconsidering-ban-on-elephant-hunting.

de Greef, K. (2018, September 28). Doubts mount over charity claim of "Elephant Frenzy." *The New York Times*. Retrieved November 15, 2018 from https://www.nytimes.com/2018/09/28/world/africa/botswana-elephants-poaching.html.

de Greef, K. & Specia, M. (2019, May 23). Botswana ends ban on elephant hunting. *The New York Times*, A12.

Dikobe, L., ed. (2012). *Natural Resources at the Centre of Rural Livelihoods: Looking beyond 50 years of Botswana's independence*. Proceedings of the 7th Biennial National CBNRM Conference: Botswana CBNRM National Forum, Gaborone.

Elephants without Borders (2010, March). People and elephants: Elephant conservation and community outreach farming project. Beyond borders: Research & Conservation with Elephants without Borders progress report. Kasane, Botswana: Elephants without Borders.

Fitt, N. (2013). Press release: Hunting ban in Botswana—Message from Permanent Secretary. BWgovernment@BotswanaGovernment. Retrieved November 15, 2018 from https://www.facebook.com/148228411926492/posts/press-release-hunting-ban-in-botswana-message-from-permanent-secretarythe-minist/500849569997706/.

Friedmann, V. (2018, October 8). Melania Trump: Out of Africa, still in costume. *The New York Times*. Retrieved November 1, 2018from https://www.nytimes.com/2018/10/08/fashion/melania-trump-africa-trip-fashion-fedora.html.

Garner, K. -A. (2012). CBNRM in Botswana: The failure of CBNRM for the indigenous San, the village of Xai Xai and the wildlife of Botswana. Unpublished thesis, Guelph, Ontario, Canada.

Global March for Elephants and Rhinos (2019). Botswana wildlife crisis? GMFER petitions government for answers. Change.org. Retrieved from https://www.change.org/p/botswana-wildlife-crisis-gmfer-petitions-government-for-answers.

Gujadhur, T. (2000). Organisations and the approaches in Community Based Natural Resources Management in Botswana, Namibia, Zambia, and Zimbabwe. CBNRM Support Programme Occasional Paper No. 1. Gaborone: IUCN Botswana/SNV Botswana.

Gujadhur, T., & Motshubi, C. (2006). Among the real people in /Xai-/Xai. In Rozemeijer, N. (ed.). *Community-Based Tourism in Botswana: The SNV experience in three community-tourism-projects*. SNV Report. Gaborone, Botswana: SNV.

Harris, W.C. (1840). *Narrative of an Expedition into Southern Africa during the years 1836 and 1837, from the Cape of Good Hope through the Territories of the Chief Moselekatse to the tropic of Capricorn*. London: Murray. (Originally published 1839, *Annals and Magazine of Natural History*, 4(25), 334–336.)

Hauser, C. (2018, July 14). Killing of African giraffe stirs anger at "white American savage," *The New York Times*, A9.

Hayes, K. (2019). Global outcry as Botswana considers lifting hunting ban. Daily Southern & Eastern Africa Tourism Update. Retrieved February 25, 2019 from http://www.tourismupdate.co.za/article/189513/Global-outcry-as-Botswana-considers-lifting-elephant-hunting-ban?utm_source=Now%20Media%20Newsletters&utm_medium=email&utm_campaign=TU%20Daily%20Mail%20-%20Monday&utm_term=http:%2F%2Fwww.tourismupdate.co.za%2F%2Farticle%2F189513%2FGlobal-outcry-as-Botswana-considers-lifting-elephant-hunting-ban.

Henderson, L. (2009). "Everyone will die laughing": John Murray and the publication of David Livingston's Missionary Travels. Livingston On Line. Retrieved April 22, 2013 from http://www.livingstoneonline.ucl.ac.uk/companion.php?id=HIST2.

Johnson, S. (2009, December). State of CBNRM Report 2009, Botswana National CBNRM Forum. Gaborone, Botswana: Kalahari Conservation Society.

Junker, L. (2011). Influenced: Out of Africa, safari clothing. Dressed Cinema. Retrieved June 14, 2017 from https://www.dressedcinema.com/blog/2011/01/influenced-out-of-africa-safari-clothing.

Keakabetse, B. (2012, May 11). Basarwa trusts under threat. *Mmegi Online*. 29(70). Retrieved January 26, 2013 from http://www.mmegi.bw/index.php?sid=1&aid=184&dir=2012/May/Friday11.

Kellert, S.R., Mehta, J.N., Ebbin, S.A., & Lichtenfeld, L.L. (2000). Community natural resource management: Promise, rhetoric, and reality. *Society and Natural Resources.* 12, 705–715.

Khayae, B. (2012). Three NGOS receive Japanese grants. *The Monitor.* 13(11). Retrieved January 22, 2013 from http://www.mmegi.bw/index.php?sid=1&aid=82&dir=2012/march/monday19.

Lartey, J. (2017, November 16). Trump sons' hunting in focus as US lifts import ban on elephant trophies. *The Guardian.* Retrieved June 6, 2018 from https://www.theguardian.com/us-news/2017/nov/16/trump-sons-us-lifts-import-ban-african-elephant-trophies.

Lee, R.B. (2012). *The Dobe Ju/'Hoansi.* Case Studies in Cultural Anthropology. Belmont, CA: Wadsworth Publishing. [Originally published Holt, Rinehart, and Winston, 1984].

Lindsey, P.A., Alexander, R., Frank, L.G., Mathieson, A., & Romanach, S.S. (2006). Potential of trophy hunting to create incentives for wildlife conservation in Africa where alternative wildlife based land use may not be viable. *Animal Conservation.* 9, 283–298.

Loveridge, A. (2018). *Lion Hearted: The life and death of Cecil & the future of Africa's iconic cats.* New York: Regan Arts.

Mbaiwa, J.E. (2004). The success and sustainability of Community Based Natural Resource Management in the Okavango Delta, Botswana. *South African Geographic Journal.* 86(1), 44–53.

Mbaiwa, J.E. (2018). Effects of the safari hunting tourism ban on rural livelihoods and wildlife conservation in northern Botswana. *South African Geographic Journal.* 100 (1), 41–61.

Mbaiwa, J.E., & Ogada, M. (2017). *The Big Conservation Lie.* Seattle, WA: Lens & Pen Publishing.

Mbaiwa, J.E., & Stronza, A.L. (2010). The effects of tourism development on rural livelihoods in the Okavango Delta. *Journal of Sustainable Tourism.* 18(5), 635–656.

McCloskey, J.P. (2018). Former President Ian Khama joins Conservation International as a Distinguished Fellow. Conservation International. Retrieved November 15, 2018 from https://www.conservation.org/NewsRoom/pressreleases/Pages/Former-Botswana-President-Ian-Khama-Joins-Conservation-International-as-a-Distinguished-Fellow.aspx.

Mearns, K. (2004). Community-based tourism: The key to empowering the Sankuyo community in Botswana. *Africa Insight.* 33, 29–32.

Mguni, M. (2018, September 11). Botswana starts national debate on elephant hunting ban. Bloomberg. Retrieved December 1, 2018 from https://www.bloomberg.com/news/articles/2018-09-11/botswana-starts-national-debate-to-end-ban-on-elephant-hunting.

Michler, I. (2012, November). Botswana to ban trophy hunting. Wildlife Extra. Retrieved November 30, 2012 from http://www.wildlifeextra.com/go/news/botswana-hunting.html#cr.

Ministry of Commerce & Industry (2000, May). Botswana National Tourism Plan: Final report, May 2000. Project No. 7 ACP. BT. 4/No. 6 ACP BT 44. Retrieved June 2018 from https://library.wur.nl/ojs/index.php/Botswana_documents/article/view/16030.

Morula, M. (2018, February 26). Hunting ban Stays: Economic aftermath continues. *The Sunday Standard.* Retrieved January 15, 2019 from https://www.sundaystandard.infohunting-bna-stays-economic-aftermath-continues.

Motlhoka, T. (2018, July 30). To kill or not to kill—Parliament to decide the fate of Botswana's elephants. *Independent.* Retrieved October 17, 2018 from https://www.independent.co.uk/voices/campaigns/GiantsClub/Botswana/to-kill-or-not-to-kill-pa rliament-to-decide-the-fate-of-botswanas-elephants-a8470551.html.

Musavengane, R., & Simatele, D.M. (2016). Community-based natural resource management: The role of social capital in collaborative environmental management of tribal resources in KwaZulu-Natal, South Africa. *Development Southern Africa.* 33 (6), 806–821.

Office of the President (2012, February 23). President at XaiXai. Inside the Presidency. Number 1. Retrieved January 24, 2013 from http://www.gov.bw/en/Ministrie s–Authorities/Ministries/State-President/Office-of-the-President/Tools–Services/Insi de-the-Presidency/Inside-the-Presidency-Issue-No-1-of-2012/.

Onishi, N. (2015, September 12). A hunting ban saps a village's livelihood. *The New York Times*, A6. Retrieved March 17, 2019 from https://www.nytimes.com/2015/09/ 13/world/a-hunting-ban-saps-a-villages-livelihood.html.

Piet, B. (2012, May 25). Khama urges prudent natural resource management. *Mmegi Online.* 29(77). Retrieved June 1, 2012 from http://www.mmegi.bw/index.php?sid= 1&aid=512&dir=2012/May/Friday25.

Rann Safaris (n.d.). Retrieved May 2015 from http://www.rannsafaris.com/index.html.

Roosevelt, T. (1910). *Wanderings of an American Hunter-Naturalist.* New York: Charles Scribner's Sons.

Shackleton, S., Campbell, B., Wollenberg, E., & Edmonds, D. (2002). Devolution and community-based natural resource management: Creating space for local people to participate and benefit. ODI Natural Resource Perspectives, no. 76. Program for Land and Agrarian Studies. London: Overseas Development Institute.

Smith, D. (2011,June 18). Drought and poachers take Botswana's natural wonder to brink of catastrophe. *The Guardian*, 31.

Strauss, C. (2006). The imaginary. *Anthropological Theory.* 6(3), 322–344.

Thakadu, O.T. (2005). Success factors in community based natural resources management in northern Botswana: Lessons from practice. *Natural Resources Forum.* 29, 199–212.

Twyman, C. (2000). Participatory conservation? Community-based natural resource management in Botswana. *The Geographical Journal.* 166(4), 323–335.

USAID (n.d.). Country-specific information USAID/Botswana activities. Retrieved January 17, 2013 from https://docs.google.com/viewer?a=v&q=cache:mC5yntQrc ZAJ:rmportal.net/library/content/frame/country-botswana.doc/at_download/file +hunting+quota+chobe&hl=en&gl=kh&pid=bl&srcid=ADGEESg_ ltbKqjR7wfxROPyRX78Oj6xRN4NcvPFE6ovRImz-Vahe09-u6atAm JXPRcCfD7mO5CTmXGsvHzB5gMFvjAK1W_wYa1xgwVoxkOvhSCFcuiFNVdg g2AtsP__IVn3t9iRBv6Kg&sig=AHIEtbQVIDqPkY2pzaOPJoxeUbWrLUrWBQ.

Webster, B. (2018, October 13). Duke of Cambridge backs trophy hunting in Botswana, says president. *The Times.* Retrieved November 15, 2018 from https://www.thetimes.co.uk/article/duke-of-cambridge-backs-trophy-hunting-in-botswana-says-p resident-926hl8d5l.

Western, D., & Wright, R.M. (1994). *Natural Connections: Perspectives in community-based conservation.* Washington, DC: Island Press.

Zeppel, H. (2006). *Indigenous Eco-Tourism: Sustainable development and management.* Wallingford, UK: CABI.

Contributors

Riddhi Bhandari focuses on local tourism markets in Agra, India to understand risks faced by entrepreneurs and strategies adopted by them to mitigate these. Recipient of the 2015–2016 Adam Smith Fellowship and the Institute of Humane Studies Fellowship, Bhandari interrogates how entrepreneurs mobilize their social networks and familiar relations to mitigate risks of getting clientele, unfavorable governmental regulations, and demands for bribes.

Jesse Dizard is a cultural anthropologist primarily interested in controlling processes. His research explores the impacts of prejudice and social inequality among ethnic minorities, particularly Native Americans, as well as children and women. He has conducted ethnographic fieldwork in West Africa, North Africa, Alaska, Asia, and Europe. He is currently the Chair of the Anthropology Department at California State University, Chico.

Maribeth Erb is an Associate Professor in the Department of Sociology, National University of Singapore and author of *The Manggaraians* (Times Editions, 1999) and the co-editor of *Regionalism in Post-Suharto Indonesia* (RoutledgeCurzon, 2005), *Biodiversity and Human Livelihoods in Protected Areas* (Cambridge, 2007) and *Deepening Democracy in Indonesia?: Direct Elections for Local Leaders* (ISEAS, 2009).

Brandon Melecio Fischer is a social anthropologist whose work centers on alternatives to socioeconomic development with a focus on gender, indigeneity, and different ways of configuring the modern within development practice. He holds an MA in Anthropology from the New School for Social Research and an MA in International Affairs with a concentration in Economic Development from the Milano School of International Affairs, Management, and Urban Policy at the New School. Currently, he works to support international cooperation by coordinating institutional strengthening within the civil society sector in Mexico.

Sharon J. Hepburn is Associate Professor in Cultural Anthropology at Trent University, Canada. She has been conducting research on aspects of tourism in Nepal since 1990, most recently during the civil war between the

Communist Party of Nepal (Maoist) and the Nepalese government security forces. Her tourism papers have appeared in the *Annals of Tourism Research, Fashion Theory, Food Culture and Society, Journeys*, and volumes edited by Michael Allen, Jonathan Skinner, Glenn Hooper, and John J. Lennon.

Maria Lauridsen Jensen has a Master of Science (MSc) in Anthropology and Global Studies and Development from the University of Aarhus, Denmark (2016). She has conducted ethnographic fieldwork among Mayas in Tulum, Quintana Roo, Mexico from August to November 2015. She defended her Master's Thesis, "Being Maya in Contemporary Tulum, Mexico: An Anthropological Study of Ethnicity in an International Tourist Town," in September, 2016.

Tonic Maruatona is a Professor and Deputy Dean in the Faculty of Education at the University of Botswana in Gaborone. Dr. Maruatona studies and has published on community development, non-profit management, and life-long learning in developing countries. His research on adult education, social justice, and participatory perspectives has been published in the *Journal of Education of Adults, International Journal of Lifelong Learning*, and *Education, Citizenship, and Social Justice.*

Angela Montague is Assistant Professor of Practice in Anthropology at the University of Utah. She is a cultural anthropologist and has been conducting research in Mali, West Africa since 2004. Working closely with Kel Ansar Tuareg from the region of Timbuktu, she focuses on the uses of cultural productions and tourism for social, political, and economic purposes. Dr. Montague's dissertation research shed light on issues of competing global discourses and contested nationalism in Northern Mali, particularly through an ethnographic investigation of the Festival in the Desert (Essakane). Her current research is on tourism development in post-conflict areas and theories of (im)mobilities.

Matthew Nelson is a board certified family and obstetrics physician in rural northern Arizona, USA. His most recent faculty positions include attending physician at St Joseph Family Medicine Residency Program in Denver and assistant professor at University of New Mexico's College of Nursing. His academic background resides in both medicine and the social sciences, with degrees in anthropology and public health. He attended University of New Mexico's graduate school for cultural anthropology and transitioned to medicine after interests took him in an alternate direction. His work as an anthropologist and public health researcher was primarily in the Southwest and focused on the processes that drive and reproduce colonization and marginalization.

Todd Pierce is an anthropologist who has conducted ethnographic fieldwork for over 20 years in the United States. His research focus has been on issues concerning HIV-AIDS (transmission and prevention), drug use and misuse, harm reduction, homelessness, poverty, violence (structural, symbolic, political, everyday, gender and orientation based, community and family violence), childhood sexual abuse, rape, social network analysis, ethics in anthropology, ethnographic method development and ethnographic representation. He currently serves as Director of the Isla de Mujeres Ethnographic Field School in Mexico.

Joe Quick is a dissertator in the Department of Anthropology at the University of Wisconsin-Madison, USA. His research explores the political economy and political philosophy of indigenous grassroots developmentalism in highland Ecuador. His dissertation addresses these issues through long-term ethnographic engagement with a community-based tourism organization and the quickly expanding sector of indigenous savings and credit cooperatives.

Frances Julia Riemer is an educational anthropologist who has conducted ethnographic research in the US, Africa, and Latin America. Her research has focused on women in development and sustainable community development, globalization and study abroad, and cultural difference, learning, and teaching. She is the author of *Working at the Margins: Moving off Welfare in America* (SUNY, 2001) , co-editor of *Qualitative Research: An Introduction to Methods and Designs* (Jossey-Bass, 2011), and a Professor in Educational Foundations and Associate Faculty in the Women's and Gender Studies Program at Northern Arizona University in Flagstaff, Arizona, USA.

Kgosietsile Velempini is a Lecturer in the Environmental Education unit in the Faculty of Education at the University of Botswana. He has a Ph.D. in Curriculum and Instruction from the Patton College of Education in Ohio University, Athens, Ohio, USA. His research focuses on environmental and sustainability education, tourism, community-based natural resource management, and climate change in sub-Saharan African countries. He has published in various environmental and geography related international journals.

Index

Critical Discourse Analysis 138, 139;
see also discursive practices
Critical tourism studies 64
Cruise tourism 153, 155, 159
Cultural display 36, 65, 66, 72, 75,
Cultural performance: authenticity 25,
51; indigeneity 50; staged 18; and
tourists 49, 52, 81; traditional 66, 75;
see also dance
Cultural tourism 40, 44, 49, 74, 114

Dance: competitive 33; indigenous
53–58, 61; tourist market 45, 50,
62, 75, 80, 144, 197; traditional 50
Dancers 53–58, 60
Denisen, I. 188; *Out of Africa* 188–189
Derrida, J. 74
Development: capitalist 64; economic
137, 190; goals 38; infrastructural 172;
international 54, 62; local 31, 37;
intrusive 7; social 36; state policies 1,
6, 8; tourism 3, 32, 67, 69–71, 81, 160,
175, 177–179; 184; uneven 5, 183, 184
Discursive practices 138, 142, 144–146
Disneyesque 145, 157; *see also*
McDisneyfication

Eco-tourism 4, 172, 174–175, 179, 183
Elephants without Borders 192, 193, 203
Emotion 65–66, 76, 81
Emotional cultures, *see* emotion
Enclave resort 71; colonial impact 153,
164; economic disparity 161; liminality
of 154; tourism 159, 161, 165; tourist
bubbles 157; *see also* Ness, S. A.
Entrepreneurs: artist 58; elites 184, 201;
guides 109; mediators 89; tourism 75,
87, 91, 94–105
Environmental conservation 191
Equivocations 50, 52, 61, 62; *see also*
Viveiros de Castro, E.
Ethnicity 134, 135, 181, 184; *see also*
Maya
Exotic 138; Africa 29, 30; display
74; exotification 4, 50, 120, 124;
imaginaries 64; liminal 118; marketing
32, 40; Other 39; remote 44;
self-exotification 30; setting 115, 119,
127, 144, 156, 189, 201
Experiential marketing 154, 156
Exploration narratives 188

Facebook 180, 182
Fairclough, N. 138, 139

Fantasy 154–159, 162, 166, 189; islands
157; scapes 153, 157
Fear: climate of 6, 15, 20–22, 24–26;
control by 17; culture of 18; elephants
198; tourists 16, 41, 44, 65, 81, 116
Festival 30, 156; cultural 73, 75, 76;
government 79; religious-agrarian 50,
53, 61
Festival in the Desert 29, 31–33, 36–45
Fez 108–114, 116–117, 119–120, 123–129

The gaze; colonizing 162, 166; hegemonic 6; questioning 37; romantic
158, 162, 180; tourist 4, 33, 35, 36, 40,
59, 154; *see also* Urry, J.
Geeyad 111, 116, 118, 120, 126–127
Geertz, C. 109
Global Environment Facility (GEF) 190
Global flows 8, 30, 134, 142
Global North: and development 190;
encroachment 164, 165; imaginaries
30; interaction with Global South 8,
165–166, 202; musicians from 33;
profits 159; tourists 32, 187
Globalized space 31
Goffman, E. 3, 25, 26, 30; back and
front stage 26, 30, 62; dramaturgy
25; theatrical metaphor 51
Grand Tour of Europe 1
Great Elephant Census 192
Greenpeace 191
Gringolandia 145
Guest *see* host

Haggard, H.R. 188
Harris, W.C. 187
Harvard Kalahari Research Group 199
Hemingway, E. 188
Host 4, 29, 49, 51, 74, 164; guest binary
3, 5, 16, 104; guest disparities 6, 30;
income from tourism 155, 160, 190

Identity 147; collective 58; community
179; cultural 1, 8; ethnic 135, 145,
148; global 135; hosts 74; honor 108;
indigenous 7, 61; Islam 117, 126; labor
and 176; local 183; Mayan 136, 140,
148; national 153, 165; non–local
173; politics 64; struggles over 65,
66; staging of 173; studies 1
Imaginary 4, 30, 187 189, 201
Imagined spaces 187
Impression management 42, 44
Inauthenticity 4, 5, 6, 26, 49

Printed in the United States
by Baker & Taylor Publisher Services